A HISTORY OF THE SCHOOL OF SPIRITUAL SCIENCE

A HISTORY OF THE SCHOOL OF SPIRITUAL SCIENCE

THE FIRST CLASS

Johannes Kiersch

English by Anna R. Meuss, FCIL

TEMPLE LODGE

The Publishers gratefully acknowledge the sponsorship of the translation by the Anthroposophical Society in Great Britain

Temple Lodge Publishing
Hillside House, The Square
Forest Row, RH18 5ES

www.templelodge.com

First English edition 2006

Originally published in German under the title *Zur Entwicklung der Freien Hochschule für Geisteswissenschaft, Die Erste Klasse* by Verlag am Goetheanum, Dornach, in 2005

A catalogue record for this book is available from the British Library

ISBN-10: 1 902636 80 5
ISBN-13: 978 1 902636 80 1

Typeset by DP Photosetting, Neath, West Glamorgan
Printed and bound by Cromwell Press Limited, Trowbridge, Wilts.

Knowledge of these things certainly cannot be passed on like any other subject that is taught. Following frequent, combined efforts over the thing itself, and out of shared life, it will suddenly arise in the soul—like a light ignited by a spark springing over—and continue to feed on its own resources.

Plato, 7th Epistle*

* 341 C5-D2, based on the translation into German by Otto Apelt, after G. Reale: *Zu einer neuen Interpretation Platons*. Paderborn u.a. 1993, p. 100f.

Contents

Translator's note

A number of decisions had to be made especially concerning the letters and documents which are given in the Appendix and partly also included in the chapters of this book.

Corrections have been kept to a minimum to convey at least some of the quality and 'flavour' of these elements.

Documents written in English by native English-speakers have not been corrected, except for obvious typing errors in one instance (as indicated in the relevant footnote).

Documents in English whose authors were of a different mother tongue were corrected only where confusion might otherwise arise for today's reader.

Some documents written in German were by individuals whose mother tongue was not German; in this case the translation was edited where it seemed necessary to avoid confusion, but as little as possible, to allow the quality of the originals to come through.

It would normally take nine or ten months to translate a work of this calibre. At the request of the Council at the Goetheanum in Dornach, the task had to be done in four or five months, which proved a challenge.

One stage in the translation process is to put the work aside for a time and then read it all in English for style, making sure that terminology, spelling, etc. are consistent, and finally also check it against the original, looking for omissions or excessive deviation. This task was taken on by my colleague Johanna Collis, Member of the Chartered Institute of Linguists, who did the work with admirable care, and also made some excellent suggestions for the handling of certain phrases.

The author, Johannes Kiersch, went through the whole manuscript as well, managing to pick up a handful of errors which had escaped Johanna and myself. I am greatly indebted to both of them. Without their help it would not have been possible to complete the task in such a short time.

Anna R. E. K. Meuss
Fellow of the Chartered Institute of Linguists
Member of the Translators' Association, The Society of Authors.
April 2006

Preface

The School of Spiritual Science was established by Rudolf Steiner in 1923 as an organ of initiative and as the 'soul' of the Anthroposophical Society. It has since spread to many countries around the world. The early years are now at a distance that makes them historical. Anyone wishing to join the School today and be active in it as a responsible member is challenged by the constant change in modern life to reconcile venerable tradition with a here and now that is forever new. It is particularly since the written records on which the teaching of the First Class of the School is based have been published that urgent questions have arisen which give occasion to reflect once more on the original intentions.

In view of this, Heinz Zimmermann—I had been attending his symposia on the language of Rudolf Steiner for a number of years—asked me, also on behalf of the Council and the Faculty of the School at the Goetheanum, if I would be prepared to write a history of this institution for the use of those who in collaboration with the General Anthroposophical Section of the School present the Lessons and conduct study groups for members of the First Class. I agreed to do so. As the work progressed, it became evident that the results might also be of interest to others who are deeply concerned with the destiny of the School. The book will therefore not be printed for private circulation among a set group of people but is intended to be generally available. This had to be taken into account. The aim was to find ways of presenting originally esoteric subject matter connected with the history of the School in a form that would be accessible to any unbiased reader, even those not familiar with every aspect of Rudolf Steiner's concept of the esoteric. Many questions concerning the further development of the Mystery School inaugurated for our present age by the founder of anthroposophy will be touched on but not solved in this book. The aim has been above all to come as close as possible to the sources and offer historical material for individuals to form their own opinion. The few conclusions reached at some points along the way do not, of course, represent the views of the Council and the Faculty of the School at the Goetheanum. Any errors are also the author's sole responsibility.

Right from the beginning, the research which has led to this volume has been limited to the history of the First Class. Events in the history of the Anthroposophical Society or the anthroposophical movement as a whole have only been included where they relate to the way in which the work in the First Class developed. Emphasis is on the early years, from the Christmas Conference to the outbreak of the Second World War. Subsequent developments are only referred to in summary as we look ahead. To avoid delay in completing the work, the histories of the different Sections of the School are not considered and thus also the esoteric work in individual professional disciplines with an anthroposophical orientation. May the future bring further work, perhaps by individuals who are active in the disciplines concerned.

Large parts of the investigation relate to source material in Swiss archives for anthroposophy. After decades during which each went its own way, I have found to my delight that today the staff at those centres are working together in perfect harmony. The project could not have been accomplished without their professional competence, kindness and readiness to help. I am especially grateful to Hella Wiesberger, the excellent editor of Rudolf Steiner's esoteric works, and to her colleagues Dorothea Weyrather and Walter Kugler at the Rudolf Steiner Archives in Duldeck House, to Angela and Heinz Matile at the Albert Steffen Foundation in Dornach, to Gunhild Poerksen and Peter Selg at the Ita Wegman Archives in Arlesheim, to Thomas Meyer at the Archives of the Perseus-Verlag publishing house in Basel and—last but not least—to Uwe Werner, who supported me all the way, in the Archives at the Goetheanum, with his colleagues Peter Braithwaite, Wilhelm Baumeier and Karin Rohrer. It took considerable effort to track down the documents for the chapter on Harry Collison and George Adams-Kaufmann, and for this I am much indebted to Margaret Jonas and Philip Martyn in London. J. Emanuel Zeylmans van Emmichoven and Peter Selg added much to my understanding of Rudolf Steiner's collaboration with Ita Wegman.

Many others have helped and advised me. I'd like to mention, in gratitude, Henry Barnes, Elisabeth Bessau, Friedwart Bock, Joop van Dam, Wolfgang Fackler, Ineke van Florenstein Mulder, Eginhard Fuchs, Ulrike Garrido Mendoza, Michaela Gloeckler, Wolfgang Goebel, Gudula Gombert, Oddvar Granly, Herbert Greif, Lawrence Harwood, Friedwart Husemann, Ernst Katz, Alexander Kubitza, Christof Lindenau,

Ekkehard Meffert, Paul Mackay, Magda Maier, Hans Peter van Manen, Stefano Pederiva, Sergei O. Prokofieff, Esa Ilmari Ristilae, Martina Maria Sam, Erik Schieferdecker, Roswitha Spence, Ronald Templeton, Reijo Wilenius and Elizabeth Wirsching.

A team of advisers has been available throughout, among them Virginia Sease, Bodo von Plato, Uwe Werner and Heinz Zimmermann, and Wiltrud Schmidt, Secretary to the Council at the Goetheanum. I am indebted to all of them for valuable advice, especially on the conception of the whole undertaking. I would like to thank Monika Weiss and Heike Hensel at the Institute of Waldorf Education in Witten for their untiring assistance with getting it all down on paper.

Previously unpublished documents are reprinted with the kind permission of the above-mentioned archives.

J.K.
Witten/Ruhr, Germany,
September 2005

1 Introduction

In not much more than 300 years, the way people think and do research in our technological and scientific civilization has obscured the knowledge of ancient times and even earlier human awareness of the existence of a supersensible world—the world of the 'spirit' in the language of anthroposophy. The sense-perceptible, physical conditions in which human souls find themselves between birth and death have of necessity come to the fore in the conscious mind. This has begun to change now. Movements critical of our civilization are for a variety of reasons seeking to revive the ancient knowledge and thus to come to new, authentic experiences in the sphere of supersensible perception. They will often go back to traditions from cultures outside Europe—Tibetan Buddhism with the charismatic figure of the Dalai Lama at its head, Indian teachings, the mysticism of the Islamic Sufi movement, the exercises done in Japan's Zen schools. Popularized derivatives of those venerable traditions spread far and wide, also in the media—yoga for relaxation, the martial arts of the Orient, feng shui, various alternative approaches in medicine, and many practices taken from nineteenth-century spiritualism, from the narcotics scene, and from old superstitions. Although that is not the intention, all this does largely devalue esotericism. The generally respected serious spiritual seeking of the past appears to have been taken into the sphere of superficial sensationalism and idle pastime. For people who feel committed to the European and North American Enlightenment tradition of the eighteenth century, any interest in esotericism will therefore tend to be a symptom of regressive irrationality, a flight to the unconscious, denying the ideals of enlightened humanity on which our system of rights and all social progress are based.

This being the present situation, it will be more than ever necessary for anthroposophically orientated students of Rudolf Steiner to represent actively their ideas of the nature of the esoteric, showing that these ideas can be considered in absolute harmony with the ideals and principles of modern rationality and may indeed be seen as a further development of these ideals and principles that is right for our time.[1] Rudolf Steiner saw

[1] Roeschert 1997.

the prevalent materialistic and positivist way of thinking in his time as a necessary stage of transition in the evolution of the human mind. Writing to refute Oswald Spengler's retrospective cultural pessimism, he said: 'A cold technology gives a character to human thinking that leads to freedom. The spirit to be found among levers, wheels and engines is dead indeed; but the human soul *awakens to freedom* in this realm of the dead.'[2] The exercises used in anthroposophy open up new avenues to the world of the 'spirit' for the human soul as it awakens to freedom, and this does not go in any way against enlightened modern thinking. In this they differ from the many well-meaning but problematical roads to salvation that come under the heading of 'esotericism' today.

Rudolf Steiner's anthroposophical esotericism is also clearly distinct from the earlier esotericism which has been the object of historical studies in recent decades. In the academic world it is no longer taboo to study the 'occult sciences', currents in human history connected with mysticism, hermetics and the like. It has certainly been permissible to discuss such subjects since Frances Yates published her works on Giordano Bruno (1964) and the history of the Rosicrucians (1972). A chair of 'history of the esoteric and mystic streams in modern and contemporary Europe' was established at the Sorbonne in 1979, and a chair of 'history of hermetic philosophy and related approaches' in Amsterdam in 1999. Antoine Faivre in particular has contributed to the methodological basis of such studies.[3] Investigations into the history of early modern times have shown a close connection between hermetic approaches and the origin of modern science,[4] or the highly topical epistemological perspectives which open up with this.[5] Freemasonry provided an esoteric core even for the uncompromisingly objective and rational cultural stream of eighteenth-century European Enlightenment.[6] An excellent example of the venerable tradition of a hermetic theme that had a widespread influence on civilization was given by Dietrich Mahnke in his study on 'infinite sphere and centre of all'

---

[2] Steiner R. *Oswald Spengler, Prophet of World Chaos* (GA 36 [1961], p. 85). Engl. in *Oswald Spengler, Prophet of World Chaos*. Essay of 13 Aug. 1922. Tr. not known. New York: Anthroposophic Press 1949.

[3] For a more detailed review of current studies in German see Stuckrad 2004.

[4] Faivre/Zimmermann 1979, Vickers 1984, Neugebauer-Woelk 1999.

[5] Liedtke 1996.

[6] Pomian 1990.

(1937).[7] More recent research on the history of philosophy has shown that Rudolf Steiner's concept of the esoteric came up in Plato's 'unwritten teachings'.[8] It had also been clear for some time that traces of it existed in German classical and Romantic philosophy. Steiner frequently made the connection when writing or speaking about Goethe, Novalis, Schelling and others of like mind. It is evident, therefore, that the hidden stream of esoterically-based tradition has influenced exoteric cultural life in many different ways. But the repercussions of this on esoteric life are also of significance. Thus Gerd-Klaus Kaltenbrunner, of Roman Catholic persuasion, has shown, in writing about the outstanding figure of Dionysius the Areopagite, that every significant stream in cultural history has an esoteric core, that it grows rigid and sterile without esotericism, and that on the other hand all esotericism needs to have an exoteric influence on the general cultural life if it is not to degenerate into sheer wishful fantasy.[9]

Against the background of this rich panorama in cultural history, Steiner's anthroposophical esotericism has nothing of the exotic or special to it. Yet in its philosophical basis and especially its psychology of cognition it stands out clearly against all related streams. Steiner's *Philosophy of Spiritual Activity* can be read as a profoundly esoteric work; at the same time it is emphatically part of scientific discussion in the public domain. The same applies to his writings on Goethe, his fundamental approach to the psychology of cognition in a lecture at the fourth International Philosophers' Congress in Bologna[10] and his principal work on epistemology, part of which is published in English as *A Case for Anthroposophy*. Considering these facts, we can understand more fully today than a few years ago how anthroposophical esotericism and with it the idea of the School of Spiritual Science evolved in history.

---

[7] This theme is given in *Conferences with the Teachers of the Waldorf School in Stuttgart / Faculty Meetings with Rudolf Steiner*, as an image for meditation on the relationship of the human head to the infinitely distant 'sphere' of the universe, and in *Education for Special Needs* as the central *Point-Circle Meditation*. For its esoteric significance in Rudolf Steiner's life work, see Wiesberger 1997, p. 325 ff. (not tr.).

[8] Szlezák 1993, Schefer 2001.

[9] Kaltenbrunner 1996, p. 438 ff.

[10] Steiner R. *The Psychological Foundations of Anthroposophy* (GA 35 [1965], p. 111–144).

Rudolf Steiner had the gift of supersensible perception from childhood. This was greatly deepened when—probably in his 36th year, before moving from Weimar to Berlin—he began to meditate on a regular basis. He had undoubtedly done exercises in meditation many times before this, at least in the form of reflective thought, if for nothing else then for the work on his philosophical writings. Yet what happened at this point was to go much further. Looking back, he wrote in his autobiography: '*Inner experience* led me to perceive the essential nature of meditation and its significance for gaining insight into the world of the spirit.' He compared this discovery with a phenomenon of metamorphosis in the animal world. 'The inner life which had been achieved needed meditation just as the organism needed lungs to breathe with at a particular stage of its evolution.'[11] The developmental step that comes to everyone who does not take anthroposophy in a theoretical way but applies the exercises in Steiner's books to himself with the necessary intensity came as a central event also in the inner development of the founder of anthroposophy. This significant step not only enabled him to perceive the physical, sense-perceptible world more intensely, as he described it in chapter 22 of his autobiography. Within a few years it also led to the tremendous abundance of impressions from the spiritual, supersensible sphere which is manifest in the surviving fragmentary notes taken of his esoteric lectures after the turn of the century, and was given its fundamental conceptual structure in his *Occult Science* in 1909.[12]

Anyone wishing to understand Rudolf Steiner's efforts to develop the School of Spiritual Science in its systematic and also its historical context would do well to get a really clear picture of the extraordinary process of taming, and bringing to concept, an overwhelming multiplicity of supersensible visions of which we can scarcely have an idea. The outcome of the process is that today we have the basic works on anthroposophy. A special help in this are Rudolf Steiner's writings in *Von Seelenraetseln* (partly translated in *The Case for Anthroposophy*). In 1917, the year when

[11] Steiner R. *The Course of my Life / An Autobiography*, chapter 22 (GA 28 [2000], p. 323).

[12] Daniel Hartmann has written in detail about Rudolf Steiner's unceasing endeavour to present the fruits of his spiritual investigations in clear and comprehensible terms, taking *Theosophy* as his example (Steiner 2004, preface and postscript). For fundamental studies on the problem of putting supersensible perceptions into words see Lissau 2001 and Sam 2004.

the First World War came to its turning point, he not only initiated his public work in the cultural field with this publication but also brought together the two major streams of his cultural and spiritual world which had so far been separate—one theosophical and esoteric, the other epistemological and philosophical, in a 'philosophy of the human being' arising from 'anthropology' and 'anthroposophy', empirical studies in the sense-perceptible sphere and supersensible spiritual investigations. Apart from the psychology of forming ideas relating to supersensible vision in chapter 1, it is helpful to study the inconspicuous fourth appendix to the book: 'An important characteristic of perception in the spirit'. Here Rudolf Steiner wrote how important it was to understand clearly that only sensory perceptions can be remembered. Supersensible perceptions in their full reality must be called up over and over again. This offers helpful key points for people wanting to take up the anthroposophical exercises for inner development. Summing up, Steiner wrote that one could 'gain much for the soul's right conscious relationship to the world of the spirit, exactly by carefully doing exercises to perceive the rather subtle differences appearing in the inner life: 1) developments in the soul that lead to a spiritual perception; 2) spiritual perceptions as such; 3) spiritual perceptions metamorphosed into concepts we know ordinarily in the mind.'[13]

Gaining clear understanding of these differences by doing the exercises, one becomes aware of a common tendency in present-day anthroposophical life, and that is the inclination to take the great teacher's words in a more robust sense than they are meant to be.[14] We need not even think of the popular notions concerning the nature of and events in the spiritual, supersensible world. Originally these related to Rudolf Steiner's esoteric teaching, but they have lost all their esoteric character and become a mixed collection of curios of inappropriately materialized facticity. Describing the decline of medieval civilization in the fourteenth and fifteenth centuries, Dutch philosopher Johan Huizinga has shown that the spiritual works of Christian art and the symbolistic thinking on which they were based, came to be more and more fixed, set, in that late

[13] Steiner R. *Von Seelenraetseln* (GA 21 [1976], p. 143); partly translated in *A Case for Anthroposophy*.

[14] See Rudolf Steiner's comments in the ninth Class Lesson on people having the wrong expectations concerning life in the spiritual world. (GA 270/1, p. 169). See also Lissau 2001, p. 21.

period of decline, literally assuming a mechanistic character.[15] Surely we can say much the same in many respects about current forms seen in anthroposophy? Some things are far removed today from the living reality of spiritual experiences that speak to us, for instance, in Rudolf Steiner's blackboard drawings—germinal, open configurations in colour and form. Nowhere do we feel tied down in dogma, but rather encouraged to make our own observations, think things further, reflect and investigate. As with the mantric material Rudolf Steiner created in words, with his *Mystery Plays*, with many spiritual passages in his published lectures, ideas are at the boundaries, in the terms given in *A Case for Anthroposophy*, in spheres where things are put in a spiritual way and we are challenged to leave all sense-bound images and thoughts behind. In view of this, we should always be aware of the limited validity of all conceptuality based on sensory perceptions. Statements about the 'spiritual world' in written form from Rudolf Steiner's literary estate, often even more 'set' by being in print or the electronic media, are not the 'spiritual perceptions metamorphosed into concepts we know ordinarily in the mind' of which he wrote in *Von Seelenraetseln* (*A Case for Anthroposophy*).

At the same time we can see the Lessons of the School of Spiritual Science as ever new attempts to draw the listeners' attention to 'developments in the soul that lead to spiritual perception'. No more than that. The recorded texts as such do not in any way convey the reality of supersensible experience in the spirit.

It is from this general point of view that we will in the following pages approach the historical events which may help us to discern Rudolf Steiner's original intentions in founding and beginning to develop the School of Spiritual Science. The focus will be on the history of the First Class.

---

[15] Huizinga 1975, chapter XV, p. 285 ff.

2 Early esotericism

In publishing his essay on Goethe's secret revelation in 1899,[16] Rudolf Steiner referred, as yet rather obscurely, to future forms of human community life. These will be possible when the time comes for a new way of experiencing the supersensible. Just over a year later, in a lecture on the same subject in Count Brockdorff's Theosophical Library, he had opportunity to speak in a 'wholly esoteric' way. 'It was an important experience for me,' he wrote, 'to be able to speak in terms coined out of the spirit world. Until then conditions in Berlin had forced me to let the spiritual merely shine through in what I said.'[17] It then became his main aim, pursued above all else when from the autumn of 1902 onwards he was General Secretary of the German section of the Theosophical Society, to 'set "disciples in the spirit" on the path of development'.[18] Initially this did not succeed in the way he had hoped. A firm invitation to 'practical karma exercises',[19] given to the small group of members at the very foundation meeting, was met with evident embarrassment. It was therefore to be many years before he took this elementary impulse up again.

What happened next gained its extraordinary certainty of purpose and import with a development of central significance in the life of Rudolf Steiner—he came to see Christianity in the way in which he would from then on represent it. The notebook entry, made in 1924, to which Rudolf Grosse drew attention, indicates that this decisive step had come in 1903.[20]

---

[16] *Magazin fuer Litteratur.* No. 34, 26 Aug. 1899. GA 30.

[17] Steiner R. *The Course of my Life / An Autobiography* (GA 28, Ch. XXX).

[18] Writing to Wilhelm Huebbe-Schleiden on 16 Aug. 1902. *Briefe*, Bd 2 (1953), p. 256.

[19] Lecture of 20 Oct. 1902. In *Cosmic Christianity and the Impulse of Michael* (GA 240 [1986], p. 256).

[20] '1903—the Christian Mysteries are becoming clear.' See Lindenberg's careful description of the whole situation (Lindenberg 1997, p. 443 ff.; also Lindenberg 1995). We are here following Lindenberg's interpretation relating to the autobiography. Hella Wiesberger gives a different interpretation, seeing the notebook entry of 1903 in the context of the literary works biography—a step in outwardly presenting the Mystery, personal experience of which had come a long time before this (Wiesberger 2001).

In the summer of that year, Steiner wrote in one of the first issues of the journal *Luzifer*:

> The theosophist knows that truth lies in Christianity. He also knows that Jesus, in whom the Christ was embodied, is not the guide of the dead but a guide of the living. He understands the Master's great word: I am with you always, even to the end of the world. Someone wishing to explain Christianity the way Annie Besant does, will first turn to the *living* guide, not to the historical report. What the 'living word' says even *today* for the ear that wishes to hear—this then shines into the gospel reports. Yes, He has remained with us to this day, the speaker of the Word, and He can tell us Himself how we should take the written reports of His deeds and His words. The 'good news' must be taken esoterically, that is, the living power which puts the stamp of the 'sacred' on them must first have come awake in our souls. The rational mind and the power of judgement as the great instruments of modern civilization must be freed from the bonds of grasping reality through mere sensory perception, of understanding only tangible things. The rational mind of modern humanity must itself enter into the ocean which fills them with true reverence for the spirit.[21]

As Guenter Roeschert has shown—we are indebted to him for referring us to this passage—these are things of which nothing was said in the first edition of *Christianity as Mystical Fact* which had appeared a year earlier.[22] It is highly probable that Rudolf Steiner gained his central insight into the Mystery of the Incarnation of the Christ in the body of Jesus of Nazareth and certainty of the living presence of the Risen Christ at the very time when he decided to accept the destiny mission of actively developing an esoteric school for the present age. The lectures then given in 1904 and 1905, where the first section of this school came to life and

---

[21] GA 34 [1987], p. 64 f. The image of the ocean used here reminds us of the mobile, open idea of truth at which Rudolf Steiner arrived in his *Goethe's Conception of the World* (1897): 'Truth is not a dead, frozen system of concepts capable of only a single form; it is a living ocean in which the human mind and spirit lives, and this can show all kinds of different wave forms on its surface.' (GA 6 [1963], p. 66).

[22] G. Roeschert. Mysterien der Idee—Rudolf Steiners Zugang zum Christentum. In L. Ravagli/G. Roeschert 2003, S. 420 ff.

the other two sections were being prepared, can be understood in the light of this.[23]

On 23 October 1902, at the foundation meeting of the German Section of the Theosophical Society, Steiner became a member of its Esoteric School (ES). On 10 May 1904, Annie Besant, leader of the School, appointed him Arch-Warden for Germany.[24] From then on he actively and on his own responsibility undertook the development of an esoteric school with three 'Classes'. In 1924 it was clearly in accord with this that he founded the School of Spiritual Science.[25]

To begin with, attention focused on the individual work each member did in meditation. Rudolf Steiner invited suitable individuals to join, was available for interviews, and offered individual meditations in many cases and advice in numerous letters.[26] In those first years at least, members were asked to keep a diary on the progress and results of their meditation exercises.[27] In a number of places, a Sub-Warden was responsible for things locally.[28] Rudolf Steiner himself gave Lessons on a regular basis.[29] On 5 June 1905, a first letter was sent to members in which the Esoteric School was called the 'heart of the Theosophical Society', and the current situation was characterized. The conditions for admittance were listed, including a three-stage morning meditation for the 'trial path' of at least twelve months, after which 'elevation to the first degree' could follow, and directions for the evening review.[30]

---

[23] With regard to what follows, see also Bock 1958.

[24] Lindenberg 1997, p. 375. Wiesberger in GA 264 [1984], p. 24 ff.

[25] Explaining the statutes (or by-laws) at the beginning of the Christmas Conference, on 24 December 1923, Rudolf Steiner said: 'Please do not take fright at these three Classes, dear friends. The three Classes did originally exist in the Anthroposophical Society until 1914, though in a different form.' (*The Christmas Conference*, 24 Dec. 1923; GA 260, p. 50 f.). See also Adolf Arenson about the three ritual hammer blows to open the Christmas Conference, in a letter to Albert Steffen dated 24 December 1926, Appendix 17.

[26] See GA 264, 266/1-3, 267, 268.

[27] *From the History and Contents of the First Section of the Esoteric School 1904–1914* (GA 264, p. 148).

[28] Michael Bauer in Nuremberg, Sophie Stinde in Munich, Adolf Arenson in Stuttgart. Ibid. (p. 115, note 2).

[29] As far as is known, the first ES Lessons were given on 9 and 14 July 1904 in Berlin. GA 266/1, p. 11 ff.

[30] GA 264 p. 145-8.

There are indications that preparations for developing the second and third sections of the Esoteric School were in progress in the summer of 1904. Rudolf Steiner spoke to a small group of members about the biblical myth of Cain and Abel. This is a theme from Masonic tradition.[31] Towards the end of that year, a number of further lectures on Masonic traditions were given.[32] He spoke of developments in a far distant future, in connection with Christian Rosenkreutz's mission, which would depend on the forms people developed for coming together in freedom to do spiritual work.

It is particularly important to note that Rudolf Steiner included the mission of Mani and his disciples. In the lecture he gave on 11 November 1904[33] he traced the Masonic traditions back to Manichaeism, saying how all life assumed rigid form after a time which prevented new life from developing, how one was thus able to show that evil was 'good out of time', needing to be resisted and overcome in 'gentleness' rather than 'fight' so that a higher good might arise. Faustus, the Manichaean bishop, here appeared as the representative of freedom based on one's own inner activity, Augustine, his student for a time and his great adversary, as the representative of traditional authority. It is truly astonishing how decisive Steiner was in speaking to this group of people, whom he intended to prepare for the more advanced levels of his esoteric training,[34] about the future of a Christianity the real significance of which had only come to him shortly before this. Mani, he said, wanted to prepare for 'the time when in the sixth root race[35] humanity would be guided by itself, in the light of its own soul, overcoming outer forms and transforming them into spirit.'[36]

---

[31] Lecture of 10 June 1904 in *The Temple Legend* (GA 93 [1979], p. 33 ff.).
[32] 4 & 11 Nov., 2, 9, 16 & 23 Dec. 1904 in *The Temple Legend* (GA 93).
[33] Ibid, pp. 68–71; Berlin, 11 Nov. 1904.
[34] According to notes made by Mathilde Scholl, the ideas in this lecture were later the subject matter for the third section. Ibid. Note relating to lecture of 11 Nov. 1904.
[35] I.e. when the seven periods of post-Atlantean civilization had run their course; in the words of the Book of Revelation: after the 'great war of all against all'. See lecture of 26 June 1908 in Nuremberg in *The Apocalypse of St John* (GA 104), with reference to 'those of Philadelphia with the principle of progress, of inner freedom, brotherly love, a small group made up of all tribes and nations' (p. 161).
[36] *The Temple Legend*, 11 Nov. 1904 (GA 93, p. 75).

> Mani will generate a stream in the spirit that goes beyond the Rosicrucian stream. This Mani stream goes across to the sixth root race which has been in preparation from the founding of Christianity. It will only be in the sixth root race that Christianity comes to expression in its full form. Only then will it truly have come. The inner Christian life as such overcomes any form, propagating itself through outer Christianity and living in all forms of the different confessions. Those who seek Christian life will always find it. It creates forms and breaks forms in the different religious systems. It is not a matter of looking for sameness everywhere in the outer forms, but of being sentient of the inner stream of life which is present everywhere under the surface. Something which still needs to be created is a form for the life of the sixth root race. This must be created earlier, for it has to be there for the Christian life to pour into it. This form must be prepared for by people creating such an organization, such a form, so that the true Christian life of the sixth root race can spread in it. And this outer social form must arise from the Mani intention, from the small group which Mani is preparing. That must be the outer form of organization, the congregation where the Christian spark will first be able truly to be at home.[37]

With sublime aims and esoteric activity to deepen the work, Rudolf Steiner was thus quietly guiding a small group of people, increasing their awareness of the form in which they must work together. At the same time he increased his activities in the outside world. Until then he had been mainly working in Berlin; now, from 1905 onwards, he repeatedly visited many other towns.[38] A powerful accent was set in a lecture given immediately after the Annual General Meeting of the German Section of the Theosophical Society in October 1905,[39] where he spoke firmly in favour of popularizing knowledge which had so far been occult, and of general cultural activities. With regard to this, Rudolf Steiner put emphasis on the contrast between inner spiritual life and outer organization, which must not be confused. It appears that the difference between 'movement' and 'Society', frequently under discussion in later

[37] Ibid. p. 76.
[38] Lindenberg 1988.
[39] *The Temple Legend*, 22 Oct. 1905, afternoon (GA 93, p. 199 ff.).

times, was here proving a problem for the first time.[40] The very next day and then again immediately in the New Year, first steps were taken to develop the School further.[41]

On 24 November 1905, Rudolf Steiner and Marie von Sivers became members of the Memphis Misraim Order.[42] On 3 January 1906 the contract was signed which gave Rudolf Steiner the right to run his own symbolic-ritual group within the Order.[43] From then on Lessons were given in ritual form in a number of places in Germany and also other European countries, until the war broke out in 1914 and it was no longer possible to continue working in this way.[44]

A detail worth noting is that in 1913, following separation from the Theosophical Society, Rudolf Steiner changed the rituals he had introduced, as the necessary secrecy could not be guaranteed.[45]

---

[40] More on this in Wiesberger 1997, p. 319 ff.

[41] Lectures of 23 Oct. 1905 and 2 Jan. 1906 in *The Temple Legend* (p. 215 ff.).

[42] GA 265 [1987], p. 50. Vorbemerkung von H. Wiesberger.

[43] Ibid. pp. 58 and 82 ff. Details of the problems and disputes connected with this given by Wiesberger in GA 265.

[44] For details see GA 265, also Gaedeke 1990, p. 132 ff. According to Wiesberger (in GA 265, p. 58), about 600 members had been admitted to the Memphis Misraim Service before it dissolved in 1914. Historically Rudolf Steiner connected the institution of the first section of his esoteric school with the Esoteric School of Theosophy of the Theosophical Society, the 'cognitive ritual' of the second section with the stream of Ancient York Masonry represented by John Yarker. The third section, and according to Emil Leinhas and Guenther Schubert this had only twelve members, appears to have had no historical precedent (Wiesberger 1997, p. 22 f.).

[45] Wiesberger in GA 265, p. 136.

3 The 'attempt' made in 1911

Quite independently of the Theosophical Society, as Rudolf Steiner said emphatically, a mysterious event occurred in the esoteric work of those years. In the lecture on Manichaeism in November 1904, he had spoken of the need to create a form now for the 'Christianity in freedom' that was to come in the far future. The 'life' of the new era could then 'flow' into this, an 'organization', or, as he put it more exactly, an 'outer social form'. 'That must be the outer form of organization, the congregation where the Christian spark will first be able truly to be at home.'[46] Seven years later the impulse arose again. Following preliminary talks in a small group, Steiner gave an address to an invited audience on 15 December 1911 in Berlin, at the time when the General Meeting of the German Section of the Theosophical Society was being held in that city.[47] Its contents make one feel irritated, if not embarrassed, to this day.[48] He emphasized that he was not talking of the usual way of founding a society or association for those who acknowledged the same ideals, but about a [spiritual] 'Foundation'. Note how carefully Rudolf Steiner was feeling his way in characterizing the special nature of this new way of working. What it was really about could not be put in words. Coming together in the way envisaged would only be possible if the reasons for working together 'belonged not to the world perceived through the senses but to the supersensible world'. The 'principles of an evolving process' had to be taken into account. 'It is not only that nothing at all has been founded. The fact is that it will not be possible to give a definition of what is to be done in any session, for everything must be in a continuous process of evolution.' He continued: '. . . what is to happen does not base itself on words but on human beings, and not even on human beings, but on what they will be *doing*. . . . It must never be the case that this endeavour is in any way negatively affected in its evolution because of what it is.' The

[46] *Temple Legend*, 11 Nov. 1904.

[47] Marie Steiner, see *History and Contents of First Section of the Esoteric School* (GA 264, p. 432).

[48] Ibid. The accepted text is the one revised in 1984 (GA 264, reprinted 1996, not yet translated).

new body had thus been sanctioned and given its task 'due to its own acknowledgement of our spiritual stream' and because 'in a certain way it sees the principle of sovereignty in spiritual endeavour, the principle of federalism and the independence of all spiritual endeavour, as an absolute necessity for the spiritual future, and is meant to bring it to humanity in whichever way it deems appropriate'.

Rudolf Steiner showed marked reserve here, seeing himself only as an 'interpreter' of the principles 'which as such exist only in the world of the spirit'. What is meant may be seen from the solemn statement that it was to establish 'a way of working in which, because of the very nature of the [spiritual] "Foundation", the immediate starting point for it is the figure who has from the distant past in Western culture been given the name Christian Rosenkreutz'.

In his consciously limited role of 'interpreter', someone, therefore, who presents his present, definitely momentary view, making no claim to any definite and final truth, Rudolf Steiner ascribed particular functions to the individuals he had invited to join in the new way of working, solemnly providing them with official names for these functions. Why did he use those old names when doing this 'interpretation'? To give those offices the proper weight in the face of this gathering of theosophists? For reasons of occult loyalty, as he did when formally relating to the Masonic tradition? He certainly stressed that 'no honours or special dignity' were connected with those offices, merely 'obligations'. In this sense, Marie von Sivers was 'interpreted' as 'curator' of the new body, her task being to find new members ('not by proselytizing, but merely by allowing people to approach her who are serious in their intention to join in this way of working'), then an 'archdeacon' for each 'secondary branch' of shared activity—Imme von Eckhardtstein for art in general, Marie von Sivers for literature ('provisionally'), Felix Peipers for architecture, Adolf Arenson for music, Hermann Linde for painting, and Sophie Stinde as 'keeper' ('to have an eye on this association'); Alice Sprengel as 'keeper of the seal', responsible for the 'principle of the organization'; and finally Carl Unger as 'secretary'. The Foundation was 'for the time being' given the name 'society for theosophical ways and art'. What was meant by 'ways' remained wholly open, in a 'seed state' as Rudolf Steiner put it. Concerning the term 'theosophical art', on the other hand, he said this related to something which did already exist—the performance of a number of mystery plays in Munich, the interior decoration of the house for the

Stuttgart Branch, the establishment of the Building Association in Munich. All this could be 'sanctioned as something which in a way was already tried and tested'. The words that 'the will to be a member cannot come from anyone but the individual concerned' introduced the new principle of self-appointment, connected with a reference to the need for acknowledgement.

The whole was initially given a time span until Epiphany the next year. After this, no reference was made to it for a long time. It was only years later that Rudolf Steiner made brief reference to it, saying: 'The matter was made impossible by the way in which it was considered in one particular case. It was an attempt.'[49]

It is easy to see that a number of the themes in this strange 'attempt' later reappeared in a different form at the Christmas Conference when the Anthroposophical Society was re-founded and also in the things which Rudolf Steiner said after that event concerning the School of Spiritual Science—the definite impulse for freedom, the principle of personal responsibility for particular tasks, connected with endeavours to gain community out of the spirit, the impulse of letting the work flow into cultural life in general, the question as to the connection between 'movement' and 'organization', the principle of the 'evolving process', the realization that progress made together rests not on the assignment of offices, but on actions. Would it also be permissible to consider the new School of Spiritual Science of 1924 to be a 'Foundation' in this sense?

---

[49] *From the History and Contents of the First Section* ... Lecture of 21 Aug. 1915 (GA 264. p. 435).

4 Founding and development of the School of Spiritual Science up to March 1925

It is well known among anthroposophists that Rudolf Steiner took a serious risk when in the autumn of 1923 he decided to take office as chairman when founding the General Anthroposophical Society and thus not only be a spiritual teacher but take responsibility for the organization also of all the exoteric work for the association. He could not be certain that the spiritual world would accept this decision and continue to be open to him. The historically unique abundance of inspirations which then came to him in the few months that remained of his life made it clear that his courage and confidence had been true to reality. The revelations continued to come. The anthroposophical movement and the Anthroposophical Society could be brought together. This gave the Society an 'esoteric trait'. Anthroposophy was now no longer merely taken care of in the traditional way in the Society; it could be done.[50]

The events connected with this have been presented and discussed in numerous publications.[51] They will not be reviewed in chronological order or systematic completeness. We will limit ourselves to quoting words of Rudolf Steiner which may perhaps indicate his specific intentions in establishing the School of Spiritual Science.

In the opening lecture at the Christmas Conference on 24 December 1923, he gave a first overview of the draft 'statutes' (by-laws) of the General Anthroposophical Society which was to be founded, and the names of those whom he proposed for the new Council, people who would closely collaborate with him: Albert Steffen, Marie Steiner, Ita Wegman, Elisabeth Vreede and Guenther Wachsmuth. One notes that parity between male and female was strictly maintained according to the principle which he had formulated for the early esoteric work: that the thought of bringing together powers of the male and female mind and

[50] See especially the lecture of 5 September 1924 in *Karmic Relationships 4* (GA 238 [1974], p. 11 ff).

[51] See list of literature in Prokofieff 2002, p. 1051.

spirit held within it what would be the creative element, the effective principle, of the future.[52]

Immediately on taking office he solved the problem, addressed many times from 1904 onwards, of a spiritual movement and an outward, physical organization working together. As with the [spiritual] 'Foundation' of 1911, he did without the hierarchic structure considered essential to this day in occult associations of the traditional kind and in religious communities, and also without the authority to issue directives. The Society's Council did, of course, have authority, above all—though not only—thanks to the inspiration given by Rudolf Steiner's participation. It renounced all power. Rudolf Steiner saw it as an organ for initiative, and the Goetheanum as a place where work is done, encouraging others to join in the work. The Council, he said in his opening lecture at the Christmas Conference, saw itself 'as a group of people who would say: We want to do something here at the Goetheanum, and will enter into dialogue, with individuals or groups who wish it, about one thing or another which we are doing.' This Council did not want to be anything 'but a group of people with initiative for the anthroposophical cause'.[53]

Rudolf Steiner then came to the question in his opening lecture of what form collaboration might take between the Council at the Goetheanum and anthroposophists taking initiative in the world at large. The Council would, of course, have to work from the centre in Dornach. At the same time, however, attention would be emphatically directed to relevant activities elsewhere. 'The whole thing is to come alive, therefore—not a Council which is bureaucratically scattered all over the world but people taking responsibility for individual groups who come from those groups themselves but will have occasion at any time to feel

[52] *The Temple Legend*, 2 Jan. 1906; GA 93, p. 289. Compare this with the detailed discussion of the problem of gender polarity in Masonic tradition in the lectures of 23 Oct. 1905 and 2 Jan. 1906 in that volume. A note Marie von Sivers made relating to a lecture of 9 April 1906 also relates to this: 'The future significance of Freemasonry lies in man and woman doing occult work together. The excesses of male culture must be held in check by the occult female powers.' (Quoted from Wiesberger 1997, p. 179.)

[53] *The Christmas Conference*, 24 Dec. 1923 (GA 260 [1994], p. 53). Rudolf Steiner also spoke of the 'Initiative Council' (as distinct from an administrative council) in the lecture he gave in Prague on 29 March 1924 (GA 260a. p. 183), and in similar terms in the *Nachrichtenblatt* newsletter (*Nbl*) of 6 April 1924 (appendix 1) and in the 8th Class Lesson.

themselves to be members, with equal rights, of the Council, though this be located in Dornach.'[54] He made clear what he meant by this three days later, when discussions on the statutes started, once again emphasizing the initiative function of the Dornach 'committee/council'—he spoke of 'central initiative'—and then referred to the member's pages in the weekly paper *Das Goetheanum*, which he thought would mean 'continuous, lively activity going out from the Council'.[55] He proposed a body of 'correspondents with the Council' as an organ needed for activity going in the opposite direction, from the world outside to the Goetheanum. These 'would perhaps voluntarily agree to write a weekly letter about things they find worth noting in cultural life in the world, things that might interest the Anthroposophical Society'. (Later the additional suggestion was made that Albert Steffen should publish a selection from those letters in the weekly paper, and Steffen was happy to take this up.)[56] The correspondents would 'be the Council of people outside, wholly the equal of the Council of people at the centre' in Dornach.[57] Rudolf Steiner brought an image from organic life for this, the image of the blood circulation, and this seems of great significance in pointing the way. '... You know, for a blood circulation you need not only centrifugal forces but also centripetal forces that return, as it were. And provision should be made for a number of members to connect closely in their souls with the Council in all things which concern not only the Anthroposophical Society in the narrower sense but the whole of the spiritual and cultural life of today where it relates to the work of the Anthroposophical Society; for a number of members who relate closely in their souls with the Council to communicate what is going on in the world outside. This will give us a completely free constitution, based on free and open collaboration, for the Anthroposophical Society. With this it will be possible for stimulus to come from every [probably meaning 'either'] direction.'[58] He then made actual suggestions as to who those outside correspondents might be—first of all Joseph van Leer, a merchant with international experience, who had generously supported the West-East Congress in 1922 and had just taken on important responsibilities

[54] *The Christmas Conference*, 24 Dec. 1923 (GA 260, p 56).
[55] Ibid. 27 Dec. 1923 (p. 107 f.).
[56] Ibid. 30 Dec. 1923 (p. 200 f.).
[57] Ibid. 27 Dec. 1923 (p. 109).
[58] Loc. cit. (p. 108).

connected with the developing firm Weleda,[59] and then Henry Monges, Harry Collison, Millicent Mackenzie, Karl Ingeroe, Willem Zeylmans van Emmichoven, Alice Sauerwein, Emmelina de Renzis, Charlotte Ferreri, Lina Schwarz, Ludwig Polzer-Hoditz, Carl Unger, Emil Leinhas, Hans Buechenbacher, people who stood firmly in public life and had at the same time shown themselves to be individuals who felt responsible to anthroposophy. Some of them were General Secretaries and thus members of the above-mentioned group of office-holders appointed from outside, others were not. And on the other hand not all office-holders would be invited to act as 'correspondents'.[60]

At the beginning of the Christmas Conference, Rudolf Steiner was thus thinking of two quite different groups of people who were to communicate with the central Council in Dornach and collaborate on initiatives according to the image of the blood circulation. One were the office-holders sent by national societies and other groups, the other were the 'correspondents'. What interested him in this were actual human situations in the different countries and spheres of work, anything which had been achieved, as with the 'theosophical art' of the 1911 'Foundation', and the special personal abilities of individuals who were already well known to him. This is how he solved—for the limited period of his work on earth—the problem of balancing forces between centre and periphery, a problem which was to turn virulent immediately after his death, calling again and again for new solutions to this very day.

In connection with this he explained the relationship of the three Classes of the School to the Sections,[61] stating that Council and Section leaders together—in 'consultation'—made up the leadership at the Goetheanum,[62] also explaining how Council, School leadership and School Faculty differed in their functions.[63]

After the solemn ceremony of laying the Foundation Stone on 25 December and the beginning of the Foundation Meeting, which included the presentation of national representatives and some reports, a meeting was held in the early afternoon of the proposed new Council and the General Secretaries who had come to Dornach to consider the

---

[59] M. Treichler in Plato 2003, p. 434 f.

[60] Lindenberg 1997 is in error on this point (p. 864).

[61] *The Christmas Conference* (GA 260, p. 112 f.).

[62] Ibid. p. 126.

[63] Ibid. p. 131.

'statutes' given out the day before. Willem Zeylmans van Emmichoven, General Secretary of the Netherlands, asked if individual national societies had anything to do with the applications for admission to the School of Spiritual Science mentioned in § 5 of the 'statutes'. In response Rudolf Steiner made it clear that the leadership of the School would be wholly autonomous in this respect, admission being an 'esoteric matter' and handled independently of the national societies. Their function relating to the School would be merely one of 'protection', and he envisaged that the School would have its own leadership organs for Class members in individual countries. Specifically, his words were:

> Among the things done there will also be this: that one gets in touch not only with office-holders but also with members who are doing work of some kind or another in different places. And members of the first, second and third Class of the Goetheanum will be appointed everywhere by the leaders at the Goetheanum. How they are going to become such members will entirely depend on the individual case; for that will essentially be a kind of esoteric matter, but an esoteric matter managed in the modern sense, of course. When this is in progress, it will also be found that there are members in the different national societies who belong to one of the Goetheanum Classes. A separate leadership will be appointed by the Goetheanum for them in the countries concerned, establishing territorial boundaries to prevent loss of definition. I will be discussing this further as the conference progresses. Essentially it will be taken care of by the leadership at the Goetheanum itself. You have point 7 for this: 'The institution of the School of Spiritual Science is primarily the responsibility of Rudolf Steiner, who must appoint those who will work with him and his possible successor.'[64]

The next day, another major theme came up: 'We must be clear in our minds that our Society will specifically have the task of connecting the greatest imaginable openness with genuine, true esotericism.' For this, Rudolf Steiner said, it would be necessary to avoid anything resembling the management of conventional associations, and make sure 'that hearts can be in harmony without heads being in conflict'.[65] How should one

[64] Ibid. 25 Dec. 1923 (p. 80).
[65] Ibid. 26 Dec. 1923 (p. 92).

see this? Surely all 'true esotericism' was at all times bound by strict rules of secrecy, the 'arcane discipline' of Masonry, with sacred material firmly protected against profanation? Was it not even the case—as Rudolf Steiner emphasized once again in the last Class Lesson he gave—that the efficacy of these texts in life depended on their being kept secret? Where does openness end and where does esotericism begin?

Rudolf Steiner's reference to the need for hearts to be in harmony makes us aware that this did not imply a form of division according to subject areas. A first step was taken by releasing the lecture courses on general anthroposophy for publication, though not for distribution via the book trade,[66] but this was rather a token gesture, something which could scarcely be avoided as there had been numerous instances of the material being passed on without permission and lecture notes containing inaccuracies were being freely shared. Did Rudolf Steiner think that his students should work even more intensively in what we would call 'publicity work' today than had been done in the preceding years in countless lectures, conferences, artistic enterprises and courses on inner development? Surely he had expressly rejected 'agitation' for the good cause?[67] Perhaps he was after all thinking rather of making anthroposophical institutions more accessible? Or that subjects which until then had been discussed only behind closed doors or *sotto voce* should be brought to open discussion as in the academies of churches and associations, or—more so today than in those days—in the media? And how would one 'connect' all this with esotericism?

It is a help in looking for answers to these questions to bring to mind how Rudolf Steiner brought the School of Spiritual Science to the conscious awareness of the Anthroposophical Society and also the general public domain from the Christmas Conference onwards. The School was explicitly mentioned in the 'statutes' which are a public document. Its existence was no secret, and this differed from the early esoteric work when even members of the Theosophical Society did not know of it. He spoke of its structure, with three Classes, its differentiation into Sections,

---

[66] The professional esotericism of specialist subject lectures such as the courses given for teachers, physicians and priests did for the time being continue to be available only with the request not to make the material public. (Ibid. 28 Dec. 1923; p. 152.)

[67] *To the Members* (GA 260a [1987], p. 123), with reference to the letter to members of 27 Jan. 1924.

and its leadership. (After the Second World War, information on the existence of the School, the significance and nature of its work, was completely suppressed in many places, at least in Germany. In the light of the above this appears to have been anything but in harmony with Rudolf Steiner's original intentions.) Rudolf Steiner regularly announced in the members' newsletter where he had been giving Class Lessons, also including further details.[68] Informing Dornach anthroposophists in more detail when admissions to the First Class had started, he said that the School would not be a 'secret society'. 'Care will be taken that people will always know to the fullest extent what the School is doing.'[69] A few days before that, he had written in the newsletter on the different ways of working in Society and School. In the Anthroposophical Society, he wrote, people first of all got to know the spiritual world in 'form of ideas'.

> There will be people, however, who would wish to have a part in the spiritual world presented in ideas, to rise from ideas to forms of expression taken from the spiritual world itself. And there will be others who would want to get to know the roads to the world of the spirit so that they might follow them in their own souls.
>
> For such people there will be the three Classes of the School. Work done in them will lead to ever higher levels of esotericism. The School will guide the individual concerned to regions of the spiritual world which cannot be revealed in form of ideas. For these it will be necessary to find means of giving expression to Imaginations, Inspirations and Intuitions.[70]

Rudolf Steiner was even more specific some months later, when the first eight Class Lessons had been given. He went so far as to give the contents of the fundamental Lessons, at least in outline, including the

---

[68] Thus about the two Class Lessons in Prague, saying that more than a hundred members were admitted to the Class there (*Nbl* of 13 April 1924, *To the Members*, GA 260a, p. 198) and about the two Lessons given in Breslau on the occasion of the course on agriculture in Koberwitz: 'I spoke of how work done in the inner soul can show the road to knowledge of the spirit and what the soul lives through in the transition from sense-based to spiritual vision (*Nbl.* of 22 June 1924, *To the Members*, GA 260a, p. 318).

[69] Lecture of 30 Jan. 1924, *To the Members* (GA 260a, p. 128).

[70] *Nbl* of 20 Jan. 1924, *To the Members* (GA 260a, p. 108 f.).

images and turns of phrase used, to people who were not members of the Class. The essay concludes with weighty words: 'What is said here in exoteric terms is *developed* esoterically in the School.'[71]

Again we have the polarity between developing and developed, life and form, which we saw in the early esoteric work. Rudolf Steiner was taking up something which he had stood for in the old Esoteric School:

> At the beginning of an esoteric lesson it is always good to be clear in one's mind as to what an esoteric lesson actually is. The subject matter of such a lesson does not really differ from the things we hear in an exoteric lesson. Everything explained in an exoteric lesson is also under the influence of those sublime spirits whom we call the Masters of Wisdom and of the Harmony of Sentient Feelings. But anything we experience in an esoteric lesson is under the wholly direct influence of the sublime Masters and is conveyed only under their immediate influence and in full responsibility towards them. It is therefore less important what subject matter we get to hear in an esoteric lesson but rather that our souls go through living experience. How the soul relates to the spiritual currents which there flow towards it—this is what matters. The mood of soul must be very different before and after an esoteric lesson. And it is not at all important for the soul to continue to have the living experience of an esoteric lesson immediately before it, but individuals must feel that they have lived through something and taken something with them. It must be like an electrostatic machine which is charged on one occasion and not on another. You need to bear what you have received in the esoteric lesson in your soul in the same way as you know your own name. You know your name as soon as someone asks for it, even if you don't repeat it to yourself all the time. And that is how the current of esoteric life must always rest in the soul. Esoteric life will then deepen the soul more and more, and this will be needed for the time that lies before us.[72]

Things said exoterically are established and can stay as they are; things in the process of esoteric development live on. They change in time with continuous practice. The difference with regard to thought content is not appreciable.

[71] *Nbl* of 20 Apr. 1924, *To the Members* (GA 260a, p. 203). See Appendix 1.
[72] GA 266/1 (Munich 5 Dec. 1907), p. 281.

The direction in which we should look is particularly evident in the Class Lessons themselves. At the beginning of the first Lesson, Rudolf Steiner referred to the serious mood demanded by the present situation. In the preceding years, the School had been under threat because of attempts to bring things into it that did not belong there; it was now to be given its true function again 'as an esoteric institution'. Rudolf Steiner also addressed the need for 'seriousness' in the second Lesson, together with the motif of 'being in the process of evolution' from the old esotericism. Everyone who wishes to be a member of the Class should say to himself: 'Now that the Anthroposophical Society has been founded again in a new way, isn't there something which I can do in a different way from the way in which I did things before? Could I not introduce something new into my life as an anthroposophist? Could I not change the way in which I worked earlier by bringing in something or other which is new?'[73] There was need, he said, to get 'out of the rut', to fight 'vanity', reject the many 'existential lies' in our modern existence. Efforts like these could create the 'mood' that would lend strength to the work one contributes to the Class.[74] Moral qualities and qualities of heart and mind, of inner attitude, are thus what matters in the esoteric part of the School.

In the fourth Lesson, those qualities were characterized in more detail. Rudolf Steiner used a tale from 'ancient esoteric tradition' to illustrate what he meant. He spoke of a pupil in the mysteries who had achieved a first level of inner maturity and entered into a 'relationship to the world of the spirit' where one 'receives the communications from the world of the spirit with the right feelings'. The esoteric teacher told him: 'You must meet the words which I address to you at the behest of the gods with all your thinking, all your feeling, all your will to take action. You must meet what I say to you with all the enthusiasm in your soul, all inner warmth, all inner fire. You must meet it with your full, wakeful attention, a wakeful attention which is as strong as you can ever make it in your inner life. There is one power of soul, however, to which I do not address myself in you at present, not at all, and that is your memory . . . I accept it if by tomorrow you have forgotten what I am saying to you today. . . . It should be new, fresh and alive each day.'[75] The virtue of 'modesty' was

[73] GA 270/1, p. 28.
[74] Ibid. p. 29.
[75] Ibid. p. 64.

needed for this, the ability to 'hear behind the words', the ability to be silent. '... [W]e need to develop an inner feeling that esotericism must come into its own in the soul's wordless activity before it can be considered to have matured in us.'[76]

Certain formulations in the eleventh Class Lesson are equally informative. They have to do with meditation on the mantras. 'True meditation, genuine inner practice, does not lie in the theoretical, intellectual content of a verse for meditation; it lies in its mantric nature. The mantric nature is given in that *meaning dissolves into situation and process* ...'[77] Rudolf Steiner was here clearly guiding his pupils towards the experience of the threshold. In 1917 he characterized this as follows: 'And from the reflective living experience which [the soul] is able to have with the different boundary ideas, a general sentience of a spiritual world becomes differentiated for it into many different ways of perceiving it.'[78]

Qualities of mood and of being existentially concerned thus distinguish 'genuine, true esotericism' from the exoteric 'open domain'. The exoteric activity which life demands from members of the School moves in the thought forms of a rational mind bound to the senses. This is the field of independent intellectual evaluation, of different views, of arguments with 'heads in conflict'.[79] In the esoteric field 'hearts must be able to be in harmony'. This calls for the more profound faculties of the human soul to which such emphatic reference is made in the methodical study of the Class Lessons. Where such faculties develop, we may hope the effect will be to make peace among warring heads. The soul's exoteric activity is equally indispensable. Where open intellectual discussions take place, unimpeded by centrally set ideas, esoteric work is protected from misleading fantasies, dogmatism, rigid adherence to outdated tradition, vanity, false claims and clique culture. It is exactly when they are clearly distinguished that 'greatest imaginable openness' and 'genuine, true esotericism' are not mutually exclusive. They help and strengthen one another.

---

[76] Ibid. p. 68.

[77] *Esoterische Unterweisungen* (GA 270/2, p. 41). Italics by J.K.

[78] *The Case for Anthroposophy* (GA 21, [1983] p. 22).

[79] Consider the famous notebook entry made by Rudolf Steiner: 'In the field of mind and spirit, there is nothing wrong with fighting; it is the element of life there.' (Notebook entry 1918, Archive No. NB 101. Quoted from Wiesberger H. in *Beitraege zur Rudolf Steiner-Gesamtausgabe* No. 105, Michaelmas 1990.)

The School concept was also made clear in a way worth noting when new members were admitted in the weeks that followed the Christmas Conference. At the Foundation Meeting on 28 December 1923, Rudolf Steiner had discussed § 5 of the 'statutes' in which the School, the Goetheanum, is characterized as 'one[!] centre' for the work of the Anthroposophical Society, inviting the members who had gathered there to see this Goetheanum as 'the soul of the anthroposophical movement'. He made it clear that for 'progress' in esoteric inner development it was less a matter of the intellectual or professional abilities which are otherwise needed in life, but rather of 'abilities to take in the esoteric and occult with feeling, in a direct way' and of moral qualities. As to the division of the School into Sections, this was not done in an abstract, schematic way but 'out of the spheres of existing facts', that is, in the way it was done earlier with the (spiritual) 'Foundation' of 1911. The Section leaders were introduced,[80] and then the kind of application and the waiting period preceding admission to the First Class in the 'statutes' were on the agenda. Karl Ingeroe (Norway) asked if a period of time to be determined by the leadership at the Goetheanum was an individual or general matter. Rudolf Steiner's answer was:

> Entirely individual, entirely individual. You know, if you envisage how it will come about: People become or already are and indeed have already been members of the Anthroposophical Society of their own will; for there are antecedents for most of those who are sitting here today. It says here 'on application', and that means you express your will to be a member of the School. And the leadership at the Goetheanum then decides if this can be so at that point in time, or only at a future point in time.[81]

This answer accords with the given situation, where those who attended the Foundation Meeting and the first applicants after the Christmas Conference were on the whole well known to Rudolf Steiner, so that there was no need for formal procedures. Towards the end of the Conference came a remarkably diffuse invitation to address oneself to Rudolf Steiner in person in an unbureaucratic way, 'with some kind of written or verbal

[80] *The Christmas Conference*, 28 Dec. 1923 (GA 260, p. 143 ff.).
[81] Ibid. same date (p. 146).

notice', or perhaps better a written one, a 'note'.[82] Only after the Conference was it said more precisely that it would be 'best to advise' people who had only just joined the Anthroposophical Society to be 'in the Anthroposophical Society for two years' first and then to apply for admission to the School. 'This cannot, of course, apply to the . . . veterans of the Anthroposophical Society'.[83] The two-year period was clearly not strictly imposed in these cases. 'We won't be pedantic about it, of course. Mature younger members who have the full enthusiasm for anthroposophy can certainly also be members of this First Class. It will everywhere be more a matter of the inner rather than the superficial aspect.'[84]

The applications made in the early weeks, held in the archives of the Rudolf Steiner-Nachlassverwaltung (administration of literary estate) and in the Goetheanum Archives, are thus not at all in accord with the exact requirements of later times. Often it is a single sentence, written in personal terms, merely asking to be admitted. (See facsimiles in Appendix 3.) It was only in the autumn of 1924 that Rudolf Steiner made application more stringent and formal.

It is worth noting in this context that the serious commitment to being a representative, stressed so many times later on, also in the Class Lessons themselves, only came to be mentioned several weeks after the Christmas Conference. Rudolf Steiner was evidently disappointed because many of the applications submitted were limited to the request for permission also to attend the 'Friday lectures'. On 30 January he therefore went into detail, in the form of a full lecture, referring once more to the difference in weight between membership of the Anthroposophical Society on the one hand and of the School on the other. He reminded his audience again that the Anthroposophical Society had work to do in the public domain, asking for 'widest possible greatness of heart' in admitting people to the Society, something which must not be left to the goodwill of individual office-bearers.[85] It was to be tolerated, therefore, that some worked with

[82] *The Christmas Conference*. 31 Dec. 1923 (GA 260, p. 143 ff.).

[83] *To the Members*. Lecture of 18 Jan. 1924 (GA 260a, p. 101).

[84] *To the Members* (ibid. p. 101 f.).

[85] Ibid. 30 Jan. 1924 (p. 115). During the Christmas Conference itself he had been critical of tendencies to patronize members. 'I got to know a branch, for example, where advice given to members went so far as to recommend or advise against particular books. Some people who were members already were not even permitted to read my *Theosophy*, as they were deemed unfit for this.' (*The Christmas Conference*, 28 Dec. 1923; p. 154.)

the teachings of anthroposophy by themselves, whilst others involved themselves more in the life in the branches. Beyond this, one could 'not really' make any 'direct' claims on people regarding representation.[86]

There was also need, however, to take care of the teachings, and this was a matter, he said, for Class members. It needed two things—being prepared to work together with the School leadership on a basis of trust, and being prepared to represent anthroposophy in the world; indeed, doing so in a truly 'representative' way. 'Individuals cannot, of course, represent it in its totality—this is neither necessary nor useful—but they can do so in one field or another. They must then, however, truly rely fully on a basis of trust, not the trust which I am saying here one needs in anthroposophy, but the trust needed for taking care of the anthroposophical cause.'[87]

It seems remarkable that here, where he spoke for the first time about the weight of commitment to being representative, Rudolf Steiner was at the same time giving similar weight to the commitment to work with the School leadership on a basis of trust. 'The leaders cannot be enslaved. They cannot be forced to work with people with whom they do not wish to work, because they cannot do so. So there has to be the possibility for the leadership of the School of Spiritual Science to say to individuals who cannot find their way to being representatives of the anthroposophical cause: You are of course most welcome in the General Anthroposophical Society, but we regret to say that you cannot be a member of the First Class.' The same, he said, applied 'when members of the School simply act against the leadership . . .'[88] And a bit further on: 'So it will not do for someone to come along in future and say: Well, we are doing things here which do not concern the Council. You can, of course, do such things, but you cannot then be a member of the Classes. It will indeed be necessary to consider the principle of being of the same mind to be as important in our School as it has always been important in all mysteries.'[89] Towards the end of his weighty lecture, Rudolf Steiner precisely stated his requirements for membership applications: The length of time for which one has been a member of the Anthroposophical Society must be

[86] *To the Members* (GA 260a, p. 122).
[87] Ibid. 30 Jan. 1924 (p. 124).
[88] Ibid. p. 126.
[89] Ibid. p. 127.

stated, and whether the applicant is 'inclined to commit himself in some way or other with regard to what I have been saying about the question of trust today, that is, truly to assume obligations as a member of the Class'.[90]

A few days later, during a discussion on conditions for admittance, Rudolf Steiner characterized the relationship between School leadership and Class members as one of a 'contract entered into freely',[91] a formulation which later came up a number of times.[92] In England, Rudolf Steiner spoke of a spiritual contract or agreement.[93] In the last Class Lesson, where he presented the subject in the context of the 'esoteric school inspired and guided by Michael himself', it finally was 'an agreement of ideal and spiritual character entered into freely'.[94]

Rudolf Steiner tended to give emphasis to the commitment involved in being a representative, and there is a tendency to overlook the condition that goes with it, which is commitment to work together with the School leadership on a basis of trust, in terms of a 'contractual relationship entered into freely' based on the School's esotericism that could be cancelled by either side at any time. As we shall see, Rudolf Steiner did, however, consider the second commitment to be equally important.

On 2 August 1924, he gave the nineteenth Class Lesson in Dornach, stating that with this, 'the first part of this First Class of the School' had been completed.[95] He indicated that a second part would follow after his visit to England, in September, and then a third. The subject matter would be the supersensible events of which he had spoken in the karma lectures of previous weeks, events connected with the destinies of the anthroposophical movement.[96] This would mean that all the nineteen Lessons are only a third of the first third of the three-level School as originally conceived by Rudolf Steiner. This is in accord with his statements concerning the three 'degrees' on which traditional brotherhoods

---

[90] Ibid. p. 130.

[91] *To the Members*. 3 Feb. 1924 (GA 260a, p. 133).

[92] *See Nbl* of 10 Feb. 1924 in *To the Members*; lecture of 18 July 1924 in *Cosmic Christianity*; Class Lesson of 28 June 1924 (No. 16) in *Esoterische Unterweisungen 2* (GA 270/2, p. 116).

[93] Lecture of 12 Aug. 1924, *Cosmic Christianity*, also in *To the Members*.

[94] *Esoterische Unterweisungen 3* (GA 270/3, p. 124 f.).

[95] *Esoterische Unterweisungen 2* (GA 270/2, p. 174).

[96] Ibid. p. 174. See the lectures in the third karma volume, especially those of 6, 8 and 28 July.

were based and the six degrees following on from these, which could not yet be fully brought to realization in the fifth post-Atlantean age.[97] The question is, though, whether the above-mentioned formulation from the nineteenth Lesson, where he spoke of the first part of 'this First Class' could not also be interpreted in a different way. Might it not be that Rudolf Steiner intended to speak of the first part of the School '*in form* of this First Class'? Hella Wiesberger refers to a note by Marie Steiner dated March 1926 where it says: 'He left us before the work he had undertaken could be completed, before he was able to give us the second and third Classes to which he had referred. In the second he intended to give us the rite which would have been in accord with the revelations of the supersensible Michaelic School that had flowed into the Imaginations from the [end of the eighteenth and beginning of the nineteenth] centuries.'[98] It appears that Marie Steiner saw it as a matter of course that the continuation of the Class Lessons in September, according to Rudolf Steiner, would not be a second part of the First Class, but the development of the Second Class, so that the contents of the First Class may be taken to be complete in themselves.[99]

On his return from England, numerous guests awaited Rudolf Steiner, hundreds of people who wanted to attend the promised lectures, and the

[97] Lecture of 4 April 1916, in *Gegenwaertiges und Vergangenes* (GA 167), quoted after Wiesberger in *Zur Geschichte* (GA 265), p. 132 f. Wiesberger also says here that the two 'cognition ritual' sections of the old esoteric school were differentiated into three and six and therefore a total of nine degrees. 'For the first three degrees, the emphasis was on the rites; in the six that followed, and tradition has it that their members were few, teaching was said to have been the main activity.' (Ibid. p. 132.)

[98] Wiesberger 1997, p. 307.

[99] For the sake of completeness, it should be added that the information, assumed to derive from written notes by Ludwig Polzer-Hoditz, that Rudolf Steiner intended to limit the second class of the School to 36 and the third to 12 members, cannot be said to have been substantiated. Christoph Lindenberg considers it a falsification (Lindenberg 1990 and 1997, p. 881), as do Heinz Matile and Andreas Meister (1997). It also goes against Ita Wegman's expectation that development of the second and third classes might have avoided the First Class being over full (IW in *Nbl* of 16 Aug. 1925, p. 129), and against the words of Rudolf Steiner quoted above that the members of all three classes who would be found 'everywhere' (*The Christmas Conference*, 25 Dec. 1923; GA 260, p. 80). On the other hand Emil Leinhas and Guenther Schubert reported that the third section of Rudolf Steiner's early esoteric school had only 12 members (Wiesberger 1997, p. 23).

courses in inner development. Many of them wanted to join the School on this occasion, but were not yet sufficiently well known to Rudolf Steiner. On top of everything else he therefore conducted a vast number of interviews, now together with Ita Wegman, in many cases making a specific ceremony of them. One of the people concerned wrote: 'On 5 November 1924 I was admitted to the First Class by Rudolf Steiner. After the handshake which was also a pledge of fidelity he then made me shake the hand of Dr Wegman, co-leader of the Class, who was sitting beside him.'[100] Ita Wegman wrote: 'Admittance interviews were held in the studio. I had to stand beside Dr Steiner, and members were brought to the studio by Dr Wachsmuth. Dr Steiner put some questions to the individual asking to be admitted, and if it proved possible to admit him Dr Steiner would say the following words: "If you are willing to keep the faith with the School of Michael, let us shake hands, and also shake hands with Dr Wegman who will be leading the School of Michael with me." This was in September, shortly before Dr Steiner fell ill. Before that, admissions took place in my presence, but I had no direct part in them, and there was not the ceremonious act of the handshake.'[101]

It was only now that Rudolf Steiner spoke unreservedly of admission to the 'School of Michael', also putting more emphasis on Ita Wegman's involvement. Behind this change in procedure lies a situation the fundamentals of which emerged in Emanuel Zeylmans van Emmichoven's three-volume Ita Wegman biography, though not yet worked up in every detail historically, nor indeed sufficiently appreciated. We must therefore at this point take a look at how Rudolf Steiner's collaboration with Ita Wegman evolved over the years.[102]

---

[100] Wolfgang Moldenhauer writing to Kurt Franz David. 15 Nov. 1972. Goetheanum Archives.

[101] IW writing to Steffen on 16 March 1926, in EZ III, p. 66. Wegman also described the situation in her letter of 25 September 1925 to Toni Voelker (see Appendix 12). In Torquay on 12 and London on 24 August 1924, Rudolf Steiner said people applying for membership of the School should turn to '[Guenther] Wachsmuth and register with me through him'. (*Cosmic Christianity*, GA 240, p. 97, and *To the Members* GA 260a, p. 347.) Wachsmuth later referred to this in his attempt to see Wegman's description in relative terms (G&C, 25 April 1930, p. 74; Goetheanum Archives).

[102] See M. Gloeckler in Plato 2003. In detail, EZ I-III, and Selg 2002, 2004, 2005 a and b. Zeylmans is currently working on a fourth volume of his Wegman biography, in which a closer look will be taken at Ita Wegman's esoteric discipleship.

This touches on subjects about which Rudolf Steiner always maintained the strictest esoteric discipline, not even referring to them explicitly when meeting with the Christmas Conference Council. They must, however, be considered here in an appropriate way unless the deeper dimensions of those events are to be wholly left aside. To gain a balanced general view it will at least have to be considered that there may have been such dimensions, even if only few indications are reliably substantiated, and that in view of our present state of knowledge any attempt to gain an overall view must of necessity be incomplete and open to dispute. It may be that in the present situation of the School of Spiritual Science and in view of the challenges we now face concerning its further development, it is not so much a question of substantiated findings but rather of questions that will take us further. Below, an attempt will be made to raise some of those questions.

At branch evenings and in many study groups of the Anthroposophical Society, the tremendous, formerly strictly esoteric, lectures are again and again discussed which Rudolf Steiner gave from the Christmas Conference onwards until September 1924 on the subject of karma, the destiny situations of the anthroposophical movement. One can sense that the people who heard those lectures were meant to be encouraged to enter consciously into their own, wholly personal destinies and thus be active as a community. All the time we hear not only of historical facts evident to the physical senses but also of events and processes before birth and after death, of active forces, conflicts, harmony and dissonance in higher worlds, in the sphere of the supersensible. For today's discerning reader, two figures emerge with special clarity in these challenging and dramatic lectures, two friends whose destinies are followed through several lives when both were on earth, who are frequently connected with crucial steps in the evolution of occidental history. Could it be that these two individuals were among Rudolf Steiner's audiences at the beginning of the twentieth century? Might the initiate's descriptions—going beyond anything familiar and movingly topical to this day—have had much more immediate intentions behind them than most members of the audience would have realized? And could it be that only very few of them perceived what this was really about?

Considering these questions in a serious way, one cannot fail to be touched by the account written by Elisabeth Vreede, member of the Christmas Conference Council, in the critical situation immediately preceding the first great split in the Anthroposophical Society in October 1934, where she described a symptomatic occurrence shortly after Rudolf Steiner's death, when the orphaned Founding Council met in his former studio. It concerned those two friends. Vreede wrote that Marie Steiner asked suddenly, referring directly to a particular individual: 'Did you have this from Dr Steiner?' Ita Wegman, she writes, answered: 'Yes indeed, Frau D[octo]r.' The report continues: 'The effect was extraordinary. In the existing situation, this answer could only be seen as one to be taken very seriously. And it was taken like that. Surprise, astonishment and even a degree of emotion were there. None of the Council members present (and all of them were indeed present) showed any doubt as to the correctness of this answer in their words or attitude at the time, and in *that* situation—humanly and factually—doubt simply was not possible. Dr W[egman] then added: I can show it to you in writing, by Dr Steiner, if you wish.'

For all who were present, in the protected space of a Council still appointed by Rudolf Steiner, a direct connection was thus made to the trail-blazing karma lectures of the previous year, and this was of immediate concern to them all. No one doubted Wegman's very simple answer. 'Even Frau Steiner,' Vreede wrote, 'was taken aback in the first moment when Dr Wegman's positive reply was given in calm certainty; she hesitated for a moment—at the time I could not understand what this was about.' Apparently Marie Steiner then managed to cope with the situation with a disparaging remark 'half joking, half embarrassed'.[103]

Meanwhile we know that the written evidence offered by Ita Wegman did indeed exist. Many of the papers are still extant. Wegman was not fantasizing, as was suggested later. Yet if this may be considered to be an established fact, how can we explain it that Ita Wegman was able to communicate her deep connection with Rudolf Steiner and the extraordinary tasks arising from this, tasks to which she felt committed, to only a very few anthroposophists? This is a key issue and we will need to consider it further.

Before that, however, there is another enigma to concern us. Why did the close esoteric collaboration between Wegman and Rudolf Steiner start so late? The date of a first meeting can be said to have been in late summer in 1902. At the time Wegman was 26 years of age. She joined the

[103] Vreede 1934, p. 9 f.

Theosophical Society and attended some of Rudolf Steiner's lectures in Berlin, but only got really interested when he spoke about Goethe's *Tale*.[104] The cosmic Imaginations behind this, which were to shine out much more clearly in Rudolf Steiner's *Mystery Plays* later on, touched her, giving her an inkling. Her question as to whether it would not be 'possible to learn more of esoteric wisdom' made Rudolf Steiner invite her to an 'esoteric lesson' at Motzstrasse 17 in Berlin. 'From that moment,' Wegman was to write on looking back, 'I knew that Rudolf Steiner was my teacher, is my teacher, and will be my teacher in future.'[105] In September 1905, Rudolf Steiner admitted her to the entry stage of the Theosophical Society's Esoteric School, and in the autumn of 1908 to a higher degree.[106] At the suggestion of Marie Steiner, Wegman studied medicine in Zurich from 1906 to 1911. There, further meetings with Rudolf Steiner took place. He took the time to go on 'long walks' with her. He also visited the Wesendonck Villa, the famous Wagner residence, with her. Another crucial event for Wegman was a talk during the Theosophists' Congress in Munich in 1907. At the time she was considering the question as to whether she should go with Rudolf Steiner or stay connected with her theosophical friends in Holland who were tending in the direction of A. Besant. 'He was in a serious mood, his eyes asking questions. Not much was said between us, we understood one another very well. I simply said, feeling that he knew of things: "I am staying with you." His eyes then shone, he took my hand, gave me the sign of Michael, and told me important things which I must not repeat. A most ancient karma which existed between him and me was renewed.' Those words, written at a time fairly remote from the situation in Munich, may be partly coloured by events in the Master's final years, yet one can sense that the meeting meant much to both of them. But still the time was not ripe. Rudolf Steiner, long since aware of the destiny background to the talks with Wegman, had to go on waiting.[107] 'The implications of this meeting,' Wegman wrote, 'only became clear to me many years later.'[108]

[104] According to Lindenberg 1988 on 4 April 1904.

[105] From the draft for a lecture in February 1933, Notebook No. 42, IW Archives. Also in EZ I, page 294 f.

[106] EZ I, p. 51.

[107] R. Steiner to IW, 11 June 1924; EZ I, p. 207.

[108] EZ I, p. 296.

When she had completed her studies and been in practice for some time, Wegman ran a small private clinic in Zurich with a woman doctor who was a friend. She moved to Arlesheim in 1921, establishing the Institute of Clinical Medicine there which is today's Ita Wegman Clinic. But it took the profound experience of the night of the fire in 1922/23 to awaken a clear idea in her of her true mission. Rudolf Steiner did most impressively connect the destruction of the First Goetheanum building with the fire that had burned down the Temple of Artemis at Ephesus. Wegman had a karmic connection with that place. And a short time after this, during the conference in Penmaenmawr (Wales) in August 1923, this led to the question for her of a renewed mystery medicine. 'I would like to have the kind of medicine which existed at the time of the mysteries.'[109] This question, to which we probably owe the decisive impulse to found not only the Medical Section at the Goetheanum but also the School of Spiritual Science altogether—comparable in importance to Marie Steiner's question in November 1901, which made the anthroposophical movement into an active reality on earth[110]—made it possible for Rudolf Steiner in discussions during the conference to consider the fundamental destiny relationships which then came to revelation in the central themes of his karma lectures the following year. 'Penmaenmawr karma fully revealed,' Wegman wrote in her private papers.[111] From then on, close collaboration developed on an esoteric basis. Over the following months, Ita Wegman received special exercises and instructions for doing them from Rudolf Steiner, sometimes weekly, and above all a number of mantras. She began to live with these. Work on the introductory part of the medical 'vademecum', for which Rudolf Steiner had been hoping for a long time already, was connected with this, ultimately to be published as *Extending Practical Medicine. Fundamental Principles based on the Science of the Spirit.* In the woodwork building next to the ruins of the First Goetheanum, Rudolf Steiner would always start their work on the book with meditation and prayer. He would attend Wegman's consulting hours at the clinic in Arlesheim whenever possible to give his advice. Seventy-six such visits are recorded between October 1923 and August 1924.[112] In

[109] Notebook No. 57, IW Archives. After EZ I, p. 146.
[110] Wiesberger 1988, p. 115 ff.
[111] Notebook No. 1, IW Archives. Facsimile in EZ I, p. 319.
[112] EZ I, p. 156.

letters written in loving inwardness, Rudolf Steiner showed how much working together with Ita Wegman was a blessing to him, a gift of destiny. He began to address her by her mystery name Mysa in those letters. The polite form of address changed to the trusting, familiar one during the summer of 1924. He addressed his friend as 'disciple of Michael', the disciple 'who must walk by my side for "time and eternity" in the realms of the spiritual world'. Now the obstacles which had so far prevented closer collaboration could also be seen for what they had been. 'Your life's experiences are also karmic in origin. And anything which had to be karmically resolved beforehand, simply had to be resolved first.'[113] Even when physically apart, he felt her to be at his side. 'You are walking beside me when I lecture.'[114] 'I share in meditating your meditation and am supported by your love.'[115]

This was not, however, a purely personal relationship. Rudolf Steiner developed a way of working together with Ita Wegman which did open up completely new opportunities for insight and taking action not only for himself, opportunities which then proceeded from the sphere of intimate esoteric experience to earthly, exoteric reality and became socially productive at the Christmas Conference and the events which followed in 1924. What it was all about would emerge during Rudolf Steiner's last visit to England. The karma lectures had prepared the ground to some extent, and at the conference in Torquay, organized by D. N. Dunlop and friends and attended also by Marie Steiner and other friends from Dornach, Rudolf Steiner gave an impressive, imaginative description of scenes from around the Temple at Ephesus in pre-Christian times, where the kind of collaboration he was practising with Ita Wegman was foreshadowed in wholly different states of consciousness. 'And in those ancient days the pupil would learn from the teacher, and the teacher from the pupil. For the revelations were in spirit and soul on the one hand, and in soul and spirit on the other. A conversation which took place in this way . . . provided the most sublime insights in human togetherness, in shared human experience.'[116] A few days later Rudolf Steiner went beyond those hints and referred to the present day. He described the

[113] Rudolf Steiner to IW; 11 June 1924. IW Archives. After EZ I, p. 206.
[114] Ibid. p. 207.
[115] Rudolf Steiner to IW; 14 June 1924. IW Archives. After EZ I, p. 209.
[116] Lecture of 14 August 1924. *True and False Paths* (GA 243 [1969], p. 89).

'spiritual anatomy' that had to be developed where it would be possible to expand the medical mind to conscious apprehension of the planetary spheres and from there progress to scientific descriptions like those in the book on which he was working with Wegman. 'What matters is that it all goes through the living human being. Why? Because these things can only be retained if we do so with the powers which arise also in shared human endeavour, the powers, as it were, which people have in them from previous lives on earth, using these powers above all to retain these things.'[117] Rudolf Steiner endeavoured all his life to 'retain' the fleeting impressions of supersensible vision in suitable concepts. New abilities and possibilities for this arose for him in working together with Ita Wegman. Insight into karma is the basis for this.

Soon after this, Rudolf Steiner affirmed this insight in Dornach. This time there were a few people in the audience who had at least an inkling of what he was aiming at. 'Investigations in particular which seek the gates that lead in the right way from the physical to the spiritual human being will only give promising results if done in the right way. For the kind of work we are speaking of, one therefore uses not only the investigative powers of the present time but specifically also powers of investigation which are found when we take up the karmic threads that arise from the story of human evolution. One has to work with the powers of karma, as it were, to discover the secrets which are involved there.'[118]

In the few days which remained before Rudolf Steiner fell seriously ill, an exemplary step could be taken in developing the School of Spiritual Science. The audience on 14 September 1924 included a number of physicians attending the Christmas and Easter Courses for 'young doctors' and were also admitted, together with the young theologians of the Christian Community, to the Pastoral Medicine course. Following the Christmas Conference, these very young people, some still in the process of taking final examinations at medical school, had been introduced to the special professional esotericism of anthroposophical medicine. As Peter Selg has shown with the lively correspondence preserved in the Ita Wegman Archives, these beginners in the medical profession, full of the most sublime ideals, did initially have enormous problems not only in

[117] Lecture of 21 August 1924. *True and False Paths* (GA 243, p. 212 f.). See also Selg 2002, p. 54.

[118] Lecture of 14 Sept. 1924. *Karmic Relationships 4* (GA 238 [1974], p. 83).

harmonizing those esoteric contents, wholly new to them, with the academic subjects they were studying, but also in coming together in a spiritual life and work community of people who were geographically apart.[119] Under the influence of the lectures heard in Dornach in September, their common endeavour was now clearly reaching the level Rudolf Steiner had long been hoping for, not least probably thanks to the firm intervention of Ita Wegman who resolutely challenged two of them: 'The wisdom of Mercury wants to incarnate. Create a vessel for this!'[120] Seven of them (two more were considered to be likely candidates) were brought together as the 'esoteric core' for the Medical Section at the Goetheanum. This was the first time a group was established for a Section in the history of the School. It was done explicitly, with solemn reference to the need to relate consciously to the 'source of effective action' said to be given at the Goetheanum with the collaboration between Rudolf Steiner and Ita Wegman. A genuine feeling of belonging together was indispensable for this.[121]

We thus have a clear picture in the special field of professional ethics. Does it also throw a light on the question, not adequately answered until now, as to what Rudolf Steiner meant when he referred to Ita Wegman as 'co-leader' of the First Class? He only did so twice in the Class Lessons given until the summer, but then in every one of the seven Repeat Lessons he gave in September. It is not very probable that he was merely thinking of the function of a 'secretary', as people would often suggest later on. On several occasions, Wegman—in agreement with Rudolf Steiner—issued her own directions relating to the First Class, namely to Lili Kolisko, Ludwig Polzer, Anna Gunnarsson (see below, Chapters 6.1., 6.5, 6.11). It was very evident that Rudolf Steiner did not see her merely as a co-signatory of his announcements nor as a secretary—Guenther Wachsmuth would have been much more suitable for this—but as a fully responsible partner, initially with the right to decide on admissions and on the passing-on of School mantras, and then also in issues concerning the content and form of Class work.

This is not to say that Rudolf Steiner appointed Ita Wegman leader of the School or of the First Class in case of his death. Without his own

---

[119] Selg 2005 b.

[120] IW to H. Walter on 25 Aug. 1924. After Selg 2005 b, p. 129.

[121] *Pastoral Medicine* (GA 318 [1994], p. 165 f.). See Selg 2005 b, p. 145 f.

involvement on earth, the leadership question could only be solved by consensus among free individuals. He himself must not intervene and prejudice the necessary social process of searching for an esoteric 'harmony of hearts'. As to how Wegman would have been able to take her role of 'co-leader' forward in a new form if this 'harmony' had been achieved remains an open question.

The intensive, close collaboration between Rudolf Steiner and Ita Wegman was, of course, more than just guessed at by Marie Steiner. She suffered the pain of it dramatically in her soul. Rudolf Steiner talked with her about it. Shortly before his death he thanked her for the 'understanding' she had struggled to gain.[122] Nor did the new way of working with Ita Wegman in any way affect his loving interest in Marie Steiner's activities. Not only did he give her Section the Eurythmy as Visible Speech and Eurythmy as Visible Singing courses in 1924, and the Drama course in September of that year, and again and again act as a consultant during rehearsals. His letters show that in the last weeks before his death he cared about even the smallest detail in her work as an artist, her initiatives for the life of the Anthroposophical Society, and her personal well-being. In his will she continued to be the sole heir of his estate. How far was she, however, able to have 'understanding' for the new situation? Clearly not enough to grasp the extraordinary significance which Rudolf Steiner attached to his collaboration with Ita Wegman for the further development of his possibilities for spiritual investigation and its social consequences; nor indeed to fully appreciate the karmic preconditions for this, or the leadership in partnership which Rudolf Steiner envisaged for Section and School. The best Marie Steiner was able to do was to acknowledge the rights of Ita Wegman by speaking of separate spheres of work.[123] This did not, however, provide a secure basis for the future. Nor had by far the greater majority of Society and School members understood what it was all about. Only a few had realized, when Rudolf Steiner died, that he had entrusted Ita Wegman as 'guardian of the mantras' with

[122] Rudolf Steiner to MSt, 27 Feb. 1925. *Correspondence and Documents* (GA 262 [2002], p. 450).

[123] Characteristically she wrote in a letter to Steffen immediately after Rudolf Steiner's death: 'So the best thing will be a personal talk between Mrs Wegman and myself. I think each will be able to prove to the other that she has certain rights and also has cause not to be presumptive about them.' (MSt to Steffen, 5 April 1925. MSt 1981, p. 99.)

important tasks for the future. Over-eager admirers of Ita Wegman reinterpreted the spiritual authority she had been given into a claim to earthly leadership. The distorted images we know from Hermann Poppelbaum's memorandum of November 1934 and, even more extreme, the notorious memorandum of 1935, thus came about among the people around Marie Steiner.[124]

All these situations made themselves felt long before Rudolf Steiner's death; latent tensions, unspoken concerns and fears meant that prospects were poor for a future without the great teacher.

In view of the large number of new members, Rudolf Steiner decided on his return to Dornach in early September 1924 not to go on with the further development of the School of which he had spoken before he went away. He repeated the earlier Lessons in rapid sequence, with the same mantras but in a somewhat different order and with mostly new, much briefer elucidations. His karma lectures in July and then in England in August on the spiritual background to the anthroposophical movement gave those Lessons an even greater solemnity and the greatest intensity. Ritual elements, 'sign' and 'seal' which conclude every Class Lesson to this day, now appeared like a light shining in from the future development of the School. At the same time the conditions for admission gained their final form.[125] The seventh Repeat Lesson marked the end of this new resumption of the work. Rudolf Steiner fell ill and was unable to take the development of the School forward. Until his death, admissions were then in written form only.[126]

[124] See also Chapter 6.11 in this book. Both documents are in EZ III, p. 232 ff. and 259 ff. Zeylmans sums up the accusations against Wegman in the same volume (p. 53 ff.). He then makes a detailed critical assessment of the accusations. See also E. Vreede, W. Zeylmans, L. Polzer-Hoditz and O. Schmiedel on the subject in the same volume.

[125] Most complete version in the Second Repeat Lesson (GA 270/3, p. 45).

[126] IW to Steffen, 16 March 1926. EZ III, p. 66.

5 Developments up to the Second World War

Rudolf Steiner's early and wholly unexpected death on 30 March 1925 brought a sudden and dramatic change in the situation of the evolving School. The remaining members of the new Anthroposophical Society's Founding Council were also members of the School's Faculty and the Board of the Goetheanum Building Association.[127] The 'statutes' had made provision for Rudolf Steiner appointing his 'possible successor' (§ 7). This had not happened. The orphaned Founding Council found themselves wholly dependent on their own judgement. Above all they had to clarify how leadership of the School, until then almost exclusively based on Rudolf Steiner's decisions, should be taken forward, separate from the very different leadership and decision structures of the Anthroposophical Society. Now, without Rudolf Steiner's advice on which they had come to depend, the finding of clear, practicable solutions to the leadership question depended above all on how consensus could be reached in both Council and Faculty. At the Christmas Conference, Rudolf Steiner had brought together a group of people from widely differing spheres of destiny and activity who now faced this unexpected task. They had had just over a year to get to know each other more fully and test their capacities for cooperation. Would they now manage to cope with one another without their great teacher and helper and develop competence in unified leadership?

Initially, the sympathy which came to the remaining five Council members of the Anthroposophical Society from the 'periphery' was unanimous. People were everywhere full of hope and trust that the developmental processes initiated at the Christmas Conference in 1923/24 could be taken forward to good purpose by the competent individuals chosen by Rudolf Steiner. There was, however, also an expectation connected with this of which only very few people were really aware, an expectation bound to put those involved under calamitous pressure if a crisis were to arise. In the last year of his work, Rudolf Steiner had again and again referred to the new Council as 'esoteric'. Because of his active

[127] For the different functions this involved, see EZ III, p. 19 ff.

involvement, the counsel and help flowing directly from the spirit world—and this is what the term signified—had been a shared reality. An authority justified by his life's work as well as his character and approach to his work gave his decisions a certainty that reconciled all life's contradictions and put people's minds at rest. Many of the members, probably the great majority, now expected the Council appointed by Rudolf Steiner to continue to be 'esoteric'—guided from the spirit world, working not in the way of a conventional association but out of 'genuine, true esotericism' of the kind practised so far in the School, sustained by personal connections of a living kind with members all over the world, and above all being of one mind in the harmony of hearts that had been spoken of so insistently at the Christmas Conference. Only a body of this kind could be expected to have the leadership quality on which the anthroposophical movement was so dependent at that time. Doubts in the 'esoteric' nature of the Council would therefore only too easily be felt to be a threat to the movement's existence. The image of the 'esoteric Council' seemed inviolable. What would happen, however, if this Council were not immediately able to achieve unanimity? If it had to cope with differences of opinion? Surely in that case the view that the Council continued to be 'esoteric' would prove to be mere assertion or dogma without solid foundation? Everyone was entitled to hope that the Council would receive inspiration from the spiritual world—at times at least, or at special moments. Could such a hope, however, be said to justify a lasting claim to authority?

Three particular views were dominant in the difficulties which arose after Rudolf Steiner's death in this respect. One was that Rudolf Steiner's words continued to be valid and that the individuals he called to serve on the Council were an 'esoteric' body in the sense of a 'spiritual succession' even though he was no longer on earth. This view arose from a sense of tradition like that connected with the 'apostolic succession' in the ordination of clergy—which Rudolf Steiner himself also fully respected in the religious context. The second view was based on the conviction that Rudolf Steiner was continuing to give impulses and to guide the group he had appointed even after crossing the threshold of death. The third asked for a fundamental review, circumstances having changed completely. It did not exclude the continued influence of the great teacher, now from the spirit world, but people did not feel that any claim could be based on this.

When open controversy first arose, Emil Leinhas, who had worked for many years with Rudolf Steiner and was deeply committed, put the problem in simple words: 'The statement that Rudolf Steiner is working through the Council in Dornach is dogma and I therefore do not accept it. (As to the statement that it is possible for Rudolf Steiner to work through the Council as a whole, I accept this as little as I would accept the statement that rain is possible the day after tomorrow.) The question of whether and how and through whom Rudolf Steiner is working, can only be met with one thing: profound silence.'[128] Few thought like this, however. And this meant that under the pressure of hidden expectations there was no possibility for open, reflective discussion on the problem which had arisen with Rudolf Steiner's death, as to whether the Council—and, things being as they were, also the leadership of the School—might still be considered to be 'esoteric'.

The newsletter brought a provisional declaration that the Council considered it to be its duty to 'continue in its functions and go on working in the spirit of Rudolf Steiner, knowing him to be always in their midst, as their guide.'[129] With regard to the continuance of the School, it merely said that applications for admission to the First Class should be sent to 'Dr I. Wegman, the Secretary'. Unfortunately we do not know so far if the Council or the faculty of the School had other, fuller discussions, searching for solutions, responsibility for which would be shared. The existing documents suggest rather the opposite. Developments during the year after Rudolf Steiner's death were thus driven initially by spontaneous decisions and actions which would only too quickly end in dissension and strife. Reference to the 'esoteric Council' was common until the 1930s,

[128] Open reply to Dr Rittelmeyer and all who are willing to hear. Christmas 1926 (in German), p. 5. Goetheanum Archives. Concerning further discussion of the concept 'esoteric Council', see esp. J. v. Grone's letter to Steffen, 10 Dec. 1926; the 'proclamation' in Kolisko 1961, p. 158 ff.; and MSt: Gespensterschau (25 Feb. 1927), Goetheanum Archives; also the verdicts of H. E. Lauer and K. Ingeroe at G&C on 25 Apr. 1930, pp. 54 and 64 ff., Goetheanum Archives.

[129] *Nbl.* of 3 May 1925. Elisabeth Vreede wrote later that the declaration had been requested by Guenther Wachsmuth, but had proved difficult to write. 'Steffen did not want to be seen as chairman and we kept asking him again and again; Dr Wachsmuth had used the handsome phrase "We consider Rudolf Steiner to be and remain our first chairman", which Marie Steiner considered a mystic eccentricity, and it was changed to the effect that we continue to know him to be among us as our guide.' (Vreede 1934, p. 7.)

and partly beyond, though it had soon become an empty phrase.[130] Mutual reproaches led to a severe crisis as early as the winter of 1925/26, which spread far among the membership. Protracted discussions—a relieved Steffen hailed them as effective 'catharsis' in the newsletter[131]—brought only passing and superficial relief. Inexorably, a disastrous chain started of 'evolving cliques', as Rudolf Steiner would have called it, driven and made more acute by concerns for the future and need for authority in smaller and larger groups of members; alliances kept changing, misunderstandings and hurtful words determined the destiny of the anthroposophical movement until the end of the twentieth century. It is neither possible nor necessary to go into detail about this in the present context. Its only relevance to our present subject is the effect on the way in which work in the School of Spiritual Science, particularly the First Class, developed.

Another problem which remained equally covert at first was the tension between Marie Steiner and Ita Wegman. The destiny constellations from which the problem arose have been considered in the last chapter. Marie Steiner was closely connected with the founder of anthroposophy, having been his closest collaborator in the early years of the twentieth century, his soul mate and wife. At that time, her question about the need 'to call into life a spiritual movement in Europe' had initiated the whole of his work for the anthroposophical movement.[132] He had entrusted his estate to her alone. Her position had been outstanding in the days of the early esotericism, and she had brought new life to speech art and drama and played a major role in the development of eurythmy. She was held in the highest regard in the whole anthroposophical movement. Rudolf Steiner's collaboration with Ita Wegman had not put any of this in question, but it did present it in a different light. Marie Steiner, for three decades the closest confidante of the initiate, had to put up with the fact

[130] Even in post-war times, the idea of the continuing 'esoteric Council' persisted here and there. Emil Leinhas wrote in evident bitterness: 'We have an "esoteric Council". Eventually it consists of three people, with the chairman publicly declaring that he is no longer able to work with one of them. On 24 June this year it has been 4, spelled out "four", years since this "esoteric Council" last met.' (*Aus meinem Dornacher Tagebuch.* Private publication. Spring 1947. Goetheanum Archives.)

[131] Nbl. of 28 Mar. 1926, p. 56.

[132] Wiesberger 1988, p. 116 f.

that another individual was then evidently equally close to him, opening up possibilities for his work that went far beyond anything he had endeavoured to do until then. This affected not only her private sphere but touched also on her position in the anthroposophical movement, her dignity. As Rudolf Steiner's letter of February 1925 shows, she honestly tried to meet the difficult new situation with understanding. For several weeks after Rudolf Steiner's death she looked for ways of fruitful collaboration with a destiny partner whom she found so hard to bear, but did not achieve a lasting result.

Ita Wegman was inwardly in a very different situation. Her esoteric talks with Rudolf Steiner—she was the only one with whom he could have them in this form—gave her an overwhelming awareness of a sacred spiritual mission. She could hope that the other members of the 'esoteric Council' might develop an inner relationship to the spiritual teacher who was now working from the other side of the threshold, one that would be of a similar kind to the one she continued to feel with all her soul to be real. 'Nothing has changed, really,' she still said to Martin Muench in Berlin in October 1925 when he asked if her 'involvement in the admission of Class members' by Rudolf Steiner had 'testamentary character'.[133] This does not have to mean that she was referring to an official appointment, as was later suggested. The answer came from the fullness of her heart, in intuitive certainty of being in harmony with Rudolf Steiner's intentions. At first she was therefore confidently expecting that the 'esoteric' Council, too, would continue to work in a common spirit. In her essay in the newsletter on 26 April 1925, published wholly on her own responsibility, with no consultation with her colleagues on the Council, she went so far as to consider Rudolf Steiner still the 'first chairman'. She cannot have been unaware that legally this view was untenable, but robustly averred the hoped-for unity of the Council in this way. She wrote: 'To us, whom he had chosen to be the Council, it was clear that we must stand firm; it was clear to us that if we intended to take seriously what the master had conveyed to us from the world of the spirit, it was a sacred duty to stay gathered around him so that he can work among us and in us, even though physically he is no longer among us. This was the mood that lived in us. And so we do still regard Rudolf Steiner as the first chairman in the midst of our Council, and see all

[133] M. Muench to Steffen, 14 Feb. 1926. Goetheanum Archives.

members of the Council in the functions to which Rudolf Steiner appointed them.'[134]

In her newsletter articles, soon so greatly in dispute, in which she followed Rudolf Steiner in starting with the formula 'To the members', she stood energetically for the urgent tasks of the immediate future which could be taken on with courage on the basis of this unity. She was far from wishing to claim sole leadership of the School in this, rightly insisting that she had always only signed 'on behalf of' the leadership, the whole 'esoteric' Council, which to her mind had the leadership function. Her way of handling admission was also in accord with this—at least for the time being.[135] All that mattered to her were the things which now had to be done together. The Goetheanum building which was then being built was a 'stronghold of Michael' to her.[136] A 'Michaelic stream' wants to 'come into its own ... in earth evolution through anthroposophy'. Human intelligence must be saved. 'A mighty image, illumined by the new Michaelic impulses, must arise out of all the knowledge of the spirit in anthroposophy. It must be lifted out of sectarian activity to be the all-encompassing world-activity which is always connected with Michael. There must be no isolated islands in the Anthroposophical Society where anthroposophy may well be taught yet people forget to stress that this knowledge is filled with the power of Michaelic impulses.'[137]

Surely the young doctors had been an example of the kind of result which could be achieved with the trust in the Goetheanum which Rudolf Steiner had hoped for and considered absolutely essential? Did not Willem Zeylmans in Holland, Norbert Glas in Vienna and the young physicians in Arlesheim gain a remarkable increase in powers for their work in the outside world because of the esoteric work relationship with their Section leader? Could one not also expect something similar from the remaining members of the 'esoteric Council'—energetic esoteric work with the mantric wisdom entrusted to them, unreserved trust in one another and in

[134] *Nbl.* of 24 Apr. 1925, Appendix 8.

[135] Thus to Marna Engels on 5 May 1925: 'I will present your application for membership of the First Class to the Council and you will hear more in due course' (IW Archives). It had nothing to do with Wegman's fundamental attitude that W. J. Stein and Kolisko asked Albert Steffen in June 1925 to acknowledge her as sole leader of the School (see Appendix 10).

[136] *Nbl.* of 3 May 1925, p. 70.

[137] *Nbl.* of 17 May 1925, p. 79.

her as 'co-leader' of the Section, based on a clear idea of karmic connections, decisive actions in the world also for anthroposophy as such?

It must have been difficult for Ita Wegman to understand why she met with resistance. Why was she unable to gain the hearts of the members of the Anthroposophical Society and the School for her sincere impulses? Did she have to fight the inertia in human hearts, as Rudolf Steiner had also found so often, or insurmountable difficulties of the general situation at the time? Or did the problems which were steadily growing in 1925 also have something to do with her way of working? Elisabeth Vreede was to recall ten years later that her feeling about the essay in the newsletter of 26 April had been that it was severely 'biased'. 'Marie Steiner,' she wrote, 'must feel excluded from the Council by these words, however true they may fundamentally be, and indeed she must literally feel that she has been ridden over roughshod with regard to her decision to stay on the Council when her attempts to make changes had failed. With the essay she published *on her own*, with no prior discussion in Council, Dr W[egman] had, as it were, made herself the representative and speaker also for the other members, though these did not know the essay in detail.'[138] There are various reports that Wegman did not always find it easy to perceive the impression she made on others. Oskar Schmiedel who worked with her in a committed way wrote that it took a talk of several hours with Rudolf Steiner to persuade him not to give up collaboration with her.[139] Emanuel Zeylmans, her biographer, was critical of her 'vague way of putting things, statements that had not been thought through and lack of form in other ways,' a tendency to get into a rage, and an authoritarian leadership style.[140] All these character traits are balanced out by the way in which she would always stand up for the faults and failings of her staff, her extensive social commitment, and her certainty about the future ('I am for moving ahead!'[141]). On the other hand we cannot overlook an almost naive blindness to certain social situations. Rudolf Steiner had formulated the Motto of Social Ethics for Edith Maryon: 'Healing only comes when, / in the mirror of the human soul / we have the image of the whole community; and when in the community / there lives the strength of each

[138] Vreede 1934.

[139] O. Schmiedel in EZ III, p. 434 ff.

[140] EZ III, p. 26.

[141] Selg 2002.

individual soul.'[142] Ita Wegman was active with the whole strength of her great soul in the community of the 'esoteric Council' and the Anthroposophical Society; what she found difficult was to let the *image* of the community arise in the mirror of this soul.

Thus she caused serious discomfort in the Anthroposophical Society with her 'To the members' letters. Later attempts at justification, however convincing in themselves, did not mend matters.[143] Above all many members got irritated by the powerful subject matter of her essays. Members resident in Dornach and a few others who had attended the lectures in September 1924 may have realized that they had heard these things from Rudolf Steiner—about the karma of different anthroposophical streams and their opponents, about the secrets relating to Arthur and to the Grail, about shared experiences in the supersensible sphere before their incarnation, and about the Michaelic mysteries. Written records of those lectures had by then only been passed on to a few chosen individuals. It would be a long time before they became the subject of work in branches of the Society, taken as a matter of course, as they are today.[144] For by far the largest part of the membership, the subject matter presented by Ita Wegman was completely new. Very few people had realized that Rudolf Steiner was inviting his listeners to gain self-knowledge and consciously take hold of their common karmic impulses. Others tended more to suspect that Wegman was with much phantasy presenting a puffed-up private mythology to pursue her personal intentions, wanting to gain followers and thus endangering the development of the united will that was so urgently needed in the 'esoteric' Council. During that summer, rumours spread that she was making special claims by referring to earlier incarnations,[145] and thus her honest efforts fell into discredit, and her enthusiastic impulse was poisoned.[146] Ita Wegman ended her great endeavour to make the contents

---

[142] *Truth-Wrought Words*.

[143] *Nbl.* of 28 June and 19 July 1925.

[144] As J. E. Zeylmans van Emmichoven discovered, there are ten passages in Wegman's essays where she used material from mantras which Rudolf Steiner had entrusted to her personally in the last year of his life (EZ II, p. 119).

[145] EZ III, p. 77 f.

[146] Marie Steiner probably helped quite a bit to deepen the distrust by making diffuse allusions in some of her items in the newsletter in the late autumn of 1925 and after the disputes in the spring of 1926. (*Nbl.* of 11 and 25 Oct. and 8 Nov. 1925 and of 28 Mar. 1926; see also EZ III, p. 52 f.)

of Rudolf Steiner's last karma lectures known to the members of the Anthroposophical Society and thus encourage them to become active together, with an intimate, almost lyrical look at the historical events surrounding the Artemis Temple at Ephesus, a subject Rudolf Steiner had touched on in his Torquay lectures the year before.[147] It appears that she included some things not only from the records on the lectures but also from personal talks with the great teacher, and perhaps also a few impressions of her own from an earlier life. After this she published only reports in the newsletter, mainly on the work in her Section. She did, however, definitely continue in her role as Secretary to the Council and hence the Faculty of the School. She saw to it that applications for admission—again and again directed to other Council members—came to her, took care that the Society offices in the different countries received lists of Class members, and was responsible for the relevant correspondence.[148]

Ita Wegman must have felt deep dismay as the year 1925 progressed and she realized that many members of the Anthroposophical Society, including highly respected and important ones, could not relate to her impulses, and that others, who were her champions, had not grasped the very heart of her concerns. Meanwhile the differences between herself and Marie Steiner could no longer be bridged. Even in the early weeks following Rudolf Steiner's death all efforts to achieve mutual understanding and collaboration, made on both sides, had come to nothing, not least due to the oppositional activities of adherents on either side. The way this happened is not without significance for developments relating to the First Class. Let us therefore take another look at the critical period of transition in the early summer of 1925.

From the historical distance we have gained today, two traits of the two significant female figures shine out—Ita Wegman's courageous confidence concerning the future of the anthroposophical cause, and Marie Steiner's sober clarity in assessing the new situation which had arisen, though she also had a sense of overwhelming tragedy.[149]

---

[147] *Nbl.* of 25 Oct. 1925.

[148] IW to J. v. Grone, 20 Nov. 1925. IW Archives. Appendix 13.

[149] In his reflections on the 'esoteric archetype of the Founding Council' Sergei Prokofieff gives a lively description of the different characters of the members of Council. In the terms of Rudolf Steiner's words in Torquay (21 Aug. 1924, GA 243) he characterized Marie Steiner as representative of the Moon and Ita Wegman as representative of the Saturn way to the Sun sphere (Prokofieff 2002, p. 380 ff.).

A document symptomatic of this sobriety may be seen in the important letter which Marie Steiner wrote to Eugen Kolisko immediately after the deeply upsetting event of Rudolf Steiner's death.[150] First she firmly said that the Council was not continuing in the way Rudolf Steiner had envisaged: 'I have clearly perceived that the way it is now, our Council has been orphaned in its childhood and is a nothing.' She herself wanted to withdraw from this body and devote herself to her Section work. Maria Roeschl, leader of the Youth Section, was to join the Council in her stead. Eugen Kolisko was to take first chair. Leadership of the School would be best taken on by Lili Kolisko. The same day Marie Steiner wrote in a similar vein to Albert Steffen, saying she proposed that Maria Roeschl be elected to the Council in her stead, and then: 'It has pleased me greatly to have discovered a way in which you [Steffen] can be retained on Council and at the same time have some of the load taken off you. This would be if Kolisko were to come and work in Dornach and be first chair. He is able to speak, to be firm, to lead; he has shown himself to be vigorous and experienced. He has penetrated deeply into the history of the [Anthroposophical] Society; he is subtle and tactful. Thus he could be a bulwark for you, and if you do not gain this we'll all be lost. He is the only one and will therefore do it. The Research Institute was due to be attached to Dornach anyway and could therefore be moved. Mrs Kolisko's valuable strength would also be urgently needed here.'[151]

Initially one may be inclined to take these two letters as a spontaneous reaction to the tragic events of the preceding days that need not be taken too seriously. Those events had been her late arrival at the deathbed, the funeral the day before [she wrote], and above all the ugly dispute in the car from Basel to the Goetheanum over the proper place for the urn.[152] Considering this in more detail we can with good reason see it rather as evidence of extreme presence in mind and spirit

[150] MSt to E. Kolisko, 4 Apr. 1925. In Kolisko 1961 p. 104 f. Also in Marie Steiner 1981, p. 92 f. See Appendix 5.

[151] MSt to Steffen on 4 April 1925. Goetheanum Archives. The letter is erroneously dated 4 March. Similar formulations in Notebook No. 20, Lit. Estate Archives, here in Appendix 6.

[152] Emil Leinhas's summing up of these events (MSt 1981, p. 89 ff.) has since been greatly added to and made more complete by Heinz Matile (2003) using Albert Steffen's diary entries. Further information in Vreede 1934.

that was surprisingly appropriate to the situation. In the significant letter he wrote to Marie Steiner on 27 February 1925, a few weeks before his death, Rudolf Steiner had once more lovingly confirmed the deep connection with his life partner, also referring to a particular quality in her which he had come to appreciate in the years of close collaboration: 'To feel and think together in forming a judgement—this I can *only* do with you.'[153] He wrote these words on his sickbed in the studio where Ita Wegman was looking after him, possibly in her presence. If we take the way he put it seriously, we must after all suspect that he was referring to a quality of soul which he did not find in that form in his medical friend. Surely these important words lead us to see the letters which Marie Steiner wrote the morning after the funeral as an expression of greatest competence in making a judgement. Might it not be the case that the events had shaken her so deeply that she was receptive to ideas that were absolutely to the point, even if initially they went against the thoughts and feelings of the figures concerned?

Eugen Kolisko was not only an established medical practitioner and active Waldorf teacher, a productive writer, but one of the most outstanding representatives of anthroposophy in the public domain—just consider how courageously he spoke up for Rudolf Steiner's impulses at the West-East Congress in Vienna. He was among the first seven members of the esoteric 'core' of the Medical Section, and a close confidant of Ita Wegman. At the same time he had Marie Steiner's full respect, which is remarkable in view of his relatively young age, as is evident from her letter to him. Almost more than anyone else, he would have been in a position to mediate between them with tact. Lili Kolisko had worked closely together with Rudolf Steiner for many years in the field of science and he had on many occasions praised the spiritual decisiveness in her research projects. She had been the only one to be specially given the task by him to read Class Lessons, and had proved her worth in this. Maria Roeschl had been called to the Faculty of the School by Rudolf Steiner to lead the Youth Section, and was already in touch with the Council members through her work. In historical retrospect, Marie Steiner's suggestions for the new assignment of roles on the Council appear remarkably astute. This also applies to her assessment of Albert Steffen's situation, for she foresaw unbearable burdens for him and

---

[153] *Correspondence and Documents.*

wanted to protect him from these.[154] Developments in the years that followed proved her right especially on this point, regrettably so. She was also objective and accurate concerning her own capabilities. Selflessly working on administrative tasks from the beginning of the century, to the detriment of her own work as an artist, and completely overburdened, she could now have concentrated wholly on the leadership function in her Section, largely avoiding the problems of communication and decision-making which were evidently on the horizon. The possibility cannot be ruled out that if her surprising suggestions had been taken up unanimously, they could have led to relatively calm, constructive further development work.[155]

In another letter to Steffen, Marie Steiner added the thought that with Kolisko not taking sides it might be possible to neutralize, with his help, the above-mentioned doubtful notion of Rudolf Steiner continuing to act through the 'esoteric Council'. She would only, she wrote, stay on the Council 'if truth prevails and not cliquism and surprise attacks, a strictly serious approach and no sentimental comedy. This will only be achieved if apart from the other reasons which I have given, a non-partisan individual like Kolisko joins the Council, and people do not address themselves to a first chair who is a spirit seen by each individual according to their own mind and spirit'.[156]

Although his wife and Elisabeth Vreede were to deny this many years later, Eugen Kolisko was certainly prepared initially to take up Marie Steiner's suggestion, on the condition, however, that this had the unanimous support of the other Council members.[157] Once it became

[154] 'And for the most subtle spiritual flow there is only Steffen now. We must protect him from the brutal outside world.' (MSt to E. Kolisko, 4 [April.] 1925. In MSt 1981, p. 92).

[155] Emanuel Zeylmans van Emmichoven, Ita Wegman's biographer (EZ III, p. 145 f.), is also inclined to think this, wholly in accord with Rudolf Steiner's suggestion that historical studies should also include possible developments that did not come to realization in the course of events (GA 181, 1979, p. 76). Modern historians here speak of 'counterfactual scenarios' (Ferguson 1997 and 1999).

[156] MSt to Steffen, 5 Apr. 1925. Goetheanum Archives.

[157] Albert Steffen wrote in his diary on 5 Apr. 1925: 'He [Kolisko] says he would only join if the Council was unanimous in accepting this.' (Archives of Albert Steffen Foundation.) See also MSt 1981, p. 109, about 'the condition set by Dr Kolisko', and the note: 'At the time K[olisko] said he would take the chair if the whole Council agreed to this.' (Notebook No. 20, Lit. Estate Archives.)

clear that such unanimity could not be achieved, the idea of the need for the 'esoteric Council' to continue, later presented as the sole motif by Lili Kolisko, gained the upper hand.

It was probably due to fears that Marie Steiner's withdrawal from work on the Council would cause considerable concern to the majority of Anthroposophical Society members that Albert Steffen and then also the other members of Council—with the exception of Ita Wegman who, as we have seen, had quite different reasons for wanting to see the continued existence of the 'esoteric Council'—took fright and rejected Marie Steiner's proposal. Steffen replied the same day that this proposal was 'quite impossible to adopt'. 'The evident intention of Dr Steiner' as regards the composition of the Council must be met. 'When in obedience to your request I presented your proposal to the people on the Council, it was said to be unthinkable even before I gave my own opinion. We beg you to desist.'[158]

This massive vote, given by all other members of Council together, ultimately meant that Marie Steiner continued formally on Council but nevertheless pursued her plan of working mainly for her Section and the estate. In the months that followed she would thus be absent again and again from Council meetings, for reasons of health or overwork, and this led to constant problems of communication, misunderstandings and accordingly efforts at justification, and this did much to continue and aggravate the dissension of the early days after Rudolf Steiner's death.

Marie Steiner stuck to her idea of getting the two Koliskos to come to Dornach for a remarkably long time. As a result, a second opportunity arose to find a way out of a situation that had by then gone seriously awry. On 12 April she had a talk with Ita Wegman and Albert Steffen about the continuance of the First Class. Initially she repeated her suggestion of 4 April that Lili Kolisko, who had shown her worth in Stuttgart, be entrusted with giving the Class Lessons for which members were feeling such a pressing need. Ita Wegman felt quite unable to agree to this. She was, however, looking for a feasible way out and suggested a kind of division of labour: She could surely read the Lesson texts, and Marie Steiner speak the mantras. Steffen felt that this made sense. It would be 'a nice symbol', he said, of harmonious collaboration before the eyes of the members. Marie Steiner did not want to accept this proposal immediately

[158] Steffen to MSt, 4 Apr. 1925. In Marie Steiner 1981, p. 93 f.

but also did not reject it completely. She asked for time to think it over.[159] Two weeks later Wegman's essay, which we considered above, appeared in the newsletter, which, as we saw, made Marie Steiner feel that she had been completely ignored. Her letters of 4 April to Kolisko and Steffen seemed now as if they had never been written, her objections to the dubious notion of Rudolf Steiner continuing to be active as first chair on the Council considered irrelevant. She did not refer again to the suggested compromise for resuming Class Lessons. Yet it appears that she continued to adhere to her proposal to change the composition of the Council. It was only by the end of May that she finally let go of the idea that Eugen and Lili Kolisko should join the work in Dornach.[160]

It is highly probable that what tipped the scales was the attempt made by Walter Johannes Stein and the two Koliskos, unacceptable to her in both form and content, to convince her that Rudolf Steiner had intended Ita Wegman to take on the leadership of the Society and the School. The way in which this came about clearly shows that when the leading individuals could not reach agreement, their followers on both sides took the initiative. With the situation seeming more threatening to them than it truly was at the time, they let themselves be carried away and took precipitate action.[161]

Wegman's essay in the newsletter of 26 April in which she showed that problematic confidence was then followed on 17 May 1925 by her first letter 'To the members' with additional guiding principles (leading thoughts). This may have been taken note of in Stuttgart on the day preceding publication. Shortly before this, Johanna Countess Keyserlingk, staying in Dornach at the time, had become convinced that

[159] Steffen wrote in his diary: 'Meeting of Marie Steiner, Dr Wegman and myself about the Class Lesson. Marie Steiner suggested Mrs Kolisko. This hurt Dr Wegman. It is actually not possible. People should indeed come together around the Council. Finally Dr Wegman said she'd leave the mantras to Marie Steiner, whilst she herself would make reading the Lessons her business. I added: it would be a nice symbol. But Marie Steiner asked for time to reflect. She was afraid that it would lead to a spiritual stillbirth.' (12 Apr. 1925. Albert Steffen Foundation Archives.)

[160] MSt to Steffen, 28 May 1925. In Marie Steiner 1981, p. 107.

[161] What follows is based on Kolisko 1961, p. 107 f.; MSt 1981, p. 108 ff.; Vreede 1934; J. v. Grone's report on events in Stuttgart on 18 May 1925, in EZ III, p. 161 ff.; MSt to E. Pfeiffer, 11 Mar. and 5 Dec. 1948, Lit. Estates Archives; Phoebe Colazza to MSt, 14 May and 9 June 1948, Lit. Estate Archives.

Marie Steiner's position in Germany needed to be strengthened. She induced Count Keyserlingk in Koberwitz to send a telegram to Stuttgart in which he suggested that Marie Steiner, who did not know of this, be offered the honorary presidency of the Anthroposophical Society in Germany. As agreed with the Countess, Mieta Waller-Pyle, friend and companion of Marie Steiner for many years, went to Stuttgart to support the initiative. The telegram arrived in Stuttgart on 17 May. Carl Unger considered it necessary to make the proposal known immediately to all branch leaders in Germany, also by telegram. Juergen von Grone, Walter Johannes Stein and Eugen Kolisko rejected the idea. Kolisko was upset because Unger had made absolutely no reference to Ita Wegman's important letter to members at the branch evening, whilst he himself had spoken about it for two hours. 'It is flowing! It is flowing!' he is said to have called out, according to Marie Steiner's critical report. Eugen and Lili Kolisko and Walter Johannes Stein probably went to Dornach immediately on Monday, 18 May, to convince Marie Steiner of Ita Wegman's justifiable claim to leadership. They talked for five hours the next morning.[162] The sources offer no information on detail. Nor do we know if the spontaneous visit had been discussed with Ita Wegman beforehand. This is not very likely. There is no authentic evidence that Wegman ever claimed to have been appointed sole leader of the School by Rudolf Steiner. As we have seen, she assumed that even with the Master no longer physically present, the 'esoteric Council' would be of one mind with her; at least she had trustfully hoped that it would be. Nor did she ever refer to the intimate talks with Rudolf Steiner concerning their shared karma. It would never have occurred to her to base claims to power on this. (When English friends later suggested she make use of notes relating to this, she firmly rejected doing such a thing.)[163] She thus had no occasion, really, to put Marie Steiner under pressure.

This is, however, exactly what those three young visitors did on that calamitous morning. We may assume that they, or at least Walter

[162] According to Colazza, who recalled this more than 20 years later, they only talked in June. This is, however, contradicted by Marie Steiner's letter of 28 May to Steffen in which she unequivocally broke with the Koliskos. Steffen's diary entry of 21/22 May (see below) and L. Kolisko's statement that the rumour of the offer of that honorary presidency had been the cause for the trip to Dornach, also suggest a date following close on 17 May.

[163] Selg 2005, p. 161.

Johannes Stein as the most passionate among them, argued their case in a way similar to the one he and Eugen Kolisko used a good two weeks later with Albert Steffen, which was after Wegman's first Dornach Class Lesson. Steffen carefully noted Stein's and Kolisko's key formulations in that talk which followed so closely in time, keeping them separate from his own comments: that Wegman 'was leader not as Secretary, but was the effective esoteric leader', that authorization to give Class Lessons could only come from her, 'and not from the Council', and that because she conducted the School of Michael, she was also 'the spiritual leader of the Society' (see Appendix 10). The same or very similar formulations are likely also to have played a key role in the talk with Marie Steiner. Stein and Kolisko felt they had to take definitive action because the general situation appeared to be getting more and more critical, and especially because of Count Keyserlingk's intervention, whom Carl Unger had tried to support in such a spectacular way. They did not realize that they must inevitably scotch Ita Wegman's hope for a 'harmony of hearts' in the 'esoteric Council' that would hold promise for the future.[164] Stein's attempt to legitimize his ideas by referring to the karmic links between Rudolf Steiner and Ita Wegman probably only played a secondary role. 'This does not impress me in the least,' Marie Steiner later said her words had been. Yet she did feel very much under pressure from the enthusiasm and zealousness of her three visitors. In tears, she asked Lili Kolisko once more to take on giving the Class Lessons in Dornach. (It is possible that by this time it had already been agreed in Council that Wegman should read a first Class Lesson in Paris and then also do so in Dornach. We will go into this later.) Mutual understanding was not achieved.

Marie Steiner wrote a 'personal communication' to the members of the Anthroposophical Society, dating the final version 19 May, the most probable date for the talk with her visitors from Stuttgart.[165] She wrote, referring to the decision she had made on 4 April: 'It is not my intention to take an immediate, active part in Society leadership. Younger people are available for this.' Her plan was to concentrate on work in her Section

[164] In the draft for a letter to Marie Steiner at a much later date, W. J. Stein regretted his thoughtlessness: 'We somehow wanted to achieve something which only Rudolf Steiner's wisdom and goodness could bring to realization.' (30 Mar. 1948. In MSt 1981, p. 142.)

[165] She had been working on a draft on the days preceding the visit. The item was published in the newsletter of 31 May.

and on taking care of Rudolf Steiner's literary estate. She did not accept the honorary presidency offered to her. (In a diary entry of 21/22 May[166] Albert Steffen called this decision a 'moral victory for Marie Steiner'.) In the days that followed, probably also under pressure from a further 'To the members' essay by Wegman in the newsletter of 24 May, which she felt to be 'demagogic', the idea that the whole was a plot grew ever stronger in her mind, a clever conspiracy of the Stuttgart 'super-council', as she now put it. The further talk among Council members on the karmic links mooted by W. J. Stein, reported by Elisabeth Vreede who thought it took place at the 'end of May', no doubt increased the feeling. At the end of May she therefore finally dissociated herself from the two Koliskos.

Anything she said and wrote over the following months turned more and more into distorted, emotionally highly charged stereotypes which prevented any unbiased perception of efforts and developments on the opposite side. The capacity for objective judgement which Rudolf Steiner had characterized so lovingly and which had shown itself so impressively only a few weeks earlier became more and more obscured. In the light of modern conflict studies, a level of discord had been reached which could not be undone without third-party help.[167] Subsequent events seem to have been inexorable.

In December 1925, after much hesitation, Albert Steffen took office as first chair of the Anthroposophical Society to meet the requirements of Swiss law governing associations. He explicitly stated that this did not mean he was also taking on leadership of the School of Spiritual Science, 'for this is made up of its Sections. There each must be responsible for himself.'[168] This did nevertheless raise the issue of the School's leadership again.

In January 1926, Wegman tried once more to get consensus by proposing that in addition to the 'School of Michael', to which she continued to feel Rudolf Steiner had appointed her, Marie Steiner could bring the esotericism of the early years to life again. 'There would be immediate

---

[166] Albert Steffen Foundation Archives.

[167] According to F. Glasl, this is the 'demonized zone' of conflict escalation (Glasl 1990, p. 284).

[168] Preliminary meeting for G&C on 29 Dec. 1925, quoted from I. Werbeck, *Zur Krise in der Anthroposophischen Gesellschaft*. Private printing, Hamburg 1927, p. 4.

peace if she were to gather all those around her again who were involved at the time, and also those whom she would wish to have with her as well. The whole Society would immediately be firmly united if the esotericism which flowered in the past and the intended aim of the School of Michael can exist peacefully side by side, mutually supportive and helping each other bear fruit.'[169] Yet soon, in early February, she unreservedly acknowledged Albert Steffen as leader of the School. At the turbulent meeting of Class members in Dornach on 7 February 1926, where she found herself confronted with massive reproaches, she said: 'I would like to say clearly and definitely that I fully acknowledge Mr Steffen in his function as first chair of the Society, with all his rights and responsibilities, and that I consider it a matter of course that he will from now on lead the School of Michael and also bear all responsibility for it.'[170] In accord with this she—initially—passed all applications for membership on to Steffen.[171] From April onwards, the blue membership cards of the School were signed by Albert Steffen, Marie Steiner and Ita Wegman together as 'the members of the Council who give the Class Lessons'.[172]

If we take a closer look at the dramatic course of events, we can see how the new form of Class Lessons evolved. Ita Wegman, clearly unhappy at not having been consulted when the programme for the first Easter conference to be held at the Goetheanum after Rudolf Steiner's death was planned, complained to Albert Steffen that unlike the year before, no provision had been made for a Class Lesson. 'The members', she wrote, 'expected this; it would have been perfectly possible to read one of Rudolf Steiner's Class Lesson lectures.'[173]

This makes it apparent that people had by then begun to take it as a matter of course that Class Lessons would be read. In notes Ita Wegman made in preparation for Class Lessons which she gave outside Dornach in the summer of 1925, this is made even clearer: 'Reading the Lessons is the only way, dear friends, for in that way the Michaelic

---

[169] IW to Steffen, 22 Jan. 1926, Goetheanum Archives.

[170] Meeting of Class members on 7 Feb. 1926, p. 4. Goetheanum Archives. Also Steffen's diary entry of 7 Feb. 1926. On 13 February, Steffen wrote: 'Dr Wegman has resigned her leadership of the School of Michael and thus also all rights to the Class Lessons.' (Archives of Albert Steffen Foundation.)

[171] See e.g. Walter Aerni(?) to Steffen, 22 Feb. 1926. Goetheanum Archives.

[172] Minutes, Council, 14 Apr. 1926. Goetheanum Archives.

[173] IW to Steffen, 11 Apr. 1925, in EZ III, p. 57.

words is [are] given to you unchanged, as Rudolf Steiner spoke them.'[174] She provided no further arguments for her reasons. Her words reflected the general sentiment which had by then developed among members, in piety remembering the glory of 1924, and perhaps also the impressive readings by Lili Kolisko. No one realized that this could turn into a problem, though Wegman went on to write: 'A law has thus been broken for the first time, in that esoteric material was written down directly. It has never been the custom, not even in earlier times, to pass on esoteric wisdom in writing. It was always made known orally.' Not a word from her that Rudolf Steiner did to the last absolutely refuse to hand the transcripts of the Class Lesson over for people to read, let alone read aloud to others, nor that in the Lessons themselves he had repeatedly decreed that written notes should be burned after a week at the latest.[175] It was only in the letter of 16 March 1926, in which she justified her actions to Albert Steffen, that reference was made to the fact that Rudolf Steiner's reaction to requests from several people to be permitted to read the texts aloud, like Mrs Kolisko, had been in the negative.[176]

The thought that a Lesson of the School might draw on Intuition gained when present in the spirit in the esotericism which had been so alive in the early years and also the Class Lessons themselves, which assumed ever new forms in the Repeat Lessons and when given outside Dornach, went wholly into the background behind the possibility, relying on the past, of basing oneself on hallowed tradition with the texts that had survived. It was only years later that Ita Wegman admitted thoughts of a different kind that would take one forward. The only possibility for her at the time was to read the texts with as much inner feeling as possible. 'We must therefore approach these Class Lessons with much warmth, with much enthusiasm, so that what now exists in writing may come alive again, as it once was when it came from the great Master's lips and was given to us. And so I would appeal to your warmth of heart, your greatest enthusiasm, to take part in this Lesson in the right way and mood, letting it come alive in you.'[177]

---

[174] EZ III, p. 63.
[175] GA 270/3, pp. 45, 63, 83, 103, 122, 127.
[176] EZ III, p. 66.
[177] Ibid. p. 63.

A similar discrepancy between the practice of reading the Lessons, which was felt to be the only possibility, and Rudolf Steiner's original intentions was evident in Marie Steiner's case. It was probably in the spring of 1926 that in preparing for an address to Class members she wrote in her notebook: '... he was utterly against these written notes being given to anyone to read, including the most prominent carriers of the work abroad when these came to Dornach for a short time and wanted to read them in our house: "They simply do not exist"—he would say very firmly. Thinking about what these words mean to me, I come to the following conclusion: It was not in line with his intention that these lectures should merely be read.'[178] Looking at the reflections which follow, not so far published, one sees the efforts made by Marie Steiner to reconcile Rudolf Steiner's abrupt rejection with her memories of everything he had told her about working in the right way with the Class mantras (see Appendix 7). Nevertheless, at the time she saw the practice of reading the Lessons as the only possible way.

Ita Wegman's decision to read a Class Lesson for the first time for members of the School on 25 May 1925 in Paris, when the national Society had its annual general meeting, must be seen in this context. According to Elisabeth Vreede she informed her colleagues on the Council immediately before her departure that she intended there to 'give a Class Lesson, as a form of practice, as it were, for a small group of people who were in sympathy with her'.[179] She certainly met with no resistance from her colleagues, including Marie Steiner, when on her return she decided to read in Dornach as well. Albert Steffen, who—as emerged

[178] From notes for an introduction before reading the Class Lessons. Notebook No. 20, see Appendix 7. The word 'not' from the last sentence is missing in the reproduction of this text in GA 270/1, p. XII.

[179] 'Unfortunately,' Vreede added, 'only after Marie Steiner had already left the studio.' She, Vreede, did however think that she must have heard of it from Steffen or Wachsmuth, 'otherwise she would not have said anything about it later, nor given permission for the first Dornach Class Lesson [given by Wegman], which she attended in a mood of considerable protest'. (Vreede 1934, p. 15.) Correspondence with Alice Sauerwein (A. Sauerwein to E. Vreede, 8 May 1925, IW to A. Sauerwein, 14 May 1925, IW Archives. Also in EZ III, p. 165 f.) shows that Marie Steiner did at least consider going to Paris with Wegman, and that the Class Lesson was not read in the heart of the meeting but rather in the periphery, as well as a lecture by Elisabeth Vreede.

later—had marked reservations, introduced her with kind, neutral words to the members gathered in the woodwork shop on 4 June 1925, emphatically not as leader of the School but as 'secretary' (the audience could not tell if this meant of the School or the Council).[180] This made reading established practice also at the centre of the School. We learn from a talk which Emil Leinhas had with Walter Johannes Stein probably as early as May 1925 that the Council was said to have decided 'that every member of the Council, except for Dr Wachsmuth, who is too young, will be entitled to give Class Lessons in his Section'.[181] Marie Steiner very probably gave her first Class Lesson on the first anniversary of Rudolf Steiner's death, and she included ritual elements from the early

---

[180] Goetheanum Archives. See Appendix 9. Steffen formulated his reservations more clearly in a letter to Friedrich Rittelmeyer written more than a year later: 'In making that declaration before the gathering of members I specifically used the term "secretary" and this has been taken down in shorthand. Later on I was always of the same opinion. I have *never* considered Dr Wegman to be the leader of the School of Michael, but always the Council.' (Steffen to Rittelmeyer, 7 Dec. 1926, Goetheanum Archives.) A light is also cast on the human situation in which Ita Wegman gave her first Class Lesson in Dornach by the fact that Walter Johannes Stein and Eugen Kolisko did immediately afterwards come up to Steffen, criticize the way he had done it, and ask him to enquire of the Council if Wegman 'was autonomous as leader of the Class', that is, Steffen added, 'if the School of Michael can be kept separate from leadership of the Society, i.e. the esoteric Council'. (Steffen at a meeting of Class members on 7 Feb. 1926. Goetheanum Archives.) Diary entries by Steffen show that Kolisko and Stein made massive demands on him concerning Wegman's entitlement to leadership which would have excluded the Council from any share in the responsibility. Steffen could not accept this. A discussion in Council concerning the matter on 20 August did not result in adequate clarity on the leadership issue. (See Appendix 10.) Two days after the talk which Steffen had with Kolisko and Stein, Marie Steiner wrote to Steffen: '[T]oday I do have hope, after all, that the two gentlemen's sally will have no further consequences as far as you are concerned, for they will surely be able to say to themselves that no obstacles were put in Dr Wegman's way, and that she has the possibility to say what she wishes wherever she wishes and gain the position she wants. That if they were, however, wanting to force us to obey their (the two gentlemen's) commands, everything would go wrong.... It has also come to my mind that Dr W[egman] was innocuously natural during the concert of the young people, but restless and weeping during the slide lecture. She had probably talked with the gentlemen between the two events.' (MSt to Steffen, 6 June 1926, Goetheanum Archives.)

[181] W. J. Stein to IW, undated, IW Archives.

esotericism.[182] Albert Steffen probably started in early April 1926. He had been given the texts of the Class Lessons by Marie Steiner on 8 March[183] and was now ready—after some hesitation—to read the first Lesson during the Easter conference: 'I read the words, without the signs.'[184] Wegman mentioned in a letter to Steffen that in the spring of 1927 it had been agreed in Council that Steffen should read for all Class members present at conferences at the Goetheanum, Wegman and Marie Steiner only in their respective circles. Steffen, she wrote, had, however, cancelled this division into spheres by 4 April.[185]

In early February 1926 Steffen still said that one reason for his hesitation in taking on leadership of the School and being a reader was that he was not adequately informed on the esotericism of the youth group in Stuttgart,[186] the core group of the Medical Section, and the faculty of teachers at the Stuttgart Waldorf school. 'I can only take on leadership of the School if I am able to see everything clearly. The secret groups where I do not know what they are doing. Without insight I cannot act freely.' Surely Rudolf Steiner's words applied here that 'all esotericism must gradually become part of the School of Michael'. Ita Wegman, he said,

[182] See GA 265, p. 485 ff. This attempt to pick up on Rudolf Steiner's early esoteric work clearly was not taken further. A member who had been present at the teaching events of all three degrees of the Esoteric School in 1907/1908 said she was utterly taken aback by it. (M. Langen-Strachwitz to Steffen, 5 Apr. 1926. Goetheanum Archives.) Steffen was also critical of the attempt. In his diary (Albert Steffen Foundation Archives) he noted: 'A memorial meeting on 30 March. The walls of the woodwork shop had black hangings. Three altars to the east. On one of them Rudolf Steiner's tools (dividers, measuring rod and hammer, which he had genuinely used in life). A vessel with fire. A tall candle on each. Mournful music. / Marie Steiner read the mantras, with hammer strokes in between. Now the metre, now the number of staves. / She was exercising the rights of a Master. Dr Wachsmuth lit the candles' (end of March). 'When Marie Steiner arranged the event, I did not know that she was going to use the ceremonies of various degrees. I am not familiar with such things. It really is an aberration to use them without informing me beforehand. . . . She has therefore mixed in things that should be strictly avoided lest souls get in conflict with themselves' (during or after the Easter conference, 2–5 April 1926. Paragraphs marked with /).

[183] Diary entry, Steffen, 10 March 1926. Albert Steffen Foundation Archives.

[184] Steffen diary, end of March. Albert Steffen Foundation Archives.

[185] IW to Steffen, 4 Apr. 1926. Goetheanum Archives.

[186] See Haid 2001, p. 88 f.

'was a state within the state, as was the esotericism of the Waldorf school and of the Independent Society'.[187] At the meeting of Class members held that day he put it like this: 'I can only take on leadership of the School of Michael if I have a clear picture of all esoteric elements in the Society.'[188] With remarkable boldness Albert Steffen, normally so cautious and sensitive—at least concerning himself—was even at this early stage of developments considering a radical final conclusion: 'From now on there must not be any esotericism. Everything can be made public. Everything has been revealed.'[189] Such thoughts did not arise in any kind of passing, perhaps pessimistic, mood. Steffen reflected on the matter for some time and connected special hopes for the future with it, as is evident from a diary entry made in 1928: 'The Section which Rudolf Steiner claimed for himself, spiritual science as such, research and esotericism, is now orphaned. / The content (the Cl[ass] lectures) no longer has the same effect because of these incidents ((Boos),[190] the mantras being taken to Russia and falling into Soviet hands,[191] the antipathies, claims to power, etc.). They should be published. This would remove the false authority. And esotericism would then once more be able to grow in its true soil, hearts illumined and full of warmth into which the Christ has entered. / Then a new content might perhaps shoot and sprout up for the General Section, something for which it could indeed stand. These lectures would

---

[187] Steffen diary, 7 Feb. 1926. Albert Steffen Foundation Archives.

[188] 7 Feb. 1926. Goetheanum Archives.

[189] Diary, 7 Feb. 1926. Albert Steffen Foundation Archives. Steffen's talk with Marie Steiner about making the Class Lesson texts available, which she referred to in a later letter, may have taken place at the same time (see GA 270/1, page XII).

[190] Roman Boos interrupted a Class Lesson given by Ita Wegman in Dornach on 1 January 1928.

[191] According to Walter Johannes Stein, 'the Class mantras were confiscated when Mme Vassileieva was arrested' in 1927. He also wrote that Olga von Sivers' archives and 'both libraries and many single lectures' were confiscated (Stein to IW, 22 Sept. 1927. IW Archives) According to information from Sergei Prokofieff, the lady in question was Elisaveta Ivanovna Vassileieva, née Dmitrieva (1887–1928), co-founder and leader of the St Petersburg branch (1913) whom Rudolf Steiner had appointed 'guarantor', i.e. she was permitted to admit people to the Anthroposophical Society (S. Prokofieff to J. Kiersch, 29 Apr. 2005). It is possible that comments made by Marie Steiner about the failure of J. van Leer and Ita Wegman in this respect relate to this (MSt 1981, p. 350).

then have to be made accessible to all members. And individual, more advanced members might speak in this Section. I myself will start with such a lecture. Then the Class will have content again. The subject matter of this lecture must be: About the mood to be gained in the heart before one wants to do investigations.... (In the first esoteric lesson I am going to give I then intend to speak about the difference between Abraham's and Melchisedek's sacrifices.)'[192]

Ita Wegman herself was also reading Class Lessons in Stuttgart,[193] Cologne,[194] Hamburg, Prague and Vienna[195] in 1925, and regularly above all in England from 28 June 1925 onwards, in continuous communication with Harry Collison and George Kaufmann, the local representatives,[196] and at the same time also in Holland. As a central theme in these activities we have her statement that it was now above all a matter of 'guarding' the wisdom received and 'repeating' Rudolf Steiner's actual words. In the newsletter of 14 June 1925 she thus wrote: 'It was clear to us [the Council] that for the time being it was a matter of guarding the esotericism which had been given, and let the powers that lie in it come alive and take effect in the members through repetition.'[197] For the first Lessons in Prague and London she noted: 'We were aware that as we thus continued the esotericism, it could not be a matter of giving something new. Continuing it had to be seen as a way of guarding the wisdom that was given in the right way; with Class Lessons that have already been given repeated in the right way.... Because of this situation, it behoves me, in agreement with the other members of the Council in Dornach, to guard and repeat the things which Rudolf Steiner had communicated to the members of the First Class of the School of Spiritual Science.'[198] In a first letter of justification to Albert Steffen in August 1925, we see also the compelling reason for the attitude she was initially taking, looking back, rather, and protective: 'As Rudolf Steiner said, and

---

[192] Diary, 28 January 1928. Albert Steffen Foundation Archives. Paragraphs marked by /.

[193] IW to J. van Leer, 9 June 1925. IW Archives.

[194] *Nbl.*, 12 July 1925.

[195] EZ III, p. 62 ff.

[196] A list in the London archives of the Anthroposophical Society in Great Britain refers to 35 Lessons up to 22 Nov. 1931.

[197] *Nbl.*, 14 June 1925, p. 96.

[198] EZ III, p. 63 f.

repeated many times, that the School of Michael had been *instituted out of the spiritual world* and was *not a human institution*, I felt I had been appointed by the spiritual world and had absolutely no right to let there be changes after Rudolf Steiner's death. For me, the question was just this: Can I, as second leader, now that the main leader was no longer able to lead in an immediate way, guard the School as such and continue leadership by repeating the wisdom of the School of Michael, which Rudolf Steiner gave in Class Lessons (in the School of Spiritual Science)?'[199]

It is difficult to say whether, in instructing stenographer Helene Finkh to pass on the written-up Class texts to Ita Wegman,[200] Rudolf Steiner wanted to keep the possibility open for a more distant future when not only Lili Kolisko, but also the 'second leader' he had appointed might communicate the esoteric lessons by reading them out, and perhaps also other individuals.[201]

For some years, then, the communication of Class material by reading became established in several European countries—in England and Holland mainly through Ita Wegman, in Scandinavia above all through Marie Steiner, in Germany through both. A special event in the history of the School was the summer conference in Ring, Hedemark (Norway) in 1934, at which Marie Steiner read all nineteen Class Lessons.[202] At the urging of several members, especially Helga Geelmuyden in Norway, talks were held early in 1930 to consider if the texts should be given out to a greater number of people for reading aloud. Marie Steiner was in favour of including at least four people who had proven their value and whom Rudolf Steiner himself had asked to communicate the mantras—Adolf Arenson, Harry Collison, Helga Geelmuyden and Anna Gunnarsson Wager. Ita Wegman on the other hand was decidedly more for reducing

---

[199] IW to Steffen, 21 Aug. 1925, EZ III, p. 59.

[200] GA 270/1, p. 197 ff.

[201] For the sake of completeness, let it be said that initially Wegman was not given all the texts, as some had already been passed on to Marie Steiner who was away on her travels. 'Afterwards Marie Steiner did also give me the missing Class Lessons.' (IW to Steffen, 16 Mar. 1926, EZ III, p. 67.) In December 1925, Wegman asked Lili Kolisko to let her have the texts for the 10th and 11th Lessons, which she had not so far been able to obtain from Marie Steiner (IW to L. Kolisko, 19 Dec. 1925, IW Archives).

[202] Helga Geelmuyden to MSt, 18 Feb. 1934, on her plan to gather as many members of the esoteric school ... 'in a rural location for three weeks, to work through all the Class Lessons'. Lit. Estate Archives.

numbers and limiting the privilege of reading—for this is how it was considered then—to the members of the Council in Dornach.[203] Yet Marie Steiner had already given a number of Class Lessons to Anna Gunnarsson in Sweden, to prepare translations and then in 1929 also to read them. Helga Geelmuyden in Norway had probably heard of this and a largish group of Class members in Stuttgart had asked for authorization for Adolf Arenson.[204] It therefore was not possible to limit the privilege to the members of Council, which Ita Wegman wanted.[205] Marie Steiner passed the texts on to individual people in charge of classes,[206] and later on Ita Wegman also did this.

---

[203] Concerning the misunderstandings and differences which arose from this, see Chapter 6.9 below, footnote 348, also Albert Steffen's report on the Council meeting on 19 Feb. 1930 with the minutes, and the correspondence relating to this, esp. with Lili Kolisko and Ludwig Polzer (Goetheanum Archives).

[204] See Chapter 6.

[205] See MSt to Steffen, 17 Mar. 1930. Lit. Estate Archives.

[206] The term 'Class reader' widely used today was not used in Rudolf Steiner's day. Nor did anyone then refer to 'lectors', a term for the office which only came into use in the 1980s. Both terms refer to *reading*, an institution which Rudolf Steiner had only been in favour of on a single special occasion. Compared to the early years after World War II, this adequately describes only *one* of several functions in looking after a Class in the School. The term 'lector' also has the problem of religious significance. In the Roman Catholic Church it refers to a particular lower order, people who in earlier times had specific functions, but today represent merely an intermediate stage on the way to higher 'orders'. The individual who leads the prayers or reads at a Roman Catholic mass is also called a 'lector' or 'reader'. The School of Spiritual Science does not have a hierarchy of orders or devotional readings. It therefore seems questionable to refer to people who communicate the mantras of the School or look after the First Class, as 'lectors'. For the Class Lessons she gave in England from 1925 onwards, Ita Wegman used the term 'representative'. She wrote 'Here in England, Mr Collison is the first representative.' Helga Geelmuyden wrote to Marie Steiner in 1926 of 'mediators' of the 'Class Lessons', and as late as 1930 still of 'group mediators'. [Some individuals in England used a literal translation of the German for 'representative' and wrote 'person of confidence'.]

6 The first 'mediators'

As we have seen from the course of events up to March 1925 (see Chapter 4), Rudolf Steiner developed the School of Spiritual Science, and with it also the First Class step by step, having observed how the individuals concerned worked together. He even wanted the 'statutes' of the General Anthroposophical Society which was due to be re-established, statutes he presented for resolutions to be passed at the 1923/24 Christmas Conference, a policy document formulated with extreme care, to be taken merely as a kind of 'narrative',[207] a description that might change at any time of something which was continually arising anew in active cooperation between 'centre' and 'periphery'. When the First Class was evolving in 1924, he thus made immediate provision for the inclusion of Class members unable to attend Lessons in Dornach. Initially the focus was on personal meditative work, as it had been when the Esoteric School developed at the beginning of the twentieth century. Without any kind of formal agreement or resolution being made, Rudolf Steiner, sovereign leader of the School, asked a number of people whom he knew and could trust to pass on the mantras given in the Class Lessons in Dornach to members of the School locally, to see to it that the strict rules concerning these mantras were observed, and also to pass on applications for membership of the School with appropriate recommendations to himself or Ita Wegman. Further ways of handling the situation were to be added in due course—but this was then no longer possible.[208]

In the newsletter of the Anthroposophical Society, Rudolf Steiner wrote in April 1924, when the Class had progressed as far as the Sixth Lesson, about how this might have been done: 'This institution [the

[207] 6 Feb. 1924, GA 240, p. 236; 16 Apr. 1924, GA 260a, p. 212; 18 Apr. 1924, GA 270/1, p. 146 f.

[208] See esp. the essay by Rudolf Steiner in the *Nbl.* of 17 Feb. 1924. (Also in GA 260a, p. 143 f.) According to Guenther Wachsmuth, Rudolf Steiner intended 'after some time to send letters to members of the School in which the contents of Class Lessons were to be given in a suitable form'. (Wachsmuth to Andreas Koerner, 4 June 1924. Goetheanum Archives) See also reference to this in Class Lesson of 18 Apr. 1924 (GA 270/1, p. 149).

School] cannot come about on the basis of abstract thoughts from "above". It must arise from the needs of our members, from "below".' The Council at the Goetheanum would thus have to establish 'harmony' between the different initiatives in the Anthroposophical Society. It should not 'act like an authority "from above",' not give 'orders' but 'advice', and this applied particularly to everything 'to be done for the School of Spiritual Science'.[209] In Stuttgart, where Lili Kolisko had started a few weeks earlier, with his permission, to read her transcripts of the Dornach Lessons to the faculty at the Waldorf school, Rudolf Steiner was at the same time endeavouring in an exemplary way to encourage this near-by initiative, giving it his kind attention. 'Another group of people wishing to have the Lessons conveyed in this way is also forming here in Stuttgart. Isn't that so, Mr Arenson? (Mr Arenson gets up and says Yes.) And if such groups develop in the immediate future, the necessary steps will be taken in Dornach to find the relevant material and ways of conveying it.'[210] The more or less marginal entry in the minutes containing this remark clearly shows the careful attention Rudolf Steiner gave to initiatives 'from below' during those first weeks of the School's development, and his kind interest in welcoming such initiatives.

Marie Steiner and Ita Wegman had certainly taken note of the fact that individuals were being asked to convey the mantras. Marie Steiner made a note for herself, presumably in 1926, of 'what he himself gave as a guideline for the work of the group who wanted to live with the mantric verses together. The person who spoke the mantras should work out for herself or himself what he or she would say with reference to these verses. He therefore intended a form of independent work on the verses, based, of course, on received wisdom. Above all, however, living experience of the verses themselves.'[211] And Ita Wegman wrote to Albert Steffen in March 1926 that Rudolf Steiner had refused to give anyone but Mrs Kolisko permission to read the transcripts of the Class Lessons, but: 'Rudolf Steiner did give some people whom he knew well permission to speak the mantras before Class Members and give some explanations relating to them.'[212]

---

[209] *Nbl.*, 6 Apr. 1924. Also in GA 260a, p. 159 f. and in Appendix 1 in this book.

[210] From the minutes of a meeting with representatives in Stuttgart on 10 Apr. 1924, GA 260a, p. 480.

[211] From Notebook No. 20, GA 270/1, p. XIII. See Appendix 7.

[212] IW to Steffen, 16 Mar. 1926, EZ III, p. 66.

The modest activities of the first 'mediators'[213] were, however, apparently considered provisional by everyone concerned. They involved no formal appointment or particular status. Anyone asked to do it in the way described would be known in this function only by people immediately connected with them. There was no communication from region to region. Any questions or problems would almost always be communicated directly to Rudolf Steiner. This alone makes it possible to understand that after Rudolf Steiner's unexpected and sudden death, the activities of the first 'mediators', which he had inaugurated, were wholly marginalized by leading individuals in the School as well as by members. If that modest, quiet work had been taken up consistently and developed further, seeing that it was in fact going on in quite a number of places outside Dornach, would developments have taken a very different course from the one which they then did take? Would a completely different life have developed for the School if the esotericists appointed by Rudolf Steiner in the 'periphery', people who were competent in many ways and actively involved, could have had closer contact with one another, and if their initiatives had been given more attention at the 'centre', with those people taken seriously as individuals who shared in the work? With questions like these, it seems well worth while to look at the work done by those inconspicuous first 'mediators' in detail, in so far as traces still remain.[214] As we shall see, this is not a marginal historical episode but a wide field of pioneering activities which may well have been much closer to Rudolf Steiner's original intentions than we have been able to think until now.

6.1 Lili Kolisko

Lili Kolisko (1889–1976) was one of the pioneers of scientific research taken further through anthroposophy. Directed by Rudolf Steiner, who valued her greatly, she worked for years on investigations of the activity of

---

[213] The term was probably first used by Helga Geelmuyden in her letters to Marie Steiner. See 6.4 below.

[214] In the passages quoted below, words underlined in the original are here shown in italics, with the author's additions in square parentheses. To get a fuller picture, the work of the first 'mediators' will be considered also beyond the years 1924/25.

exceedingly small entities, developing epoch-making methods for understanding the sphere of life in connection with the cosmos.[215] Together with her partner Dr Eugen Kolisko, the first school doctor in the young Waldorf movement, she also took a lively interest in the evolving destiny of the German Anthroposophical Society, which from 1919, the year of the threefold commonwealth campaign, had its focus in Stuttgart. Able to attend the first Class Lessons in Dornach in February 1924, she asked Rudolf Steiner's permission to take these down, so that she might pass the contents on to members of the School of Spiritual Science in Stuttgart. Looking back later on in life, probably with the help of diaries which unfortunately are not so far available for research, Lili Kolisko wrote: 'Having attended the Lesson, I was extraordinarily impressed and asked myself: How about all the other members who do not live in Dornach and therefore cannot hear the grand Lessons given by Rudolf Steiner? Might there be a way in which the contents of these Lessons could be made available to other members? I put my question to Dr Wegman, Secretary of the Society. "Well, what do you imagine?" she said, and I replied that one might perhaps be permitted to tell at least a small group in Stuttgart about it, perhaps one like the Group of Thirty. Dr Wegman promised to ask Rudolf Steiner, and then Rudolf Steiner asked me to see him. I want to put this down as accurately as possible. Rudolf Steiner said: "Dr Wegman has told me of your intention to pass the Class Lessons on to a group of members. I like this intention very much. But why does it have to be the Group of Thirty? The Group of Thirty is not a body I can work with esoterically." I answered that I was not particularly concerned with the Group of Thirty and had merely referred to it to demonstrate my wish to convey the contents to at least one relatively small group of people. Rudolf Steiner then went on to say: "Would you not be prepared to pass it on to the faculty at the Waldorf school?" I was, of course, perfectly prepared to do this, and Rudolf Steiner promised to make out the necessary membership cards for the whole faculty right away. That is how this institution started for the Stuttgart teachers. Rudolf Steiner asked me if I would be prepared to do this, and I was happy to accept his proposal. The appointment meant that I would go to Dornach every week to attend lectures for members and Class Lessons. Of course, I had many questions about conveying the contents. I did not consider

[215] Ch. Haid in Plato 2003.

myself capable of giving them in my own words and asked Rudolf Steiner if he'd permit me to take them down. He did give me permission, though no one else was permitted to take them down. Let me stress, "no one else".'[216] A few days before the Lessons started, the faculty of the Waldorf school had had a lengthy meeting with Rudolf Steiner when he first visited them after the Christmas Conference in which they had asked for clarification as to how the Waldorf school related to the newly founded School of Spiritual Science, with almost all of them asking to be admitted to the First Class.[217] In the early months, about 60 people attended, among them some guests.[218]

In a letter to Ita Wegman, Lili Kolisko wrote of deep-reaching influences on the soul and spirit among the group of young teachers. The Class Lessons, she said, had 'created a warm bond among the whole faculty'. Rudolf Steiner had once told her that the faculty should develop into a core group from which something could then shine out. She thought that this core was now developing 'more and more strongly'. 'No doubt you also know', she continued, 'that the anthroposophical teachers meet almost every Sunday after the service [worship based on the general Christian teaching in the school]. There, too, something is in the air which one feels to be most satisfying. Many issues can now be discussed which they could not have discussed before Christmas. Something is slowly evolving from the chaos, and it has strength and life.'[219] Lili Kolisko also experienced a profound influence on herself. 'I would also like to tell you', she went on, 'how remarkable my relationship to the teachers has become since I have been permitted to pass on the Lessons. Not a night passes when I do not dream of one member of the faculty or another. Even people from whom I'm otherwise remote will appear. In Holland I dreamt the whole [Stuttgart] meeting, e.g. in the night from Tuesday to Wednesday. It is held on Tuesday evenings and I had it

[216] Kolisko 1961, p. 90 f. Here Kolisko did not take into account that Helene Finckh had been asked by Rudolf Steiner to take the Class Lessons down in shorthand (see explanations in GA 270/1).

[217] Meeting on 5 Feb. 1924, GA 300/3, p. 116. Rudolf Steiner's famous words: 'The conference in Dornach was the second part of a hypothetical conclusion. The first part is: If anthroposophists wish it, one thing or another will be initiated from Dornach...' were spoken at that meeting (p. 111).

[218] G&C, 25 Apr. 1930, p. 88. Goetheanum Archives.

[219] L. Kolisko to IW, 2 Nov. 1924. Ita Wegman Archives.

confirmed that I had experienced a real mirror image of the meeting. The night before, a very strange dream image arose together with Mrs Stein, Dr Haebler and Miss Mellinger. It seemed to refer to earlier lives on earth.'[220]

By October 1924, Lili Kolisko had completed a first sequence of all nineteen Class Lessons.[221] The question she had previously discussed with Ita Wegman then arose again as to whether perhaps all Class members in Stuttgart should be invited when the readings were repeated. It would now be possible, she wrote to her revered friend, to unite them.[222] Did this mean that the Stuttgart members admitted to the Class by the leaders of the School should be invited as well, or was it a matter of uniting with the School group led by Adolf Arenson (see Chapter 6.3)? At any rate, Ita Wegman was happy to agree, presumably with Rudolf Steiner's consent.[223] 'It is a tremendous gift which is thus given to all Stuttgart members', Kolisko wrote back. 'All Stuttgart, I think, will give a sigh of relief, as though freed from a dreadful nightmare, when they learn that it has been possible to obtain this permission.' She wrote that she intended to start at the Stuttgart Branch building on Thursday 13 November.[224]

In view of the tensions that existed among Stuttgart members it is remarkable that the resulting extension of Lili Kolisko's reading activities was supported by all the different factions. Carl Unger made the announcement at a Branch meeting that readings would begin on Thursday, 20 November.[225] An announcement was also made at the Michael (formerly Kerning) Branch led by Toni Voelker.[226] And so it was

---

[220] L. Kolisko to IW, 2 Nov. 1924. Ita Wegman Archives.

[221] It appears that initially she used her own transcripts, partly incomplete (see details given in GA 270/1, p. 202). A year later she wrote to Wegman: 'Enclosed are the 1st and 3rd Class Lessons. I'll need the fourth this Thursday. You must then be so kind and let me know when you need the fourth, perhaps sending me the 5th then.' (Kolisko to IW, 7 July 1926, IW Archives.) This suggests that from her third sequence onwards she used Helene Finckh's transcripts borrowed from Ita Wegman.

[222] Kolisko to IW, 17 Oct 1924. IW Archives.

[223] IW to L. Kolisko, 29 Oct. 1924. IW Archives.

[224] L. Kolisko to IW, 2 Nov. 1924. IW Archives.

[225] Kurt Dannenberg in his application for membership addressed to Rudolf Steiner, 18 Nov. 1924, Goetheanum Archives. Numerous letters of this kind in November and December 1924.

[226] Julie Hauser to Rudolf Steiner, 19 Nov. 1924, Goetheanum Archives.

that 174 members attended the first Lesson, among them Carl Unger and his wife, Emil Molt, Friedrich Rittelmeyer, Emil Bock. Visitors from outside Stuttgart would often attend, among them Ludwig Polzer and Moritz Bartsch, and Marie Steiner and friends from Dornach for the 14th Lesson. The total number of names in the list of attenders which is now in the Goetheanum Archives was 397.

Lili Kolisko read at weekly intervals, with a first sequence of 19 Lessons for the larger audience completed in early summer 1925. Then there was a 'relatively long pause', probably because of the crisis in Dornach, and after a further sequence another pause lasting two years, for health reasons.[227] In the spring of 1930, when the Council's reading privilege was under discussion in Dornach, misunderstandings aggravated the talks about starting again, but permission was then given from Dornach.[228] In 1934, Lili Kolisko and her husband went to England. It is not so far known if she did still give occasional Class Lessons in Stuttgart until they were banned. She did, however, go there for regular further readings from 1950 to 1969. Gisbert Husemann, who attended her Lessons at the time, wrote: 'During the Lesson she gained in greatness; she would then have a mighty voice, and could speak in a very intimate way. Emil Leinhas was deeply moved, did not hide this, putting it in words: That is exactly how Rudolf Steiner would speak to us in his lectures in those days.'[229] Friedwart Husemann wrote: 'Emil Leinhas's impression carries twice the weight, for he was not one of the followers of Kolisko, being wholly connected with Marie Steiner and the Literary Estate Association.—My father would often look back on the different ways in which Albert Steffen, Marie Steiner, Ita Wegman and Lili Kolisko read the Class Lessons. Albert Steffen and Ita Wegman "modest, as though on this side of the threshold", Marie Steiner and Lili Kolisko on the other hand "powerfully, deeply moving, as though from beyond the threshold".'[230]

The impressive way in which Lili Kolisko took up the task given by Rudolf Steiner no doubt contributed greatly to the fact that this form of conveying the Lessons was generally felt to be exemplary even in 1924.

---

[227] Eugen Kolisko at G&C, 25 Apr. 1930, p. 89. Goetheanum Archives.

[228] See the detailed discussion of events at the G&C, 25 Apr. 1930, p. 79 ff., and L. Kolisko's explanatory letter to G. Wachsmuth, 23 Mar. 1930, Goetheanum Archives. Appendix 22.

[229] Husemann 1978, p. 53.

[230] F. Husemann to J. Kiersch, 16 Mar. 2003.

We may ask ourselves why Rudolf Steiner did not give others the right to read Class Lessons (the provisional arrangement for Prague being an exception). A possible reason may be that Lili Kolisko was the first ever to ask for it, doing so in February 1924, for the specific purpose of passing the mantras on to people she knew in Stuttgart.[231] He was following the principle of developing the School 'from below', according to members' needs, and therefore gave a loving response to Lili Kolisko's request. It is unlikely to have been his intention to make this a generally binding principle, as will be evident.

6.2 Hans Eiselt and his group in Prague

On 3 and 5 April 1924, during an Anthroposophical Society conference in Czechoslovakia, Rudolf Steiner gave two Class Lessons in Prague. These were taken down by Hans Eiselt and two other members.[232] Initially, these transcripts were read a number of times by Ludwig Polzer at four-week intervals, with Rudolf Steiner's consent, whilst waiting for further directions from Rudolf Steiner.[233] Eiselt reported in 1930: 'Rudolf Steiner, asked directly if the lectures might be taken down, had immediately said "Yes". He also knew that the lectures would be transcribed in typescript from the shorthand record, knew that they would be translated into Czech, and in retrospect—this was then actually in the summer of 1924—gave his approval, sending the reply by Dr Wachsmuth that he agreed, and he even—if I am not mistaken this was in the late summer of 1924—gave permission for these lectures to be read also in Bruenn [Brno], using the transcripts we had made.'[234] From November 1924, this provisional arrangement was replaced, again with Rudolf Steiner's agreement, by Count Polzer's free renderings (see Chapter 6.11).

[231] Another factor may have been that at the time, Lili Kolisko had got a study group going in Stuttgart with some who had attended the young doctors' course in January 1924, where she read parts of her transcripts of lectures from the course which were not available then in any other form (Selg 2005b, p. 35).
[232] GA 270/1, p. 198.
[233] Eiselt in G&C, 24 Apr. 1930, p. 77 & 90. According to Polzer the Prague transcripts were initially read by Hans Eiselt and others at two-week intervals (Polzer to Council, 27 Feb. 1930. See Appendix 21).
[234] G&C, 25 Apr. 1930, p. 77. Goetheanum Archives.

6.3 Adolf Arenson

Adolf Arenson (1855–1936), author of a guide [in German] to Rudolf Steiner's lecture courses, was a merchant in Chile, then a freelance composer in Hamburg and Stuttgart-Bad Cannstatt. In 1904, he and his later son-in-law Carl Unger became esoteric pupils of Rudolf Steiner.[235] Two years later he took on a leading role in Stuttgart as 'Sub-Warden' of the Esoteric School (see Note 28 above).[236] He played a major role when the Stuttgart Branch House was built, with a special room for the teaching events of that School. It is not surprising then that in 1924 Rudolf Steiner encouraged him to take a part in developing the School of Spiritual Science. Yet in the spring of 1924, Lili Kolisko had already started, with Rudolf Steiner's permission, to read her transcripts of the Class Lessons given in Dornach to the faculty of the Waldorf school, and there were signs that the audience might expand to include all Class members in Stuttgart. Arenson thus found himself in a difficult position. Tensions between younger and older anthroposophists had erupted in Stuttgart after the Goetheanum fire. Rudolf Steiner had made the surprising suggestion to let the young people find their own way in an 'Independent Anthroposophical Society' in search of their own ideals. These tensions had only been bridged temporarily and still created a heavy atmosphere in Stuttgart. Arenson later wrote to Albert Steffen that he and Carl Unger had been asked by Rudolf Steiner who 'might be considered for reading the Class Lessons' in Stuttgart. 'I understood it to mean', he added, 'apart from Mrs Kolisko.'[237] They had proposed 'a truly neutral person' such as Dr Rudolf Maier. But Rudolf Steiner did not agree. The next day, Arenson thinks he remembers, he did, however, say in a meeting with Stuttgart members: 'I thought of Mr Arenson for Stuttgart. You would agree, Mr Arenson?' Mr Arenson wrote that he then got up and said 'Yes'. In a note in the minutes of that meeting, which is clearly not a complete record but allows us to give the date of the meeting as 10 April 1924, we read: 'Thus for instance, Mrs Kolisko is always conveying the lectures of the Class Lessons to the faculty of the Independent Waldorf School and some friends. Another group of

---

[235] R. Templeton in Plato 2003.

[236] Wiesberger in GA 264, p. 115, Note 2. Also Arenson to MSt, 22 Feb. 1930, Lit. Estate Archives.

[237] Arenson to Steffen, 28 Feb. 1930, acc. to minutes of G&C, 25 Apr. 1930, p. 69 f., Lit. Estate Archives.

people seeking to have the lectures conveyed is now evolving here in Stuttgart. Isn't that so, Mr Arenson? (Mr Arenson stands up and says "Yes".)'[238] The question to which Mr Arenson replied may sound different in this note than it does in his later report to Albert Steffen, but Rudolf Steiner's intention to address Arenson as the central figure in the new initiative is equally unmistakable.[239]

It is not so far known how the group which according to Rudolf Steiner was 'evolving' under Adolf Arenson developed after this; nor even if it actually ever started work in Rudolf Steiner's lifetime. Arenson certainly gave much thought to how it might proceed. It almost seems as if he saw the task which he accepted with his succinct yet solemn 'Yes' as encouragement in a highly individual development—the 'attempt' of 1911—in which he had also been involved because of a decision made by Rudolf Steiner (see Chapter 3). He certainly felt compelled two years later to put his thoughts on the subject to members of the School in a circular, thoughts that had come to him in view of the completely changed situation after the death of their spiritual teacher. In May 1925, Ita Wegman had started to give Class Lessons in which she read the Dornach transcripts. In the spring of 1926, Marie Steiner and Albert Steffen had followed suit. In view of this, Arenson now wrote about the Class Lessons: 'They are conveyed to members of the First Class by reading out the transcripts.... In future times, however, our work relating to them must go beyond this. They, too, must be a spiritual seed to which we give soul quality through our own creative work.'[240]

---

[238] Notices of the meeting with Stuttgart representatives, 10 April 1924. In GA 260a, p. 480.

[239] Arenson's report on Rudolf Steiner's request is also mentioned in Steffen's clarification of 28 Feb. 1930 and the correction relating to this (Steffen to Council, 28 Feb. 1930 and 1 Mar. 1930, Goetheanum Archives). MSt also quoted it in her letter to Arenson of 10 Oct. 1930, Goetheanum Archives.

[240] Circular to members, October 1926. Appendix 15. The reservations Arenson evidently had concerning the new practice of reading the texts aloud, and his search for ways of working that would bear fruit for the future was seen as a massive attack on Rudolf Steiner's spiritual legacy by some of the younger anthroposophists who had by then become attached to Ita Wegman. About the resulting controversies, see Kolisko 1961, p. 158 ff.; J. v. Grone, An die Zweigleiter und Mitglieder der deutschen Landesgesellschaft (17 Feb. 1927), Goetheanum Archives; L. Werbeck-Svaerdstroem, *Zur Krise in der anthroposophischen Gesellschaft*. Private publication 1927, Goetheanum Archives; MSt, Gespensterschau. Zur Orientierung fuer die Mitglieder 1927, Lit. Estate Archives.

It is possible that Arenson and a few of his friends worked quietly for years, without having the Dornach transcripts to hand, to find ways of developing meditative work on the School mantras on those terms. Independently of Lili Kolisko, he sent recommendations for membership applications to Dornach, which means that he was seen there as a representative for matters concerning the School.[241] In 1930 he wrote to Marie Steiner strongly protesting against the rumour that he had asked Rudolf Steiner's permission to read the Class Lessons and been refused. He wrote that he had not even considered asking for this, adding: 'I will tell you other things, when we meet, which are wholly in accord with the fact that Rudolf Steiner one day said to me, without being asked, that the prohibitions issued by him about passing on the verses from the Class Lessons did not, of course, apply to me. And also that he later sent me the message that he fully agreed to Margarete Kreuzhage conveying to me the contents of the Class Lessons read by Mrs Kolisko.'[242]

Is it permissible to conclude from this that Arenson did not only pass on applications for membership and interview people for this, but that like the other 'mediators' appointed by Rudolf Steiner he ran a group for meditation or study where they worked with the Class mantras in a free way, also drawing on the pointers from Lili Kolisko's lessons? He was certainly one of the four people for whom Marie Steiner repeatedly spoke up in the discussions on the reading privilege in Dornach in 1930. In a letter to Albert Steffen she listed the people 'Rudolf Steiner had named for esoteric work with the members', H. Collison for England, Mrs Ge[e]lmuyden for Norway, Mrs Gunnarsson for Sweden, and at the top of the list, 'Mr Adolf Arenson for Stuttgart'. 'These are the people who were asked to do this work by Rudolf Steiner himself.'[243]

Steffen also received a letter signed by 85 Stuttgart members of the School, asking him to let Arenson have the Class Lessons.[244] He sup-

---

[241] See e.g. Arenson to Council, 23 Aug. 1925, Goetheanum Archives.

[242] Arenson to MSt, 22 Feb. 1930. Lit. Estate Archives. A letter from Mrs Kreuzhage to Ita Wegman of 23 Dec. 1924, in which she asks to be permitted to tell the contents of the Lessons read by Lili Kolisko 'in their fullness' to Arenson (he already had the mantras from Carl Unger), bears a comment in Rudolf Steiner's handwriting: 'Is good that she does it R St.' (Kreuzhage to IW, 23 Dec. 1924. Goetheanum Archives.)

[243] MSt to Steffen, 17 Mar. 1930.

[244] G. Herberg and others to Steffen, 17 Mar. 1930, Goetheanum Archives.

ported the letter by speaking in favour at the meeting of General Secretaries and Councils in April.[245] It appears that it was several months before a decision was made on the application from Stuttgart. In October, Marie Steiner wrote that Arenson should decide for himself, since she herself, Steffen and Wachsmuth were in agreement, but Wegman and Vreede were not.[246] Arenson evidently decided to accept the offer, and he then received the texts. At the end of January 1931 he wrote, with relief, to Marie Steiner: 'People feel most grateful that at last they will have the opportunity to get to know the whole text of the Class Lessons.'[247] Does this not also imply that he had already passed on part of the text, i.e. the mantras?

A last record of Adolf Arenson's reading activity is found in a notice from 1932: 'Class Lessons start again on Saturday, 17 September, at 5 p.m. Adolf Arenson, Stuttgart, Landhausstrasse 70.'[248] The significant esotericist was then in his 78th year. He escaped Nazi persecution by dying on 26 December 1936, during the Holy Nights.

6.4 Helga Geelmuyden

Rudolf Steiner first went to Norway in 1908, and then visited the country almost every year until 1913. Apart from his public lectures, work in the Esoteric School started relatively quickly and on a broad basis in Norway. Helga Geelmuyden (1871–1951) played a key role in this. The profound friendship between her and Marie Steiner continued until the death of the latter. She translated *Knowledge of the Higher Worlds* and other works by Rudolf Steiner into Norwegian and worked in the editorial offices of the journal *Vidar* established in 1915, as well as having responsibility in the Oslo Branch and the national Society.[249] At the Arnhem Conference in July 1924, Rudolf Steiner asked her to pass on the mantras of the School to the more than one hundred Norwegian Class members, though he did not provide her with the transcripts of the Dornach Lessons. 'But it will go

[245] Minutes G&C, 25 Apr. 1930, p. 68.

[246] MSt to Arenson, 10 Oct. 1930, Goetheanum Archives. See also MSt to Steffen, 10 Oct. 1930, Goetheanum Archives.

[247] Arenson to MSt, 25 Jan. 1931, Goetheanum Archives.

[248] Goetheanum Archives.

[249] Terje Christensen in Plato 2003.

really badly', she said to Rudolf Steiner, as Joergen Smit told the story many times. 'Yes, of course,' was the answer, 'but it will get better as time goes on.'[250] In the months that followed Geelmuyden made all necessary preparations. Members admitted to the School were then invited to the first Class Lesson in Norway, to be held on 14 March 1925.[251] Geelmuyden later expressed the wish to Marie Steiner to attend the Lessons in Dornach, 'where it is also permitted to convey the words Rudolf Steiner said concerning the mantras'. 'For', she continued, 'Rudolf Steiner asked me to use the mantras as texts and speak about them, which is a tremendous responsibility, since I was only able to attend some of the Lessons.' She immediately added the plea, made again and again to the leaders of the School in Dornach or to Marie Steiner in person, whether she could not be given help in some way in this difficult situation. She also felt that she shared responsibility for developing the work of the School further from the centre. 'If there were to be a meeting again in Dornach to find ways in which the work of Rudolf Steiner may be taken forward in a fruitful way, will the mediators of the Class Lessons also be admitted to the inner circle?' At the same time she was concerned about developments in Dornach in the winter of 1925/26.[252]

In the spring of 1927, Helga Geelmuyden was able to feel that the difficult task set by Rudolf Steiner had for the moment been achieved. 'We progressed slowly, but the last mantras will be conveyed by me in mid-February. I will then have fulfilled the promise made to Rudolf Steiner—to convey the mantras to the disciples he had recognized.' She did not consider it possible to continue the work because of tensions in working together with Karl Ingeroe, General Secretary of the Anthroposophical Society in Norway. 'I do think that it is wholly necessary to

[250] Oddvar Granly to J. Kiersch, 30 Dec. 2002.

[251] 'Til de norske medlemmer av første klasse av den frie høiskole for aandsvidenskap. Første klasse av høiskolen holder sin 1ste time i Norge lørdag den 14de mars kl. kvarter over seks precis i Oscarsgate 10. Notisbok medbringes. Det blaa medlemskort forevises ved indgangen. Dørene stenges precis! Helga Geelmuyden' (Oddvar Granly).

[252] Geelmuyden to MSt, 22 Feb. [1926], Lit. Estate Archives. In the same letter she wrote that her correspondence with the leaders of the School was in Rudolf Steiner's lifetime mediated by Guenther Wachsmuth, but had later at his request gone to Ita Wegman, since—as Wachsmuth wrote—'Rudolf Steiner has expressly appointed Dr Wegman leader of the esoteric work.' Wachsmuth's letter to this effect is not known to date.

have an objective approach that goes beyond anything personal in working esoterically. . . . If I were to continue to run Class Lessons, *my way of conveying them* would have to be given more space [i.e. probably extending her commentaries on the mantras] than would certainly be possible under these conditions. Rudolf Steiner's mandate was the only justification I had in doing esoteric work in the group. I was given it because members here would otherwise not have been able to have the mantras. I would not wish to go beyond this under the difficult conditions that exist.'[253] Geelmuyden reaffirmed her decision in March 1927 and was hoping that Marie Steiner might visit them so that the Class work might continue.[254] It is not known if she herself did start again after all in the two years that followed.

She gained new impetus when Anna Gunnarsson-Wager in neighbouring Sweden was at Whitsun 1929 empowered by Marie Steiner and Albert Steffen to read two Class Lessons in the original words of Rudolf Steiner (see Chapter 6.5). Geelmuyden did not refer to this, though she had, of course, heard of it. From then on she pushed with increasing intensity for the Council in Dornach to seek a fundamentally new way of arranging things. At first she was none too happy when Marie Steiner started considering whether Anna Gunnarsson-Wager should not take on the School work for the whole of Scandinavia. She openly said, though with restraint, that as someone appointed by Rudolf Steiner himself and appreciated by Norwegian members she did not intend to accept this. 'Here the wish is that I continue to give the Class Lessons, and I consider it necessary to give newcomers the first mantras as a basis. I therefore put the question which you had discussed with me on your visit to the leaders of our group. The question, therefore, whether people here would agree to having Mrs Gunnarsson from Sweden read the Class Lessons for the *whole* of Scandinavia. A definite wish was, however, expressed that since there was someone here who until now had given the mantras at the behest of Rudolf Steiner, this person should also be in a position to continue this work when it was decided to provide the *valuable* aid of the authentic texts. It was said that more than a hundred members here have the wish to hear the Lessons in their own language. Concern was also felt that it would involve a costly journey if members here had to depend on Mrs

[253] Geelmuyden to MSt, 8 Dec. 1926, Lit. Estate Archives.

[254] Geelmuyden to MSt, 10 Mar. 1927, Lit. Estate Archives.

Gunnarsson who is little known to them. This would no doubt affect the regular rhythm of Lessons.

'I would be glad to know the Council's decision, for if Mrs G. were to continue the work here, I would prefer to withdraw now. I would certainly do so if people in Sweden were given the transcripts and we would not be in a position to have them here.'[255]

The suppressed indignation evident in these lines may have grown when months passed and there was no reply. In December 1929 she wrote to Helene Finckh, the stenographer of the Class Lessons who worked closely together with Marie Steiner, expressing her concern over collaboration between the 'esoteric Council' and the 'mediators of the esoteric material'.[256] Three weeks later she directly asked the Council in Dornach to trust her with the transcripts of the Lessons so that she might read them to members.[257] Ita Wegman, reminding the Council of this, used the opportunity to plead for limiting the reading of Lessons to Council members.[258] The decision was delayed. Marie Steiner thought that reserving reading privilege for the Council was no longer tenable.[259] No decision was made for the time being, not even as regarded the reading activities of Adolf Arenson, Lili Kolisko and Ludwig Polzer.[260]

Geelmuyden then decided to broach the subject openly at the meeting of General Secretaries and National Councils at the end of April 1930. She raised it as a matter of principle, proposing that people still appointed by Rudolf Steiner himself to do the work of the School in the periphery should be included in the decision process. Her words, spoken off the cuff in German—a language in which she was not entirely fluent—and deeply committed, give a richly coloured picture of the situation at the time, especially as regards the difficult and as yet unclear relationship between 'centre' and 'periphery'.

She started by speaking of the position of the 'esoteric Council'. 'People have talked of it as though it was a matter of having uniformity of opinions there. This is not the case, of course, nor can it be. But I would say emphatically that an esoteric council can never be a rigid structure. It

[255] Geelmuyden to MSt, 8 Sept. 1929, Lit. Estate Archives.
[256] Geelmuyden to MSt, 22 Dec. 1929, Lit. Estate Archives.
[257] IW to MSt, 19 Apr. 1930, Goetheanum Archives.
[258] Albert Steffen on Council meeting of 19 Feb. 1930, Goetheanum Archives.
[259] MSt to Steffen, 17 Mar. 1930, Goetheanum Archives.
[260] Minutes of Council, 15 Apr. 1930, Goetheanum Archives.

was called to life out of the world of the spirit at a particular moment by Rudolf Steiner. This is what we are told. Well, he was there at the centre. But surely it is a matter of such a structure having to grow, develop and thrive. And from what source shall it be fed? It can feed on trust. And it must be filled with the life of truth and trust. There are signs of disease which must be taken very seriously, so that we may indeed ask: Is there the possibility of healing from inside, or is the position such that there would have to be surgical intervention? This question, I think, should really be asked in all seriousness and in a feeling of great responsibility by each individual here, and above all, of course, by each member of Council. I am in a position to be sentient of the fact that the situation as it is does not help the work, the esoteric work, in the countries. I mean, how should it be at all possible to take the esoteric work forward after Rudolf Steiner's death. There has to be an understanding among those whom Rudolf Steiner himself asked to do the work. The way things are now, there is really no consistent work. And one can say that the claim has been made that it was Rudolf Steiner's wish that apart from the mantras, the esoteric material he has given should not be passed on by others, but that work be done on the esoteric content in such a way that perhaps personal activity would be cultivated after all in the work. That is how I saw it from my position, and what I have tried to do.—But in the way in which matters were then taken further by the Council, these principles were not adhered to after all. The position now is that the individuals who were closest to Rudolf Steiner and should be in the best position to develop this work actively, that it is really they, being in the best position to take full responsibility, who have after all had to face the fact that too many difficulties were in the way. They have not adhered to Rudolf Steiner's principles. And then there is the fact that others who were less in a position to take full responsibility, did try to do so after all, in all modesty; they would be very much aware of this contradiction. And I think something must come from the chair of the Dornach Council, for it is he who must take the initiative here, something must be done on his part which ensures consistency in the work, not a consistency where everyone says the same and gives the same, but which in accord with Rudolf Steiner's spiritual work means that something comes from individuals. If we are to trust that what is needed to take the work forward will come from the different individuals, then this would have to be looked for first and foremost in the Dornach Council. If we were to remain at the point where we feel a lack of trust in continuing to believe in this possibility from the world of the spirit, then the representatives in the different countries must be called.'[261]

As the debate continued, now concerning the issue of School leadership and Ita Wegman's competence as leader, Geelmuyden spoke movingly of her difficult position. 'It really seems to me that the greatest responsibility would lie not in having the right to read the papers, but really in that a heavy responsibility was given to us by Rudolf Steiner when he asked us to speak to the mantras on the basis of our own work! I am not saying that I would be able to accept this responsibility if from Rudolf Steiner's point of view I had seen it being the case that he would actually no longer have the opportunity to come to us and make further arrangements. At the time I saw it as a task given to me because I was there, had initiative, and said that it would be so important to me—when he said [probably in giving the task to Geelmuyden in Arnhem in July 1924, see above] he would not be able to come right away—if one of the Council members were after all to be permitted to copy down the mantras. Rudolf Steiner then said, putting the list aside: You are permitted to do it; you should give it to all members admitted to the Class in your area. And I asked him: How should this be done? And he said: You should take the mantras and speak about them. This responsibility was much greater than my abilities are to carry it. But I have tried always to work with the greatest truthfulness through something which I had to recognize as having come from the processes of initiation, given as such in the mantras. Then the difficulties really kept on growing. They grew also because things were done differently, with the things which Rudolf Steiner had given being read again and again, and yet in the Society, that is how it often is, recognition is not easily given to anything coming from individual effort, and one does not always adhere exactly to Rudolf Steiner's words. I therefore made the attempt, repeatedly so: Having once abandoned the principle that the transcripts were not available, we, who really had need of more help, should have been given help. I think that it really is too great a burden of responsibility for us who never worked with Rudolf Steiner to that extent, and what does the Council in Dornach know about what is said with reference to the mantras! It might also be that the things said are not correct. So I think that if one considers us

[261] G&C, 25 Apr. 1930, p. 41 f. Goetheanum Archives.

altogether unworthy of the task, we should either stop doing it altogether or you must help us. You must somehow help us! The transcripts exist, therefore, and definitely are not the private property of Dr Wegman, and if they may be read by members of Council then it must be that people appointed by Rudolf Steiner may also read them.'[262]

Geelmuyden was not only speaking for herself here, as is evident from the words of E. A. K. Stockmeyer, the well-known teacher at the Stuttgart Waldorf school, who spoke next: 'I would like to ask if the Council will discuss this, and we may be informed if steps can be taken in the immediate future concerning the needs of these members who live far away, with regard to passing on the Class Lessons by either reading them or giving free renderings. We would really ask for this, for surely the situation is that the people who so far have permission, in one form or another, are not enough yet to meet the need, and it seems to me that an important task waits for us here considering the importance of the First Class when it comes to taking the Society forward.'[263] Other speakers then asked for the reading privilege to be extended. At the time, the Dornach Council—inwardly in dispute as it was—could not bring itself to take up these urgent demands from the 'periphery' in a constructive way.

Geelmuyden was, nevertheless, given permission by Marie Steiner to read the transcripts of the Class Lessons for herself during a stay in Dornach. She assumed that Ita Wegman was in agreement with this. 'She did say of her own accord that although in her view the transcripts could not be copied for the group mediators—an enquiry had come from Mr Smitt in Bergen—I should study them myself, seeing I was here [in Dornach].' 'And so', she continued, 'as Albert Steffen has evidently also agreed, it seems that all the people who set the standard are prepared to help me.'[264] In fact this did not yet mean that Geelmuyden had all the Class Lesson texts in her possession. In July 1930 she sent a tentative enquiry, asking for permission if necessary to take them down when Marie Steiner would be reading them in Norway.[265] The longed-for opportunity to read the Class lectures, at least in exceptional situations, finally came in October. Marie Steiner had to cancel the trip to Norway. 'Could I be given per-

262 Loc. cit. p. 75–77.
263 G&C, 25 Apr. 1930, p. 93.
264 Geelmuyden to MSt, 28 [?29] May [1930], Lit. Estate Archives.
265 Geelmuyden to MSt, 19 July [1930], Lit. Estate Archives.

mission,' Geelmuyden then wrote, 'to *read* Class lectures in this exceptional case, where four Lessons have been promised? With *free* renderings I must have much more time to prepare for each Lesson.' In the same letter she mentioned that she had in the meantime received a number of the lectures so that she might prepare for her work of interpreter in Marie Steiner's Lessons.[266] A few days later, she thanked Marie Steiner and Albert Steffen for the desired 'permission to read Class Lessons', which meant in her own translations.[267] It gives us food for thought that a few months later she wrote to her revered friend: 'We must be infinitely grateful to have permission to receive the texts of the Class Lessons; no fear then of personal elements becoming a disruptive influence, though the need to do my own work at that time did prove very helpful for me.'[268]

It may also be mentioned that the work of the old Esoteric School, where Helga Geelmuyden—as well as Richard Eriksen, Marta Steinsvik and Ole Reitan—had leading roles as 'supervisors', was with Rudolf Steiner's consent cultivated further for many years even after the School of Spiritual Science had been established. The first lesson, connected with the Memphis-Misraim rite (see Chapter 2) had been given in Oslo (then Kristiania) on 16 May 1909. By 1914 thirty-two people had been admitted to the three divisions, three of them in the third degree. The first lesson of the Esoteric School (ES) was given on 16 June 1910.[269] That same year, Norway had *c.* 50 ES students, more than half of the Theosophical Society membership at the time. Rudolf Steiner had solemnly dissolved the group following those rites in December 1921,[270] but he permitted Nanna Thorne to continue the lessons of the Esoteric School, with summaries of the old lessons made available to her from Dornach.[271] Geelmuyden wrote to Marie Steiner: 'In the last talk I had with Rudolf Steiner in Arnhem, after enjoining *me* to convey the *Class Lessons*, he said with regard to my question concerning Miss Thorne: Miss Thorne may continue her activities *for the time being; let those who go to her go to her, and those who come to you come to you.*—I found this difficult, thinking that a

266 Geelmuyden to MSt, 7 Oct. [1930], Lit. Estate Archives.
267 Geelmuyden to MSt, 12 Oct. [1930], Lit. Estate Archives.
268 Geelmuyden to MSt, 23 Apr. [1931], Lit. Estate Archives.
269 GA 266/2 p. 56 ff.
270 GA 265, p. 451.
271 Oddvar Granly to J. Kiersch, 30 Dec. 2002 and 2 Jan. 2003.

split would be harmful. Hoping that Rudolf Steiner would still visit Oslo to arrange the esoteric matter I did not mention this, and merely said: Miss Thorne may certainly continue. I also found it good that this work was going on parallel to my own, for I did not have the texts and was truly facing a difficult task.

'Now the split will perhaps happen after all, possibly involving personal emotions because of lack of awareness, what do I know. There should be more discrimination at an *objective* level. As I told you earlier, I do not think it a good thing that Miss Thorne gives as many of the older mantras as *possible*; these are to be written down, and the students have books for these lessons. It is quite confusing, with the Class verses often not taken seriously enough because people can't cope with it all.

'Otherwise I appreciate the way in which Miss Thorne presents earlier esoteric lectures with great personal warmth.'[272]

In a later letter, she added: 'I really gained the impression that Rudolf Steiner permitted these lessons for the time being more out of regard for Miss Thorne and kindred souls rather than because it was the right thing once the School of Michael existed.'[273]

6.5 Anna Gunnarsson Wager

Anna Gunnarsson Wager (1873–1957) was a central figure in Sweden's anthroposophical movement.[274] She was actively involved in founding the national society in 1913, having attended the Theosophical Congress in Budapest in 1909, where a Christological lecture by Rudolf Steiner left a deep impression. As a member of the national council, and from 1930 also General Secretary, she had far-reaching responsibility for the anthroposophical work in her country, organized events, including the *Christ and the Human Soul* lectures for members in Norrkoeping in 1914, ran a publishing house and a journal, and translated many texts by Rudolf Steiner. She became a close friend of Marie Steiner. Gunnarsson was one of Rudolf Steiner's early esoteric pupils. This explains her certainty and independence when, having attended six Class Lessons given by Rudolf

[272] Geelmuyden to MSt, 2 June. [?1929], Lit. Estate Archives.
[273] Geelmuyden to MSt, 23 Apr. [1931], Lit. Estate Archives.
[274] The information given below is based on F. Carlgren in Plato 2003.

Steiner in Breslau and Dornach, when she may be presumed to have been given the task by him, she started in October 1924, with Ita Wegman's permission, to pass on the School mantras in Stockholm, initially to ten members. A letter she wrote to the Dornach Council on 21 January 1926 tells of the problems which arose in connection with this. The group of ten, with whom she worked regularly throughout that winter, grew to 24, several of whom did not have sufficient knowledge of German. She knew how to help herself. 'I did, of course, adhere to it that people must make a particular effort and write them [the mantras] down ALSO in German and try to read them, but to help them I added a translation / with Dr Wegman's consent[275] / and would always speak about the preceding one, explaining it, when we met the next time, so that they would have worked with them on their own in the meantime. Always reading the mantras in German slowly and reverently, starting with "Human being, know ..." / never letting them take things down / conclusion with "Human soul", esoteric version [evidently indicating that the three angelic hierarchies were called upon in the Christmas Conference version of the *Foundation Stone Meditation* which had not yet been published]. I drew the signs, as given, on the blackboard, but never did them in front of the members, for I had never myself seen them done by Rudolf Steiner, and was not sure at the time if they were to be considered to be mirror image, or IN FRONT OF the human being.'[276] She stopped the work in the summer of 1925—'it was also not my intention to continue'—but at the members' request decided to start again, with 20 new members joining. She gave supplementary lessons in Malmoe and Norrkoeping. 'We are starting with about 10 new members on 31 Jan. [1926] in Stockholm—with older members able to attend again if they wish.'

Finally and with truly delightful openness she came to the 'real purpose' of her letter: 'If the esoteric school is to be WHOLLY meaningful for us, opportunity must no doubt be given to us that we may sooner or later take part in Rudolf Steiner's explanatory lectures, which may be by letting us

[275] Wegman wrote to Gunnarsson on 16 Oct. 1924: 'You might indeed give translations of the mantras into Swedish to members who ask for them and do not know enough German. One should, however, try and convey the mantras in German, because the rhythm has such a great influence. Members who do not know German can meditate using the translation.' (IW Archives.)

[276] Gunnarsson to Council, 21 Jan. 1926, Lit. Estate Archives.

have direct transcripts, circulars, by instructing selected individuals in each country, e.g. that they might read the lectures in Dornach and make notes, or in some other way. In the long run it is not enough to have Class Lessons given only in Dornach—even those of us who understand German and are able to make the journey will in this way have them at most 2 or 3 times a year—nor that someone comes to us from Dornach, perhaps every 10 years, and gives them in German—though we would, of course, like to ask for this *as well*, for a very special occasion.

'If we were to have the actual transcripts, for example, everyone who knows German will, of course, wish to hear them read in those words / and the others too. / It does, however, seem equally natural to me that those others are given the content in their own language. I would add here that if the task were given to *me*, I would not commit myself to doing a written translation and reading this out, but only to an exact, free rendering of the content. The translation is dead and much more likely to cause misunderstanding than a free rendering of summary content. It is, of course, different for the German text, for this has the occult content of the speech sounds.'[277]

Anna Gunnarsson was thus voicing problems with the further development of Class work at an early stage. Other 'mediators' may well have felt the same. In the years that followed she continued to insist on practicable arrangements being made by the leaders of the School.

It is not known so far if the Dornach Council responded to her suggestions. In April 1926, Gunnarsson wrote once again, this time to Marie Steiner, asking for directions concerning problems with Class members who lived some distance away.[278]

In October 1926, Marie Steiner informed her that the Council had decided not to make the Class Lesson transcripts available, in spite of a 'request' from Harry Collison, at least not for reading out. She wrote that Ita Wegman had, however, made an exception in two cases, to make *interpretation* possible. As she was about to visit Sweden, she intended to entrust four of the lectures to her, too, for the purpose of translation only and for no other use, so that she might prepare for the necessary interpreting work at the meetings which were due to be held.[279] Gunnarsson

---

[277] Loc. cit.

[278] Gunnarsson to MSt, 30 Apr. 1926, Lit. Estate Archives.

[279] MSt to Gunnarsson, 27 Oct. 1926, Lit. Estate Archives.

thanked her and was happy to agree.[280] Further letters show that Marie Steiner did give Class Lessons in Stockholm and Norrkoeping, probably in early June 1927, where she would read and Gunnarsson interpret, using notes she had made in preparation.[281]

With reference to a talk in Norrkoeping, Gunnarsson sent an important letter to Marie Steiner in the autumn of 1927 in which she—as a 'suggestion'—outlined her ideas how a 'Rudolf Steiner Association' might work; this had evidently just been founded. It is not yet known if the impetus for this new association had come from an attempt Marie Steiner made, just over a year earlier, to introduce elements of the earlier esotericism in her Class Lessons (see footnote 182). Gunnarsson certainly intended to use such elements—'from the first three degrees'—as well, though, 'seeing we no longer have our leader' there was need now to appeal more strongly to members' awareness of freedom and personal responsibility.[282] 'Miss [?Lisa] Svanberg' was here referred to as 'chair of the R-S Group'. It did, however, take more than a year until the esoteric work of the new group started in earnest. From Gunnarsson's reports it can be concluded that Nils Nordin, a relatively young anthroposophist, gave a fairly long address at the first meeting on 26 November 1928, and that Rudolf Steiner's first Class Lesson was then read out, embedded in formulae from the old Esoteric School.[283]

Six months later Gunnarsson wrote that the new group had just met for the twelfth time.[284] Again she only gives hints to her dear friend, who had evidently written about her own intentions relating to the whole undertaking (letter not traced to date), and how she intended to proceed. She referred to the 'leader' who had given the group detailed directions. Would this be an unknown person whose identity was known to Marie Steiner from earlier conversations? The term 'leader' was used by Gunnarsson for Rudolf Steiner in the letter she wrote in the autumn of 1927. Could it be that she felt that he was still acting as 'leader' from beyond the threshold of death? The instructions given by this mysterious 'leader' are certainly detailed and quite specific. A further meeting was to be held only

[280] Gunnarsson to MSt, 1 Nov. 1926, Lit. Estate Archives.
[281] Gunnarsson to MSt, 28 Apr. and 25 May 1927, Lit. Estate Archives.
[282] Gunnarsson to MSt, 17 Sept. 1927, Lit. Estate Archives.
[283] Gunnarsson to MSt, 26 Nov. 1928, Lit. Estate Archives.
[284] Gunnarsson to MSt, 16 May 1929, Lit. Estate Archives.

if Marie Steiner could join them; for the summer, each member had been set a special task to study specific lectures by Rudolf Steiner; the 'young one', presumably the above-mentioned medical student Nils Nordin, was to visit two specific places in Vaermland for 'studies in occult medical geology' (? in terms of the *Young Doctors' Course* of 1924). Finally the 'leader' had asked for 'decentralization'. 'We must not overburden Marie Steiner', meaning that she could not be expected to go to every place where she might be needed. Gunnarsson felt that this direction confirmed her own earlier view on the future of anthroposophy, drawing conclusions from it regarding strategy: It was a question of a new order not only for Sweden but also for other countries and language areas. The Council should think about this, and perhaps it would later on be possible to come to 'thinking about it in a somewhat larger group of invited people'. 'The continued existence of our Society depends on maintaining the inner work; there must be a group who will always stay together, never tire or let go.' For how long the esoteric work in the 'Rudolf Steiner Association' continued is not known. Meetings certainly resumed in the autumn of 1929 and continued at least until October 1930.[285] Anna Gunnarsson then pursued her great impulse for Dornach to provide for the maintenance and intensification of anthroposophical work in a proposal made at the meeting of General Secretaries and Councils in November 1930 that Albert Steffen be given a more comprehensive mandate.[286]

It remains to say that in view of the heavy burdens on Marie Steiner, Gunnarsson was empowered at Whitsun 1929 to read the full transcripts of Rudolf Steiner's 7th and 8th Class Lessons in Stockholm.[287] Presumably she was soon after this also given the right to read all the other transcripts. Whichever way this may be, Marie Steiner and Albert Steffen thus established a fact, more than a year before the Council had its internal debate on the reading privilege, and this no doubt had a considerable influence on the course of the debate.

---

[285] Gunnarsson to MSt, 4 Oct. 1930, Lit. Estate Archives.

[286] G&C, 29 Nov. 1930, p. 109 ff; Gunnarsson and others to Council, 15 Nov. 1930, Goetheanum Archives.

[287] MSt to Gunnarsson, 24 Apr. 1929, Lit. Estate Archives, w. confirmation by MSt and Steffen.

6.6 Johannes Leino

Johannes Leino (1868–1925), first General Secretary of the Finnish-speaking part of the Anthroposophical Society in Finland, had been connected with the anthroposophical movement from its theosophical times. He and his wife Ellen Leino-Relander had got to know Rudolf Steiner in person in 1908 and Leino had corresponded with him and Marie Steiner from then on. A professional musician and popular conductor, he established an anthroposophical study group with Edvard Selander in Viborg (Viipuri) for a time and then in Helsinki in 1912, gave introductory lectures and for many years published the journal *Antroposofia* together with Kersti Bergroth.[288] He and his wife became members of the First Class on 21 June 1924, which was probably when he was given his task. He later wrote: 'In the summer of 1924, Rudolf Steiner asked me to send on the applications for Class membership and also gave me permission to pass on the Class mantras to people who had the Blue Card.'[289] From then on he would send applications to Dornach with his recommendations and ask permission to give mantras to specific people.[290]

It is not yet known if Johannes Leino held meetings like those Helga Geelmuyden did in Norway and Anna Gunnarsson in Sweden at which the mantras were given out. The early mediators in Scandinavia knew one another, however, and so this is highly probable. Together with Olga von Freymann, Leino received the texts when attending the AGM in Dornach in 1933.[291] It is evident from a later letter that he then read the transcripts of the Class Lessons in Finnish. A protracted illness made him suggest to Marie Steiner that another long-standing member, Miss Katri Lorma, give the readings in his place,[292] but this was probably refused. Some months later, Marie Steiner wrote to him: 'There can be no

[288] E. Ristilae in Plato 2003.

[289] J. Leino to MSt, 14 Aug. 1928, Lit. Estate Archives.

[290] Thus for Olga von Freymann, who was later to give the Class Lessons in the Swedish-speaking Finnish Society (J. Leino to Rudolf Steiner, 27 Nov. 1924, Goetheanum Archives).

[291] MSt to Freymann and Leino, 2 Feb. 1933. Lit. Estate Archives.

[292] Leino to MSt, 19 Dec. 1937, Lit. Estate Archives.

question of giving permission for this to a member who is not known to us.'[293]

A charming anecdote told among Finnish anthroposophists is that when Johannes Leino spoke of how difficult it would be to translate the School mantras into Finnish, Rudolf Steiner said: 'I'll help you.'[294] The promise may have been more seriously meant than it may seem, for Rudolf Steiner was fluent in Hungarian, a language related to Finnish, at least in his childhood.

6.7 Amalie Kuenstler

The first 'mediators' chosen by Rudolf Steiner were members of the School whom he knew and trusted. This is particularly evident in the case of a person whose esoteric work can only be considered in some aspects and in general outline today on the basis of oral though well-vouched-for communications—Amalie Kuenstler (1873–1957) in Cologne. In his comprehensive work on Mathilde Scholl and the people connected with her through destiny, Ekkehard Meffert has given a loving and well-informed description of how theosophical life developed in that city with its rich traditions even before the twentieth century, spreading widely from there to the Rhineland and the neighbouring Ruhr district, how an independent anthroposophical society came to be founded there in 1912/13 on Mathilde Scholl's initiative, how much Rudolf Steiner enjoyed visiting this significant pioneer in the anthroposophical movement and her friends Eugen and Maude Kuenstler in their handsome house at Belfortstrasse 9, which served as a home for the early activities of the Cologne Branch and also the Esoteric School.[295]

Amalie Kuenstler was the manageress of a leading fashion house in Cologne. A member of the Cologne Branch from 1904 and soon also of the Esoteric School, she worked with Imme von Eckardtstein to design

[293] MSt to J. Leino, 4 Apr. 1938, Lit. Estate Archives. It is evident from the same letter that concern over the need for care in dealing with the texts had led to more definite rules: 'The Class texts must remain the property of the Council at the Goetheanum, and this must be put in writing. In this particular case the Council will agree that Miss v. Freymann is put in charge of them.'

[294] Oral communication from Reijo Wilenius, Helsinki.

[295] Meffert 1991.

costumes for the performances of Rudolf Steiner's *Mystery Plays* in Munich, and was a close friend of Marie Steiner. Like Adolf Arenson, she thus belonged to the karmic setting for the 1911 'Society of the Theosophical Way and Art'. So it probably was not by chance that Rudolf Steiner's request that she should convey the Class mantras to the members of the School in Cologne (Mathilde Scholl had by then been living in Dornach for some time) was brought to her by Felix Peipers, who had been given the field of architecture as his domain in that society. According to Gerta Petzl, who read Class Lessons in Cologne at a later time, this happened when Rudolf Steiner 'had started to give the Class Lessons', i.e. in 1924. Petzl went on to say: 'She told me that apart from the mantras she had also used parts of the old esotericism.'[296]

Summing up the situation, Meffert has written: 'Amalie Kuenstler was asked by Rudolf Steiner to give the Class Lessons in 1924. In 1925, after Rudolf Steiner's death, she received the full set of mantras from Ita Wegman, not having attended all the Class Lessons in Dornach. To contribute to their understanding she freely used material from the old Esoteric School when the Class texts were not yet available. She only received these after 1935, and then 'read' the Class with them.'[297]

6.8 Henry Monges

The only mediator outside Europe appointed by Rudolf Steiner himself was, as far as we know, Henry Monges (1870–1954). An architect

[296] G. Petzl, Erinnerungen an Erzaehlungen von Frau Amalie Kuenstler. Goetheanum Archives. Ekkehard Meffert has a report by Gerta Petzl which differs slightly from the above: 'Prior to establishing the First Class of the School, Rudolf Steiner sent a message to Mrs Kuenstler that she should read the Class for its members in Cologne. Only the mantras were then available and not the transcripts of the individual Lessons. The messenger had been Dr Felix Peipers. After Rudolf Steiner's death, Dr Ita Wegman handed the material over to Mrs Kuenstler who, as a member of the old esotericism, had transcripts from the ES which she also drew on when reading the Class mantras. She told me how she felt when reading the Class for the first time. She said she turned to Rudolf Steiner, and when she stood in front of the people she sensed something like a light-filled flow of strength coming from behind and enveloping her. She read the Class in Cologne until her final illness, which lasted 15 months. The period when the ban was imposed in the Nazi era meant that there was a break.'

[297] Meffert 1991, p. 194, with handwritten additions.

by profession, he had been interested in things of the spirit from a young age, being a member of the Theosophical Society from 1893 to 1914. Having heard of the Anthroposophical Society, he went to Dornach in September 1919 with his wife, Maud Breckenridge, and stayed for two years to learn German and hear Rudolf Steiner lecture. On the latter's advice he moved to Chicago where he had his own publishing house (later Anthroposophic Press) to represent the work of Rudolf Steiner in the United States. At Rudolf Steiner's suggestion, he became General Secretary of the Society in North America at the 1923 Christmas Conference, putting great energy into its development.[298] It appears that Monges stayed on in Dornach for a time once the Anthroposophical Society had been newly established. Joining the First Class on 12 February 1924, he probably heard at least Rudolf Steiner's first Class Lessons. His close connection with Rudolf Steiner is evident not only from the many talks he had with him concerning his plans for the USA, but also from the two personal mantras he was given, one of them two days after the first Class Lesson.[299] The mandate to pass the Class mantras on in the United States was probably given in connection with this.

In the years that followed, Monges would frequently send applications for membership to Dornach. He also asked permission to pass mantras on to individual members.[300] He went to Dornach again in April 1926. Whilst crossing the Atlantic, he wrote to Marie Steiner, reflecting on how the meetings he had since started, when he would give out the mantras, might be in future. 'Since Miss Irene Brown & Madame Ricardo already have the Sprueche [*sic*; = mantras] am I to assume that they may, if they wish, attend the meetings at which the Sprueche are given. Also do you believe we should (or could) meet regularly even after the Sprueche would be read & then a few moments of meditation thereafter. Likewise—would it be advisable[?] to give the signs at these meetings—which I understand quite well are not regularly instituted class meetings.'[301] We do not know how Marie Steiner responded to this. Another letter, undated and clearly written in

[298] H. Barnes in Plato 2003. Details in Barnes 2005.

[299] GA 268 (1999), pp. 33 & 100.

[300] Correspondence on admissions, Goetheanum Archives.

[301] Monges to MSt, 17 Apr. 1926, Lit. Estate Archives. Original English.

haste at Villa St Georg, Arlesheim,[302] shows that Monges sought Marie Steiner's permission—probably in connection with those reflections—to read the full texts of the Class Lessons whilst in Dornach.

'I do not of course wish you to make exceptions for me—but it may be a long time before I have the chance again to be here and I should like to have some knowledge of what Herr Doctor Steiner said on the work of the school.' In the first place, therefore, he appears to have been interested in the details concerning the work of the School in general, which were in the transcripts. But an exception that went even further would, of course, have been even better: 'Of course if you think it possible that I might have the actual Lectures to take with me—this [reading them in Marie Steiner's house, which was awkward] would not be necessary.' We see from a later letter to Marie Steiner that he was then in fact given permission to read the texts in her house. He apologized for making some notes on the occasion which were essential for his translation work, but said he certainly did not copy down the texts in full.[303]

In the years that followed, Henry Monges worked with growing eagerness on translations of the mantras. In the autumn of 1929 he wrote to Marie Steiner: 'I am working hard at the translations of the Sprueche—this is of course a big task which I may not be able to complete before I leave here, but before I leave I will place quite a number of translations of Sprueche in your hands for your approval.' He did not think that his own translations should be considered the only ones that were suitable. 'But in America the time has come where we must give the members of first Class an English translation.'[304] It appears that Monges was not corresponding with Harry Collison who was facing the same problem at the time in Britain.

Monges continued to work steadily on his translations. During a further visit to Dornach he reminded Marie Steiner that he had given her a copy of his attempts in 1930, knowing well how inadequate they were. Now—three years later—he had taken another look at the revised versions, together with 'Dr Frankl' [probably Otto Fraenkl-Lundborg]. Perhaps she would like to use these new versions for the two Class Lessons

---

302 The letter was found among documents from the year 1927 in the Goetheanum Archives, but it could also have been written during his visit in April 1926.

303 Monges to MSt, 18 Apr. 1933, Lit. Estate Archives. Original English.

304 Monges to MSt, 25 Sept. 1929, Lit. Estate Archives. Original English.

planned for English Week?[305] Soon after this, Marie Steiner seems to have decided to entrust the full Class Lesson texts to Henry Monges. She had by then also given them, or at least part of them, to others.[306] More than ten years after this, we learn from a letter by Lisa Dreher, later his wife, that he was now reading 'Class Lessons in his translation from time to time'.[307] According to Ehrenfried Pfeiffer, Monges was still 'the only person' to read the Class Lessons in North America in 1948.[308] In 1951 he had to give up this work altogether after a relatively long break, as his eyesight was failing. He proposed Ehrenfried Pfeiffer as his successor.[309]

6.9 Harry Collison and George Adams-Kaufmann

To understand the situation in Britain after the Christmas 1923 Conference, one has to realize that there—even more so than in Holland, where the problem also existed, and in a very different way than in Stuttgart—a latent difference existed from early on between people who were looking for a more traditional, inward-looking kind of anthroposophy and others to whom it was more important to see a worldwide influence in outer terms. Rudolf Steiner had been able to bridge the gap, which showed itself in the anthroposophical movement as a whole and also the School, by looking kindly on either group. After his death it broke open again and made itself felt as a tension between 'centre' and 'periphery'—mildly so in demands to share responsibility, something repeatedly brought up by Helga Geelmuyden and Anna Gunnarsson in Norway and Sweden, and more acutely so in the form of a conflict which started early in Britain and soon became permanent and could not be resolved.

The differences between Albert Steffen and Eleanor C. Merry, essentially still very restrained, appear to be symptomatic of this. A year after Rudolf Steiner's death this was the background to essays appearing in the Dornach newsletter. Merry was a friend who was working with Daniel Nicol Dunlop (1868–1935), at that time the outstanding figure among British anthroposophists. An occultist from early youth, successful

305 Monges to MSt, 1 Aug. 1933, Lit. Estate Archives.
306 Monges to MSt, 27 Sept. 1934, Lit. Estate Archives.
307 L. Dreher Monges to MSt, 12 July 1945. Lit. Estate Archives.
308 E. Pfeiffer to MSt, 30 Nov. 1948. Lit. Estate Archives.
309 Monges to Steffen, 12 Jan. 1951. Goetheanum Archives.

businessman and cosmopolitan, he had met Rudolf Steiner in person in 1922, put much energy and far-sighted vision into making anthroposophy publicly known, and was highly esteemed by Rudolf Steiner.[310] The initiative taken by Dunlop and Merry led to the summer conferences in Penmaenmawr (GA 227) and Torquay (GA 243) which were of great importance for the destiny of the anthroposophical movement; later, in 1928, the World Conference in London.

In April 1926, Steffen published 'Gedenkworte zum Todestage Rudolf Steiners' (memorial on the anniversary of Rudolf Steiner's death), movingly describing how he saw the situation one year after the spiritual teacher had left this earth. 'Before, we only had to go to the woodwork shop to receive new wisdom, at no great effort. Now we have to take the road to the stars ourselves.' With great poetic power he described a road of inwardly entering wholly into the secrets of the cosmos and of human history, starting from the riches which the Master had left behind.[311] Merry responded by acknowledging the merits of the essay and then writing of the wholly different situation of members in the 'periphery'. Being far from Dornach, we have always had to cope on our own in the chaos of a world inimical to things of the spirit. '*There is no Schreinerei* (woodwork shop) *to go to*. And it has been like that, not for one year, but for all the years.' No reason for complaint, however. This darkness allowed a pioneering spirit of its own kind to develop. 'The same love and loyalty for the Anthroposophical Cause animates the outposts as that which glows from the diamond-hearted Centre at Dornach; but their courage must be recognised alongside of their weaknesses and their failures; for the difficulties and the failures are, when they are honestly faced, the steps of the ladder of initiation. And I believe also the not having had the privilege of constant nearness to the Teacher, not feeling so keenly the purely personal and physical loss, the sense of the *spiritual* nearness comes to us now, very often, with a wonderful radiance of benediction, encouragement and hope.'[312]

Both moods could probably have co-existed for some time, as there was mutual regard. They did not, for claims made to exclusiveness soon

[310] T. Meyer in Plato 2003; detailed in Meyer 1996, Villeneuve 2004.
[311] *Nbl.*, 11 Apr. 1926.
[312] One year after. Some thoughts from the 'Periphery'. *Nbl.*, 9 May 1926. Original English.

gained the upper hand—not least because of escalating strife at the centre in Dornach.[313] The two 'representatives' appointed in Britain by Rudolf Steiner continued to make efforts towards fruitful collaboration for a considerable time. Their different functions—very probably expressly assigned as such by Rudolf Steiner—initially made this difficult task easier for them.

Harry Collison (1868–1945) had heard lectures by Rudolf Steiner when in Rome in the spring of 1910, and soon after this attended the premiere of the first *Mystery Play* in Munich. He became an esoteric pupil of Rudolf Steiner and joined the German Section of the Theosophical Society. During the First World War he still saw himself as a member of the Berlin Branch. He then established the Myrdhin study group in London, and translated many of Rudolf Steiner's lectures, publishing them in his own publishing house. Lecture tours took him far beyond Britain to the United States, Australia and New Zealand. As co-founder and General Secretary of the Anthroposophical Society in Great Britain he represented his country at the Christmas Conference.[314] Above all, however, he presumably played a leading role in Rudolf Steiner's Esoteric School even before the war. This made him an obvious choice as first 'representative' of the new School in Britain. Later opponents were never in doubt about this. Ita Wegman wrote in the notes for her introductory address for the first Class Lesson in London: 'Here in Britain, Mr Collison is the first and Mr Kaufmann the second representative'.[315] D. N. Dunlop at least did not reject Albert Steffen's statement that 'Mr Collison . . . as a

[313] Little more than a year before her death, Ita Wegman wrote a strange letter to Guenther Wachsmuth where she derives fruitful prospects for the future from the difference under consideration: 'Human beings have two different aspects in their nature which reflect the two cosmic movements—centrifugal and centripetal. Each has its own justification, and its function. / The difference led to the split in the [Anthroposophical] Society. Unification will only be possible if there is understanding—*binding* by allowing freedom—and this we had in the person of Rudolf Steiner. . . . I merely wish to mediate—whatever lives in those doing the Anthr. work and whatever may arise in the future, when the national societies can be built up again after the war. The Council will be better able to bind if they are able to permit freedom and to respect this differentiation and this inmost need for new forms.' (Quoted from Selg 2004, p. 124.)

[314] MSt in *Nbl.*, 6 Mar. 1938. P. Martyn in Plato 2003. In detail, Villeneuve 2004, vol. 1, p. 236 ff.

[315] EZ III, p. 64.

man of confidence in esoteric matters, occupies the first position. He is to be regarded as steward of the Meditations. Mr Kaufmann in his capacity as translator is to be regarded as a person of confidence in the School.'[316]

George Kaufmann (1894–1963) was one of the pioneers in anthroposophically renewed natural science. Son of an English mother and German father and born in eastern Galicia, then part of Austria, he grew up trilingual.[317] An active pacifist and conscientious objector, he was actively involved politically and socially. He met anthroposophy during the First World War and soon also Rudolf Steiner in person. Thanks to his linguistic skills he became his indispensable helper with the interpreting that was needed on Rudolf Steiner's lecture tours in Britain.[318] He, too, felt that Rudolf Steiner had given him responsibility for the First Class.[319] According to Eleanor Merry this was particularly in connection with language mediation.[320] He did pass on applications for membership with his recommendations to Dornach and also queries concerning work with the mantras, but for many years did not give Class Lessons himself. His activities for the First Class, carried out with dedication and most dutifully, were limited to organizing the meetings, setting dates, making the physical arrangements (see Appendix 24), and translation. Initially the

---

[316] Dunlop to Council, 19 Dec. 1927. Goetheanum Archives. Appendix 19. Original English. It should be noted that the first study group in Britain to work with Rudolf Steiner's teachings had been established by Herbert James Heywood-Smith and his wife, continuing in London for many years as the Zarathustra Group. Heywood-Smith was, like Harry Collison, among the first members of the German Section of the Theosophical Society and like Collison was considered a representative in Britain of the Anthroposophical Society when it had been founded in 1913. (Biographical documentation, Kulturimpuls research centre, Heidelberg/Dornach. In detail, Villeneuve 2004.) Rudolf Steiner gave an esoteric lesson on the premises of this group at 47 Radcliffe Square, London SW, on 16 April 1922 for all members who had received personal meditations from him (GA 266/3, p. 369).

[317] The documents referred to in this chapter all use his father's name, Kaufmann. We will therefore stay with this name, though George did decide to take his mother's name, Adams, during the Second World War.

[318] R. Ziegler in Plato 2003.

[319] 'But I do not think it right to relinquish the responsibilities which Dr. Steiner gave me in the matter of the First Class.' (To Collison, 6 Oct. 1927. London Archives.) Original English.

[320] '. . . because he was asked by the Dr to translate the mantras and enter deeply into them in the process . . .' (Merry to IW, 6 Oct. 1927, IW Archives.)

main responsibility was evidently Harry Collison's; he was not only responsible for matters concerning the School but from the Christmas Conference onwards also held the office of General Secretary. He characterized his inner attitude to his responsibilities, also being a bit of a schoolmaster in showing his level of decision-making in the right light, in writing about the First Class in the English Society newsletter: 'Frau Dr Wegman gave on Sunday morning a lecture to the First Class. It is beginning to be realised that this is quite a special matter that must be dealt with in a special way. In admitting members there is a very great and eternal responsibility both on the person who admits the member and upon the person admitted. Very great earnestness is required, and it is far better to wait patiently the time appointed by one's karma than to rush in upon it. There is no question of members of the First Class being better Anthroposophists than those who are not members. It is a question of karmic responsibility.'[321]

In August 1925, Rudolf Steiner's mandate for Collison was affirmed by Ita Wegman to the effect that she gave him the power to convey the School mantras also at group meetings.[322] Collison thanked her for the trust put in him: 'It is a great honour but a great responsibility. And I know you feel this too. But so long as my health lasts I hope to help.' He suggested, however, to wait until her projected visit in October before beginning. 'I then can learn a little more about it, and can avoid mistakes. For instance, I should like to have a good talk over the esoteric side [changing to German here:] and make and have everything clear. I am, however, wholly in agreement with your proposals and thank you so much for your kind trust.'[323] Kaufmann for his part had informed Wegman some days earlier that Collison's decision would be positive, merely commenting that the suggested weekly rhythm for the Lessons was not likely to prove possible. He also asked most urgently for a

321 *Anthroposophical Movement. Weekly News*, Vol. II, No. 30, 26 July 1925, p. 245. Original English.

322 The letter in question has not so far been found. It may be assumed that Wegman's comment in the *Nbl.* of 16 Aug. 1925 did refer to this, however: 'The best way would be for everyone to receive at regular intervals the elements for his continuous instruction; then the number of people attending individual Lessons would not be so great and the intimate nature of the Lessons could be preserved. . . . This has already proved successful in England . . .' Also in EZ III, p. 62.

323 Collison to IW, 30 Aug. 1925, IW Archives. Original English.

complete list of Class members.[324] In another letter to Wegman Collison then confirmed in December 1925 that he had started Class meetings (Wegman's visit had not taken place until November). 'We had our Meeting of the First Class this morning, and all seemed to go well, and as you wished.'[325]

It is not yet known if George Kaufmann received the mantras of the First Class for translation in Rudolf Steiner's day or only at this point, from Ita Wegman. Collison certainly turned to him about them. 'Frau Wegman has told me that you ought to give me all the 1st Class Meditations—twenty-one. I shall be content with copies.'[326] In Dornach, Collison soon took care that the membership cards included the notice to return them which has since become customary. In the minutes of the Council meeting of 18 February 1926 it says: 'At the suggestion of Mr Collison, all blue and red membership cards will in future bear the following stamp on the back: "In case of death or resignation this card is to be sent back to the General Anthroposophical Society".'[327]

At first it seemed that collaboration between Collison and Kaufmann on matters concerning the School and also the Anthroposophical Society would offer no problems. In March 1926, Kaufmann wrote of shared preparations for the festivities to celebrate the opening of the new Rudolf Steiner Hall, with guests coming from the whole anthroposophical world.[328] But the contention in Dornach during the winter of 1925/26 was now spreading to Britain. M. Wheeler, D. N. Dunlop and Kaufmann complained to Guenther Wachsmuth that they still had no news of Ita Wegman's proposed visit in early November, using the opportunity to be firm in rejecting excessive leadership claims on the part of Collison, saying that he had informed the Council of the Anthroposophical Society in Great Britain that he had asked in Dornach to be given leadership under sole control of the Council in Dornach, 'an absolute control of the First Class in England subject to the

[324] Kaufmann to IW, 24 Aug. 1925. London Archives. According to a letter of 16 Sept. 1925, the First Class had 134 members by that time (not known to Collison. London Archives).

[325] Collison to IW, 13 Dec. [1925], IW Archives. Original English.

[326] Collison to Kaufmann, 24 Jan. 1926, London Archives. Original English.

[327] Goetheanum Archives.

[328] Kaufmann to IW, 15 Mar. 1926. IW Archives.

Vorstand'. This claim must be rejected: '...we desire to place on record that we have no knowledge of such control being granted to Mr Collison by Dr Steiner, and, further, that such a contention does not accord with what we heard Dr Steiner say when he held the Class in England.'[329]

At the same time, Adolf Arenson in Stuttgart, deeply concerned about the situation in the anthroposophical movement, sent out his 'circular' (see Appendix 15), and this raised a storm of indignation among Ita Wegman's friends. Collison felt his position was strengthened by it. He wrote to Arenson that he'd been criticized for not showing Dr Wegman and Zeylmans the respect they merited when they came to the opening of Rudolf Steiner Hall. His own view was that such a building should really have been opened by the president of the [world] Society, i.e. Albert Steffen, and Marie Steiner. The compromise he had suggested was that Ita Wegman should continue her Class Lessons in Britain as appointed by the Council in Dornach, and thus not on her own responsibility. He wrote in detail to his Stuttgart friend about the complex discussions of the problem, not without the occasional swipe at the idolization he thought existed among those around Ita Wegman, 'the attitude of false personal sentimentality that is making a Sect of the Anthroposophical Movement'. Many people in Britain who were interested were studying the works of Rudolf Steiner independently, outside the Society. He felt tempted to withdraw completely, but still considered it his responsibility to give the movement form, so that it would not turn into a Dutch or English sect that was 'international' only in name.[330] Collison felt bound by Rudolf Steiner's mandate.[331] He did, however, seriously aggravate the existing tension by making his claim to leadership very apparent. In August 1927, Dunlop had still respected Collison's position in the fullest sense. Speaking

---

[329] Wheeler, Dunlop and Kaufmann to Wachsmuth, 12 Oct. 1926. IW Archives. Original English.

[330] Collison to Arenson, 7 Nov. 1926. Lit. Estate Archives. See Appendix 16. Quotes in original English.

[331] Kaufmann later wrote that Collison said 'he was altogether, as instituted by Rudolf Steiner, the leader in the First Class in England; and had been so even before the First Class was established.... The background to this was, of course, that his position in the old esotericism did as a matter of course continue to be valid for the new School.' (Kaufmann to IW, undated (?1934). IW Archives.)

to Eleanor Merry, he insisted that the Council in Britain ('Executive') had nothing to do with decisions concerning the First Class. 'All this is wholly in the hands of Mr Collison—and Mr Kaufmann as keeper of the mantric texts. Mr Collison has always considered himself to be the esoteric "head" in England, saying that Rudolf Steiner called him such.'[332]

Then, however, Collison had a highly provocative notice put in the newsletter of the national Society: 'First Class of the School of Spiritual Science. Mr. Collison finds it necessary to remind members that he is the leader of the first class and Esoteric School in England, and communications in regard to anything concerning this should be directed to him personally at 25 Hereford Square, London, S.W.7.'[333] This was not acceptable to the opposition. The rights of George Kaufmann had to be protected, and in its urgently needed activities for the spread of anthroposophy, the group around Dunlop could not tolerate any ominous authority controlling it. In a heated debate in Council ('Executive'), Collison declared this body not competent, being exoteric, asked for the debate to be postponed, as it might affect the imminent visit by Marie Steiner, and drew attention to the danger of a split in the Society, but to no avail. 'Dunlop & Kaufmann', he wrote to Wachsmuth, 'did not care, they welcomed it'. He did once again appeal to Dornach for support, referring to the mandate Rudolf Steiner had given him personally, not in connection with his office.[334] In a confidential letter to Marie Steiner he complained with acerbity about his opponent's claims to power.[335] Eleanor Merry, who in turn was keeping Ita Wegman informed, initially reacted with similar agitation and came to assume that in his stubbornness Collison 'makes every preparation to provide Marie Steiner with the opportunity for a *coup d'état*',[336] but impressive supersensible experiences then made her take a less agitated view. A split, she felt, was unavoidable and would later on lead to 'a larger unity'.[337]

---

[332] Merry to IW, 21 Aug. 1927. IW Archives. Original English.
[333] 4 Sept. 1927. Original English.
[334] Collison to Wachsmuth, 28 Sept. 1927. Lit. Estate Archives. Quote in original English.
[335] Collison to MSt, 28 Sept. 1927. Lit. Estate Archives.
[336] Merry to IW, 30 Sept. [1927]. IW Archives.
[337] Merry to IW, 6 Oct. [1927]. IW Archives. See Appendix 18.

Dunlop tried to reach mutual understanding in a private talk with Collison, also wanting to avoid a commotion during Marie Steiner's visit, for this might damage the London World Conference planned for 1928.[338] Ita Wegman also advised her friends to look for a peaceful solution. It would be best, she wrote to Merry, if two additional representatives were appointed for the First Class, in addition to Collison and Kaufmann, or if the whole Executive could take responsibility for it.[339] What is more, people in Dornach were afraid that the World Conference on Spiritual Science planned for London might cause financial problems with the inauguration of the Second Goetheanum building.[340] D. N. Dunlop finally summed up existing problems in a carefully worded status report, asking the Council in Dornach to appoint two more representatives ('persons of confidence')—Wheeler, then in office as treasurer, and himself as General Secretary.[341] It appears, however, that his suggestion was not taken up.[342] The conflict thus grew progressively worse.

Collison, seeing his position threatened more than ever, addressed himself to Marie Steiner for help. 'The only rocks upon which I can stand now are the First Class and the Publishing Company.... The First Class I must be able to give independently of the graces of Kaufmann. The Publishing rights must be reaffirmed in your name.'[343] He was even more explicit in an undated letter, presumably written at that time: 'Though I may be unable to continue for long as an Official in

---

[338] E. Kolisko to IW, 9 Nov. 1927. IW Archives. The crisis which then existed is described in detail in this letter.

[339] IW to Merry, 28 Nov. 1927. IW Archives.

[340] In her letter to Merry, Wegman wrote that the plan was now 'to make it known everywhere ... that the building can be opened at Michaelmas, and encourage people to give their all, so that it may all flow towards Dornach, rather than spend money on the world conference.' The only possibility, therefore, was 'to take a firm stand and pursue one's own initiative without asking too much if the Anthroposophical Society may not like it perhaps or be well content.... You see how everything is received with limited understanding; people are not even allowed to go there, lest they widen their horizons, keeping everything as narrow and one-sided as possible.' (IW to Merry, 19 Dec. 1927. IW Archives.)

[341] Dunlop to Council, 19 Dec. 1927. Goetheanum Archives. See Appendix 19.

[342] 'But it did not prove possible,' Eleanor Merry wrote later to Wegman (6 Sept. [1928]. IW Archives).

[343] Collison to MSt, 3 July 1928. Lit. Estate Archives. Original English.

the Society—, I hope I may be able to control the First Class and the Publishing affairs. Miss Pethick and many others are anxious for me to have the original text. Kaufmann keeps his notes, & this is illegal. The whole matter is inconsistent.'[344] Two months later he learned from Dorothy Pethick, who may well have looked in on Marie Steiner when in Dornach, that he was invited to read the Class texts in Dornach and make notes.[345] This meant that very quietly, with the other members of the Dornach Council not being informed, and in accord with the wish he had had for a long time, Collison was given a similar privilege to Ludwig Polzer even before Helga Geelmuyden and Anna Gunnarsson. Ludwig Polzer had had that permission earlier on, with Ita Wegman making her own decision (see Chapter 6.11). It may be assumed that Collison copied a great deal in Dornach. When Ita Wegman, having grown suspicious, asked him soon after this how he gave the Class Lessons, he spoke of the earlier agreement, which had been that he would speak freely, basing himself on Kaufmann's notes without reference to the latter's name. He also said that he had heard the first Lessons so many times that he had certain passages almost by heart. Discreetly, though this told Marie Steiner much, he added: 'There was no reference to any verbatim translation. She seemed satisfied. Your name was not mentioned.'[346]

At the same time polarization in the national Society in Britain reached a new stage. Dunlop resigned his office as General Secretary, with the twelve people of the Executive together taking on leadership. Heywood-Smith's Zarathustra Group separated from the national Society, making direct connection with Dornach. Collison created a Rudolf Steiner Fellowship with a group A, whose members were also directly connected with Dornach, and a group B which continued to belong to the national Society. Ita Wegman informed Albert Steffen of this development, adding: 'The Class Lesson [which she had given] went well. Mr Collison will do a repetition from time to time by speaking the mantras and adding a few words of explanation of his own. He himself told me that this is how he does it.'[347]

---

[344] Collison to MSt, undated. Lit. Estate Archives. Original English.
[345] Collison to MSt, 4 Sept. 1928. Lit. Estate Archives.
[346] Collison to MSt, 11 Dec. 1928. Lit. Estate Archives. Original English.
[347] IW to Steffen, 18 Dec. 1928. Goetheanum Archives.

The disputes on the Dornach Council's reading privileges in 1930 only touched Britain marginally.[348] The more important aspect there was that Collison took his Myrdhin Group completely out of the national Society and then re-established it.[349]

D. N. Dunlop, in the meantime again elected General Secretary, and his friends then refused to include announcements of Class Lessons in the newsletter of the national Society,[350] asking the members of the Myrdhin Group to let them know if they wished to joint the national Society again or not.[351] From June 1930 onwards, separate Class Lessons were presumably given by Collison in the Myrdhin Group, possibly in cooper-

[348] At the insistence of Ita Wegman the Council decided on 19 February 1930 that reading the Class texts should be the sole privilege of members of the Dornach Council. A first draft of the document informing Ludwig Polzer and Harry Collison, probably by Ita Wegman, said: 'To have uniformity in the way Class Lessons are given, and to avoid further spread and difficulties, we would ask that the giving of Class Lessons, i.e. *reading the texts* of the Class Lessons, be reserved exclusively for the members of Council, and that in studying the mantras with your group you will refrain from reading Rudolf Steiner's texts (except for the texts of the mantras themselves).' Marie Steiner added a critical note by hand: 'If Mr Collison is *not* reading them and has expressly told Dr Wegman so, this is surely an insult. Polzer does, however, read them.' (Council to Collison and Polzer. Draft 20 Feb. 1930. Goetheanum Archives.) The final version then read: '. . . so that, although we regret being unable to meet your wishes, your study of the mantras with your group would also have to be without reading Rudolf Steiner's texts (except for the texts of the mantras themselves).' (Council to Collison, 20 Feb. 1930. Goetheanum Archives. See also MSt's report in G&C, 25 Apr. 1930, p. 96. Goetheanum Archives.) Wegman sent a copy of this letter to Kaufmann, adding: '. . . he [Collison] appears to have asked about the text at one time, at least that is what Marie Steiner says. Where did he get the texts from? He is reading them out, isn't he?' (IW to Kaufmann, 21 Feb. 1930. London Archives.) It is possible that her suspicion was justified and that Collison had meanwhile received the complete texts.

[349] According to the draft of a letter Dunlop wrote to members of the Myrdhin Group, Collison told the Executive Council of the separation on 18 Mar. 1930 (undated. London Archives). See also Council minutes, Dornach 15 Apr. [1930]. Goetheanum Archives.

[350] Elsie Hamilton to Executive, 26 May 1930; Executive to Hamilton, 18 May 1930. Dunlop to Hamilton, 1 June 1930. London Archives.

[351] Draft, Dunlop, undated, probably June 1930. London Archives.

ation with the group around Heywood-Smith,[352] and by Ita Wegman who was assisted by George Kaufmann. Collison complained that Kaufmann refused all contact with him, and asked Marie Steiner to admit an applicant to the Class who had been refused by Ita Wegman because of her (the applicant's) differences with 'Kaufmann & Company', a sign that the former decision of the Dornach Council to admit new members together, did no longer apply.[353]

A characteristic indication of the tense situation and the discreet manoeuvres made by both sides to strengthen their position is given in Ita Wegman's advice to Kaufmann who was unsure if he should meet Collison's request[354] and let him have the addresses of new Class members she had admitted. She thought one should simply not reply to the request, accepting that the Executive, and hence Dunlop and Kaufmann, were responsible for the well-being of the First Class. The situation would, of course, be different if Collison were to be more definitely supported by Marie Steiner or Steffen in Dornach. 'Then the moment will have come for me when I no longer take part and say very firmly that I on my part cannot put my trust in him and then put it in someone else who should then also read out the texts at the same time as C. does it, e.g. reads from the text.' She wanted to avoid this for as long as possible, however. 'I don't know,' she added, 'if I have made myself sufficiently clear, for with this Class you have to be very exact, yet at the same time also not too inflexible.'[355]

In October 1930, Collison once more sought Marie Steiner's help, asking her to produce the necessary membership cards for people who attended his Class Lessons and did not want to be admitted by Ita Wegman. 'I can vouch personally for all these members, but they do not care to ask Frau Wegman, and therefore are precluded from this First Class if you do not give them a card. It becomes very awkward for me, as I still continue to read and explain the Mantrams, and they do not understand why they should be excluded from the privilege of hearing them.'[356]

[352] In April 1930, Dorothy Osmond wrote to George Kaufmann: 'I hear that Heywood Smith is giving lectures or classes at the new book-shop opened by Collison people in Westminster.' London Archives. Original English.

[353] Collison to MSt, 5 June 1930. Lit. Estate Archives.

[354] Collison to Kaufmann, 28 May 1930. London Archives.

[355] IW to Kaufmann, 21 June 1930. IW Archives.

[356] Collison to MSt, 21 Oct. 1930. Lit. Estate Archives. Original English.

Final evidence of Collison's desolate situation by the end of that year is a telegram he sent to Marie Steiner on 8 November 1930: 'Dunlop claims control first class please remind Steffen leadership given me personally by doktor Steiner not necessarily connected with secretary general many members object to new society different from the one founded by doktor Steiner and are leaving it. . . .'[357]

In the years that followed, positions grew progressively more fixed also in Dornach, so that it made it even more difficult to bridge the differences in Britain: 'Here we have out and out catholicism, no one is free any more. The latest thing is that they want to have the name Anthroposophy and Rudolf Steiner patented.'[358] In April 1933, Ita Wegman wrote to Kaufmann and complained that Collison's report on Britain published in the weekly *Goetheanum* paper gave the impression, which was completely wrong, that Collison continued to play a leading role there.[359] Some months later she wrote with acerbity about the newsletter edited by Collison: 'In the New[s] Sheets, controlled from here, I see a tremendously hostile act against the properly established Anthroposophical Society in Great Britain. All events are listed, including those in London, but only those submitted by Collison, so one gets a completely wrong picture of the situation. C[ollison] has the cheek to announce Class Lessons on Sundays. All I can say is that we must keep a very close eye on the matter and raise strong objections.'[360] Early in 1934 she insisted on giving Class Lessons again in Dornach, having refrained from this previously for the sake of peace.[361] Wachsmuth then drafted a diplomatic reply, finally giving up the fiction which had so far been maintained that the Class was run by the members of the Founding Council together. 'In your letters to Marie Steiner and Mr Steffen you stated that their views on giving Class Lessons were not authoritative. The undersigned are therefore not in a position to respond to your letter of 14 January and will not be able in future to take responsibility for your way of handling Class matters.'[362] A few days later, D. N. Dunlop refused to send the addresses

357 Lit. Estate Archives. Original English.

358 IW to Kaufmann, 24 Nov. 1932. London Archives.

359 IW to Kaufmann, 29 Apr. 1933. London Archives.

360 IW to Kaufmann, 14 Oct. 1933. London Archives.

361 IW to Steffen, 14 Jan. 1934. Goetheanum Archives.

362 Draft by Wachsmuth, marked 'agreed' by MSt. Note on copy: 'sent on 19 January 1934'. Goetheanum Archives.

of Class members in Britain to Dornach, which had been the custom until then, saying that trust, having been lost, must first be restored.[363] Wachsmuth expressed his indignation.[364] In the meantime, friends of Ita Wegman prepared a 'declaration of will' for the AGM of the General Anthroposophical Society at the end of March, and this aggravated the situation further.[365] Over the summer, the 'United Independent Anthroposophical Groups' established themselves in Britain and Holland after preparatory members' meetings, and these had their own membership cards.[366] The conflict was coming to a head with the disastrous AGM in April 1935 when members connected with Wegman and Vreede were excluded from the Anthroposophical Society.

In July 1935, Collison ('confidentially') had the name 'Rudolf Steiner' legally protected.[367] Far beyond the end of the Second World War, the two anthroposophical streams which had developed around Marie Steiner (and until the battle over the literary estate also Steffen and Wachsmuth) on the one hand, and Ita Wegman on the other, functioned separately. Harry Collison was progressively entering into tragic isolation. Something over a year before his death he sent Marie Steiner, to whom he remained unerringly faithful even in the battle over the literary estate which was now beginning, a bitter summing up of the endeavours in his last years. He wrote how Cecil Harwood had visited him some months before the Second World War, i.e. in 1939, to talk with him about his enemies at London's Park Road, the 'headquarters' of Wegman's friends. In answer to a question from Harwood, he had said that if they wanted reunion, they would have to go to Dornach and ask for it.[368] He himself could not find a way out of the dead end he had come to in life.

It remains to show how the work of the second 'representative' of the

[363] Dunlop to Steffen, MSt and Wachsmuth, 24 Jan. 1934. Goetheanum Archives.

[364] Wachsmuth to MSt and Steffen, 5 Feb. 1934. Goetheanum Archives.

[365] E. Kolisko, D. N. Dunlop and W. Zeylmans van Emmichoven to Steffen, 23 Mar. 1934, Goetheanum Archives.

[366] Open letter, J. v. Grone and E. Kolisko, 18 June 1934. Dunlop, Kaufmann, Zeylmans, de Haan, v. Grone, Kolisko, Vreede to Steffen, 4 July 1934. Goetheanum Archives.

[367] Wachsmuth to Steffen and MSt, 17 July 1935. Goetheanum Archives. Acc. to a note by Wachsmuth this was done by officially registering a 'Rudolf Steiner Association Ltd'. Goetheanum Archives.

[368] Collison to MSt, 25 Apr. 1944. Lit. Estate Archives. See Appendix 33.

School in Britain, George Kaufmann, developed following the discord between him and Collison. As already stated, Kaufmann initially limited his activities for many years to organization, recommending membership applicants, and above all to his work as a translator and interpreter. He worked closely together with Ita Wegman from 1925 until her death in 1943. She regularly read Class Lessons in London and other places in England and Scotland. Kaufmann freely interpreted the texts she read into English, probably in much the same way—summing up in three stages—as he used to interpret for Rudolf Steiner. At first he was not allowed to see the full transcripts to prepare himself, only receiving permission (in July 1927) to translate such mantras as were required.[369] More than a year later, he asked Wegman to read a Lesson to him the day before.[370] It is therefore improbable that he and Mrs Wedgwood had 'the full version' by the end of 1927, as Collison maintained.[371] Even in 1937 he only had a written translation of the first Lesson, which he had produced at Wegman's request for her to read 'many years ago', though she had then not made use of it.[372] Since Wegman firmly supported the Dornach Council's reading privilege in the spring of 1930, it is unlikely that she would have given Kaufmann the complete texts at that time.

Kaufmann continued to correspond with Ita Wegman on the situation in Britain, and about courses he gave for students in mathematics and medicine, among other things on ideas and exercises in projective geometry and the modelling of organs.[373] He was tireless in arranging for Wegman's Class Lessons in Britain, sending out invitations to these on his own, without Collison, from February 1933 at the latest.[374] Summing up

[369] 'It appears that Mr Collison plans to have further Class Lessons given during the English Conference in Dornach in August, for he recently showed me a letter in which Dr Wachsmuth (in response to his request) wrote to confirm that Mr Steffen had replied I could translate some more mantras.' Since he had not heard the Lessons, however, and would have problems translating the mantras without having heard them, he wrote to Wegman, he would ask her 'to bring the next Class Lessons with you to England (perhaps the twelfth and thirteenth as well as the eleventh), so that I can do the translations with your help, as in previous cases.' (Kaufmann to IW, 11 July 1927. IW Archives.)

[370] Kaufmann to IW, 4 Dec. 1928. London Archives.

[371] Collison to MSt, 14 Nov. 1927. Lit. Estate Archives.

[372] Kaufmann to IW, 4 Feb. 1937. IW Archives.

[373] Kaufmann to IW, 19 Oct. 1932 and 1 Feb. 1933. London Archives.

[374] London Archives.

the situation with his extensive anthroposophical work in the country he wrote to Wegman in 1932: 'I am constantly invited to visit individual branches when I am here, but I have to ask myself again and again how the work may be made fruitful. Especially in more recent times I feel more and more the need to strengthen the *inner* life among our friends. Life in the branches should be a steady preparation in the early years for membership in the School of Michael for those who are serious about it. If such preparation is not given, one has the same sad result again and again: warm initial enthusiasm gives way to disappointment, discouragement, helplessness. Anthroposophy is too much for people unless they can feel the real presence of the School. The Society is, however, in a muddle in its present state. How can we make up for it that the impulses of the Christmas Conference had not taken effect centrally, at the Goetheanum? That is the central issue. It is a matter of life and death for the present life in our Society in Britain.'[375]

When the British and Dutch groups had been excluded, the friends met at Clent in August 1935 to consider the demands arising from the new situation: Ita Wegman, Elisabeth Vreede, Maria Roeschl, Willem Zeylmans van Emmichoven, Eugen Kolisko, Juergen von Grone, Herbert Hahn, Fried Geuter, Michael Wilson and George Kaufmann. They decided that Ita Wegman should continue her readings in the anthroposophical centres in Holland and Britain (it was no longer possible in Germany by that time) and that in addition meetings of Class members were to be conducted by Vreede in Britain, and by Vreede, Zeylmans and Hahn in Holland, at which the mantras would be communicated, with explanations added in their own words.[376] Instead of the blue membership cards they would in future issue 'a more provisional form of certificate'.[377]

At the end of October, following a discussion with Lili Kolisko who had raised objections,[378] Ita Wegman was in favour of continuing to

[375] Kaufmann to IW, 19 Oct. 1932. London Archives.
[376] From July 1937, Class Lessons were given every three weeks, alternating between The Hague and Zeist (communication from Joop van Dam).
[377] Kaufmann to Wheeler, 26 Aug. 1935. London Archives. See Appendix 28. An address Ita Wegman gave to English Class members concerning resumption of esoteric work after the exclusion has also survived. London Archives. See Appendix 29.
[378] Vreede to Zeylmans, de Haan and Kaufmann, 7 Sept. 1935 London Archives. Kaufmann to Vreede, 18 Sept. 1935. Goetheanum Archives.

accept the blue cards and issue interim cards only for new members. This would also be done in Holland.[379] This kept the door open for reunion with the original centre, Dornach, without giving up co-leadership of the School, as Rudolf Steiner had appointed her. Vreede started in England with a series of Lessons from 13 October 1935.[380] It was only then that Kaufmann followed a suggestion by Ita Wegman and started to give Class Lessons himself, initially with small groups in Leeds, and from May 1936 also in Manchester.[381] When Wegman had to cancel two readings planned for 6 and 7 February 1937, she asked Kaufmann to take over for her. He was happy to do so. 'We merely have to decide how I am to present the Class in English. It does not work well to read straight from the German text in English. I would therefore either need to read the text through before giving a free rendering (as I do when you read the Class), or I would have to do a written translation beforehand and then read it.'[382] Wegman's reply was that he should make a translation and read it out.[383] She also indicated that she was thinking of letting him take over altogether in time. '... [T]he time would come when she no longer had the strength and things would have to be arranged differently.'[384] Kaufmann further told Vreede: 'Dr Wegman then gave me the texts and I had to work for 2 or 3 nights to get them translated in time. The two Lessons went well; there was—as at the earlier weekend—a serious, solemn mood, and Dr Wegman asked me some days later to come to her, when she told me I was to continue like this; destiny had brought it about in this way, and she felt that a particular guidance lay in this.' He wrote that he had accepted this, and then spoken generally about the continuance of Class Lessons in Britain. 'I told her,' he went on in his letter to Vreede, 'that you considered it right to give Class Lessons with individual explanations offering analogies—as well as reading the actual texts—supplementing them in some respects, and above all raising awareness; but that you greatly felt the lack due to not seeing the texts, and that I have been helping you to the best of my ability on the basis of my interpreting

[379] IW to Kaufmann, 30 Oct. 1935. London Archives.

[380] Invitation issued by Wheeler and Kaufmann, 9 Oct. 1935. Goetheanum Archives.

[381] Kaufmann to IW, 9 May 1936.

[382] Kaufmann to IW, 4 Feb. 1937. IW Archives.

[383] February 1937, London Archives.

[384] Kaufmann to Vreede, 13 Feb. 1937. Goetheanum Archives.

notes. . . . She then said that you must of course have access to the texts so that you can prepare.'—'I saw,' Kaufmann commented, 'that she still did not feel it was right for anyone but herself to *read* the German texts *aloud*.' Wegman had then lent him the second, third and fourth Lessons for translation; he had given the nineteenth and first Lessons back to her. 'What was especially good was that Dr Wegman arrived at this wholly of her own accord; she now also seems to be happy about it, and I have the feeling that it has brought her a degree of relief.'

Kaufmann then wrote down the whole new arrangement for Vreede. She would give Class Lessons during her regular visits to London, giving her own explanations; in the interims he would read two Lessons every four weeks in English, one on a Saturday and the other on the Sunday.[385] By the summer, Kaufmann had then translated and read the first nine Lessons, as he wrote to Wegman. This also changed the way he worked with Ita Wegman in her Class Lessons. '. . . I think when you read Class Lessons [in German] which I have already translated, it will be good to continue doing it in *c.* three stages, as before, but I would then read the Engl[ish] text rather than giving his own interpretation, as until now.'[386] From October 1937, Kaufmann also gave regular readings in Bristol,[387] and from February 1938 in Clent. He started a new cycle in London in March 1938.[388]

George Adams-Kaufmann continued to read Lessons at the request of Ita Wegman. It was only after her death that he felt himself to be fully responsible for the First Class in Britain.[389]

6.10 Willem Zeylmans van Emmichoven

In November 1923, Willem Zeylmans van Emmichoven (1893–1961), not yet 30 years of age, became General Secretary of the newly founded national Anthroposophical Society in Holland. This was at Rudolf Steiner's request. He attended the 1923/24 Christmas Conference, and it

[385] Kaufmann to Vreede, 13 Feb. 1937. Goetheanum Archives.
[386] Kaufmann to IW, 1 Aug. 1937. IW Archives.
[387] Kaufmann to IW, 20 Oct. 1937. IW Archives.
[388] Kaufmann to IW, 23 Feb. 1938. IW Archives.
[389] Adams to Karl Koenig, 14 July 1955. Goetheanum Archives. Original with Friedwart Bock, Camphill.

was probably in 1924, at the Arnhem Conference in July at the latest, that Rudolf Steiner asked him to give Class Lessons in his country.[390] One of the most outstanding physicians in the anthroposophical movement, he became a member of the esoteric group in the Medical Section at the Goetheanum.[391] Deeply moved by Rudolf Steiner's karma lectures,[392] he felt his special destiny-given mission to be not only to work as a physician but also to represent anthroposophy in the whole civilized world. Thus the return, with great energy, to the idea of a 'world school association'—Rudolf Steiner had urged people to do this in vain—became a 'campaign' to be strategically planned.[393] Later he most successfully organized 'Kamp de Stakenberg', a first great international youth meeting on the subject of anthroposophy.[394] At the same time he took on Rudolf Steiner's mandate to assume responsibility for the work of the First Class in the Netherlands, a real example of following the principle of the School, which is to combine work in the public domain with esotericism.

It seems that at first Zeylmans hesitated to begin Class Lessons. He actually started much earlier than has been thought so far, but probably not in Rudolf Steiner's lifetime. In October 1924 he first asked Elisabeth Vreede if Rudolf Steiner would consider it desirable for someone, herself for instance, to go to Holland regularly for a few days, every three months, for example, and give Class Lessons, as Mrs Kolisko did in Stuttgart (that is, reading them aloud).[395] It may be assumed that Rudolf Steiner's response was in the negative, as with all other enquiries of this kind. It was only in the autumn of 1925 that Zeylmans took up esoteric School work himself, at the suggestion of Ita Wegman. He wrote to Wegman that he intended to start on 13 September, and asked for more detailed directions concerning the form

---

[390] Van Manen 2002, see Appendix 31.

[391] Van Dam in Plato 2003; E. Zeylmans van Emmichoven 1979.

[392] Symptomatic are his letters to Grete Bockholt, 7 Oct. 1924, and IW, 1 Sept. 1925 and 19 Jan. 1926. IW Archives.

[393] 'De W.S.V. [world school association] zal zijn *geestelijk* centrum in Dornach hebben, zijn propaganda centrum in den Haag en zijn *paedagogisch* centrum in Stuttgart' (to IW, 24 Jan. 1926, IW Archives). 'Duitsland zal wel spoedig toetreden en dan kann de groote veldtocht beginnen' (to IW, 10 Jan. 1926, IW Archives).

[394] Haid 2001.

[395] Zeylmans to Vreede, 9 Oct. 1924. Goetheanum Archives.

of the planned sessions. He used the remarkable term 'Meditatie uren' [meditation sessions].[396]

On 9 September, Ita Wegman replied: 'What I meant was that you would speak the Class mantras like a meditation spoken aloud. Having thus spoken the mantras, you conclude with the Sign of Michael and the words that go with it: E D N, I C M, P S S R. You then close with the words: "We end with the Sign of Michael" and give the Sign. Once this has been said and the Sign been given, you translate the words as stated: I love the Father ... Then you give the Sign once more with the Latin words—I don't want to say much in between or talk about it, for it is my intention to make this the beginning of a ritual. Therefore, say the mantras out loud, Sign of Michael, and finish.

'If it is a pity to have all members gathered and the rite so short, one can have a pause and then either read something by Rudolf Steiner or say something of one's own. It would be better to read or say more about Michael. I think it is important that the explanations to be given for all these esoteric things come through me, out of what Rudolf Steiner has given. I think that much good will come of this arrangement and very much hope for your good will, collaboration and support.'[397]

With these detailed instructions, it has to remain open whether and how far Wegman was possibly relying on talks she had had with Rudolf Steiner at times when he gave his various commissions for conveying the mantras. Her statement: 'I think it is important that the explanations to be given for all these esoteric things come through me' is certainly remarkable, even if 'out of what Rudolf Steiner has given'. No mention of the 'esoteric Council' as the responsible organ for leadership in this communication to a familiar friend, though she often referred to it elsewhere. Equally notable is that she was thinking of 'starting a rite' with the 'act' characterized in her letter.

Apart from occasional readings by Ita Wegman, Zeylmans very probably organized regular gatherings of Class members in Holland from the autumn of 1925. After his introductory words, the mantras would be read out and affirmed through 'Sign' and 'Seal'. 'Meditation sessions' where the Class meditations were listened to and lived

[396] Zeylmans to IW, 1 Sept. 1925, IW Archives. The same term was used on the invitation to members sent out on the same day (see Appendix 29).
[397] IW to Zeylmans, 9 Sept. 1925. IW Archives.

through together'. In December 1927, he reported to Wegman that it had been possible gradually to develop a 'genuine school' ('een werkelyke school').[398]

Following the split in the Anthroposophical Society in 1935, Zeylmans invited Class members who were on the side of Ita Wegman and Elisabeth Vreede to Class Lessons that were 'study meetings'.[399] He received the complete transcripts of the texts in 1936, even before George Kaufmann.[400] He produced abridged versions in Dutch and made these the basis for his Class Lessons, given as free renderings at the time, later also passing them on to other Class holders.[401] At members' requests he later started to read out the texts. Immediately prior to the outbreak of the Second World War, Zeylmans and 'friends from abroad' arranged a week-long conference in Rotterdam where he gave the ninth Class Lesson at the end.[402] After the war he asked other people to read Class Lessons in the Netherlands—Bernard Lievegoed, Pieter de Haan, Rein van Mansvelt, Max Stibbe, Henri van Goudoever, and later also Daan van Bemmelen.[403]

6.11 Ludwig Count Polzer-Hoditz

Ludwig Polzer (1869–1945) was one of Rudolf Steiner's few personal friends for many years. Having come to know anthroposophy only after mid-life, he joined the Esoteric School in 1912, was present at the laying of the foundation stone for the First Goetheanum, would often attend Rudolf Steiner's lectures and visit the Goetheanum on many occasions. He was there the night the First Goetheanum burned to the ground.[404] In a talk on 24 September 1924, Rudolf Steiner gave him the entitlement to

[398] Zeylmans to IW, 15 Dec. 1927. IW Archives.

[399] Circular to members of the Anthroposophischen Vereeniging in Nederland, 15 May 1936. Goetheanum Archives.

[400] J. van Dam to J. Kiersch, 19 Dec. 2002. Kaufmann wrote in 1937 that Zeylmans in Holland also had the texts (Kaufmann to IW, 17 Aug. 1937. IW Archives).

[401] J. van Dam to J. Kiersch, 19 Dec. 2002. H. P. van Manen 2002 (see Appendix 31). A copy of the abridged versions is in the hands of Paul Mackay, Dornach.

[402] Invitation from Anthroposophischen Vereeniging in Nederland, Groep Rotterdam, July 1939. Goetheanum Archives.

[403] J. van Dam to J. Kiersch, 19 Dec. 2002.

[404] M. Toepell in Plato 2003. In detail, T. Meyer 1994.

convey the Class mantras to Class members in Vienna, and hold meetings for this purpose.[405] The following Michaelmas Sunday he gave his first Class Lesson in Vienna,[406] and he continued with this for years. In a further talk with Rudolf Steiner on 11 November he was also given permission to extend this activity to Prague.

In his diary he wrote: 'Arrived in Dornach today. He [Rudolf Steiner] had heard that I was in D[ornach], and asked me to come and see him. His studio had become a sickroom. He was then sitting in an armchair for the first time. We spoke of my father. Then about the matter of the Michaelic School and the Esoteric Group. When I asked how I should give the Class in Vienna and Prague, he said lovingly and with emphasis: "Do it as you wish".'[407]

A more detailed version of the talk is given in a report Ita Wegman gave at the meeting of General Secretaries and Councils on 25 April 1930, which was more than five years later. She said Polzer had asked Rudolf Steiner if he might not read the transcripts of the Class Lessons in Vienna, as Mrs Kolisko was doing in Stuttgart. Rudolf Steiner had rejected this and recommended something else: 'Out of what you have heard, out of the mantras, what you have, out of this you can develop a form of work with people who want to do it with you. Count Polzer then said: "How can I actually do this? I know too little about it." Rudolf Steiner said to him: Do what you can, and also as you will, but out of what you yourself know. As you are able and wish to do it on the basis of the mantras, with various members who also wish it. And so Count Polzer left the studio and I felt sorry for him and said to him: "Now if it is permitted, and I believe that it is permitted, and there is nothing wrong about it, you can go to Mrs Kolisko on occasion and read the text which she has; you will then recall things again and on this you can build you work again." And this is also what he did.'[408]

---

[405] Polzer to Council, 9 May 1930; Polzer's 'Declaration' of 2 June 1935. Goetheanum Archives.

[406] Meyer 1994, p. 243; Polzer to Council, 9 May 1930. In a letter to Albert Steffen he wrote: 'There were twenty-one of us; it was a really good Michaelmas mood.' (Meyer 1994 p. 243.)

[407] After Meyer 1994, p. 562. The notes which follow concerning Rudolf Steiner's intentions for the further development of the School (see Appendix 4) may not be authentic (see Footnote 99). The phrasing 'Do it as you wish' does, however, appear in other reports Polzer gave (Polzer to Council, 9 May 1930; Polzer's 'Declaration' of 2 June 1935. Goetheanum Archives).

[408] G&C, 25 Apr. 1930, p. 70 f. Goetheanum Archives.

After the disastrous AGM in 1935, this was made the occasion to complain that Polzer had not been entitled to give Class Lessons but merely to 'explain the Class mantras to a small group of people'. Polzer made it clear that this had been a misunderstanding based on Wegman's report on the talk of 11 November 1924. He said he had long since spoken with her about this and they had reached agreement. Making things more precise, he went on to say: 'In that talk it was mainly a matter of passing on the mantras which Rudolf Steiner gave in the esoteric group in Stuttgart and Dornach in 1923, before the Christmas Conference, and at Michaelmas 1923 also in Vienna, giving me permission to continue with it. Those were not the Class mantras at the time but those of the esoteric group.'[409]

---

[409] Polzer's 'Declaration' to members. Goetheanum Archives. Polzer here identified, possibly erroneously, the group of people who attended the esoteric lesson in Vienna as the 'Wachsmuth Lerchenfeld group', as Rudolf Steiner called it, which had met in Dornach on 27 May 1923, 23 October 1923 and 3 January 1924. This consisted of *c.* 15 people, among them Maria Roeschl, Marie Steiner, Harriet von Vacano, Elisabeth Vreede, Ita Wegman, Margarita Voloshin, Juergen von Grone, Kurt Piper, Otto Count Lerchenfeld, Albert Steffen, Guenther Wachsmuth, Wolfgang Wachsmuth and his wife (Wiesberger 1997, p. 229 f.). A number of visitors from Prague attended the lesson in Vienna on 30 Sept. 1923 (Wiesberger 1997, p. 300), and they consequently asked Albert Steffen to enquire of Rudolf Steiner, who was then on his sickbed, if Count Polzer could not also give Class Lessons in Prague. Mathilde Hauffen from Prague wrote to Steffen on 29 October 1924: 'Count Polzer was in Prague the other day and gave two lectures for us which connected us more strongly again with Dornach. Now I do not know if you are aware that last autumn, when Rudolf Steiner was in Vienna, Ct P. established a group with people from Vienna and a few members from Czechoslovakia, and Rudolf Steiner also made us the gift of an es[oteric] lesson in this. In this group, here consisting of Otty Schneider, Mr and Mrs Klaubek, Schiller, Dr Eiselt, Dr Reichel, Schmelkes, Prykril and myself, we met again recently and spoke with Ct P. about the Class lectures here, which at Rudolf Steiner's wish we have together with our Czech friends here once every four weeks. Ct P. told us that he is now also in charge of Class lectures in Vienna and from time to time always goes to Dornach for new spiritual material. I asked him if he could not also pass on such lectures in Prague from time to time, if Rudolf Steiner agreed. This would then, of course, be not only for the small group but for all members whom Rudolf Steiner has admitted to the First Class here.' (Goetheanum Archives.) Rudolf Steiner then agreed to this request in his talk with Polzer on 11 November. For further details on the 'Wachsmuth-Lerchenfeld Group', which we may assume Rudolf Steiner convened with a view to the coming Christmas Conference, see Wiesberger 1997, p. 298 ff. and GA 265, p. 455 ff. and GA 266/3, p. 351 ff.

Polzer added the telling comment: 'After Rudolf Steiner's death I have known times in Dornach when individual members of Council were quite uninformed on many things which Rudolf Steiner had talked about with the others, and also uninformed on what Rudolf Steiner had discussed with me, even such important matters as esoteric ones. I can only conclude from this that Rudolf Steiner did give many tasks to individuals and did not want to have a spiritual and esoteric centralism after his death.'

Polzer also said that soon after his first Class Lesson he had gone to Lili Kolisko in Stuttgart and copied the Class texts, with Ita Wegman's permission.[410] In 1930, Marie Steiner recalled: 'I later heard from Mr del Monte that Count Polzer stayed with him in Stuttgart for about five days and had at that time been copying from morning till night. Mrs Kolisko is said to have been with him once. I assume he was given the texts to read and make notes, and probably wrote much of it down.'[411]

When Ita Wegman visited Prague in October 1925, Polzer was recognized 'in the name of the Dornach Council for Class work in Czechoslovakia' in an official 'document' signed by her and Wachsmuth.[412]

[410] 'At that time, in November [1924] I then wanted to go to Mrs Finckh, so that on the basis of Rudolf Steiner's words she would give me the texts of the Cl. L., but Marie Steiner was away, and so I went to Mrs Kolisko, she then asked Dr Wegman if she might give me the texts and was given that permission. I then went repeatedly to Stuttgart and gradually made my own copies of the texts.' (Polzer to Council, 9 May 1930. Copy in Goetheanum Archives.) A different version, which must, however, be viewed with particular caution because of the tensions existing in the spring of 1935, and for which there also is no authentic documentation, was given by Albert Steffen, Marie Steiner and Guenther Wachsmuth in a kind of documentary note: 'Concerning the permission given to Count Polzer to read the texts, the situation is that Dr Wegman has denied this. She declared, though only after a considerable interval during which she kept silent about this, that the permission had only been given, at Count Polzer's request, to work with the mantras. Asked who had given the texts to the Count she declared that she did not know. Mrs Kolisko's answer was that she had given them to him for a short time so that he might read, not copy them. It was then established that Count Polzer had been a guest in Mr del Monte's home in Stuttgart for four days, and had spent all day copying down the lectures Mrs Kolisko had lent him. It was therefore not at Rudolf Steiner's behest that Count Polzer received the texts at all. The Count had obtained them second hand in the way described above.' (Copy. Concerning the letter from Count Polzer, written to Mr Jilg on 6 May 1935. Goetheanum Archives.)

[411] G&C, 25 Apr. 1930, p. 70. Goetheanum Archives.

[412] Polzer to Council, 9 May 1930. Goetheanum Archives.

According to Hans Eiselt, Polzer 'gave free renderings of the whole first cycle [i.e. probably all nineteen Lessons of the first series] (although he had the copies of Lili Kolisko's transcripts)'. 'He himself,' Eiselt added, 'wanted to give free renderings, and it was only from a particular time onwards, because the wish was presented to him again and again, that he went over to reading. He really also did this [against] his initial practice and against his will, reading the Class verses [Class Lessons] at our wish.'[413] Polzer was then given the texts of the Repeat Lessons by Marie Steiner, to copy them.[414] Polzer himself wrote in autobiographical notes, presumably in 1930: 'About every 5 weeks, except in the summer months, I gave 2 Class Lessons each in Prague & Vienna ... I also give such Lessons regularly, in sequence, in Linz, and occasionally in other places.'[415]

In this situation it was natural for Polzer not to accede to the request five years later to forgo his Class Lessons to preserve the reading privilege of the Dornach Council.[416] The reasons he gave are worth noting. Referring to the fact that Rudolf Steiner had given the Prague members permission to take down the two Lessons given in Prague in shorthand and read the texts aloud—until further notice—every two weeks, he wrote: 'It therefore seemed to me that Rudolf Steiner did not consider reading the texts to be a matter of privilege. In the talks we had on the subject, Rudolf Steiner never spoke of studying the mantras, only of Class Lessons and meditating the mantras. If there can be talk of study in this case, this seemed more justified to me for the texts rather than the mantras. Initially I gave the Class Lessons without reading out the texts, and I only did so later at the request of some members, also considering it to be more modest.'[417]

In September 1930, when discussions on limiting the reading of the texts to members of Council had led to provisional agreement, the Council declared that they agreed to 'Count Polzer giving Class Lessons',[418] which also implied reading them. This was before others (apart from Anna Gunnarsson) were given this power. In 1931, Polzer

[413] Eiselt in G&C, 25 Apr. 1930, p. 101.
[414] MSt to Council, 27 Apr. 1930; G&C 25 Apr. 1930.
[415] Notes in Goetheanum Archives, Polzer file.
[416] Minutes, Council, 19 Feb. 1930. Goetheanum Archives.
[417] Polzer to Council, 27 Feb. 1930. Goetheanum Archives.
[418] Council, 16 Sept. 1930. Goetheanum Archives.

started Class Lessons in Pardubice, continuing there until March 1938.[419] His close personal connection with this town meant that when the local branch was ceremoniously opened in December 1932, he gave a Class Lesson and an 'esoteric act'. Thomas Meyer assumes that he used mantras from the Esoteric School before the First World War.[420] Polzer had an independent way of doing things, as evident from the fact that at the anthroposophical congress in Prague in December 1931, he admitted the 20-year-old daughter of engineer Milos Brabinek from Pardubice to the First Class on his own responsibility. 'I knew,' he later wrote, 'how Brabinek had brought up his children in the spirit of anthroposophy. Maña had also been in Dornach for a year after she finished school. I was therefore able to admit her straight away, permitting her to attend right away, on 6 December.'[421]

The high point in Polzer's work may be considered to have been the speech he gave at the General Anthroposophical Society's AGM on 14 April 1935.[422] Today it seems to us a last appeal for reasonable commonsense in a conflict situation that had gone beyond redemption. The dispute between the parties in Dornach had grown in acerbity over the past year. With the AGM in March 1934[423] taking such a problematical course, followed by the founding of the 'United Independent Anthroposophical Groups' in July, when members connected with Ita Wegman and Elisabeth Vreede had announced their feeling of freedom and independence of the leadership in Dornach, though fully prepared to cooperate,[424] the differences had become very evident also in the 'periphery', especially in Britain, Holland and Germany. Hermann Poppelbaum had written a circular on the position of Marie Steiner, Albert Steffen and Guenther Wachsmuth in November 1924 that attracted much attention.[425] Some weeks before the 1935 AGM, his arguments were substantiated more fully in an extremely one-sided 'Memorandum' in which its authors agitated with unproven statements and massive

[419] Meyer 1994, p. 303.
[420] Ibid, p. 318.
[421] After Meyer 1994, p. 309.
[422] See Appendix 27.
[423] Minutes in Goetheanum Archives. Summary, EZ III, p. 213 ff.
[424] EZ III, p. 228 f.
[425] *From the history of the Anthroposophical Society from 1925 onwards*. Also in EZ III, p. 232 ff.

slander, their tone leaving no doubt as to the fatal outcome to the discussion which was due to be held.[426]

Polzer had travelled extensively in the Danube Monarchy, in Britain, France, Italy, Switzerland and Germany, meeting and making friends with anthroposophists belonging to the different factions. This meant that he would be listened to even by the majority of the audience who were resolved to 'recall' Ita Wegman and Elisabeth Vreede and exclude the groups connected with them from the Society. Polzer spoke in a calm, conciliatory tone, endeavouring to make the differences and their causes comprehensible and achieve unity at this eleventh hour. He also spoke of the situation of the School. As in a 'memorandum' addressed to the leaders of the Anthroposophical Society in 1930, and not published at the time as Marie Steiner and Albert Steffen were against it,[427] he was for leaving leadership of the 'General Anthroposophical Section' and therefore the School open, not taking the thought of an esoteric 'succession' any further, building on individual Section leaders working together in harmony, and placing responsibility for Class work wholly with local groups, the representatives of which would then work together with the independently working Section leaders. 'I consider that it will only be possible to regulate Class affairs after Rudolf Steiner's death if an individual who is prepared to take responsibility in the eyes of the spiritual world and of Rudolf Steiner, and is supported by the will of a number of people, informs the Section leaders of this and discusses the matter with them. I believe that this would maintain the necessary continuity with Rudolf Steiner. I later also informed Mr Steffen in a similar way of this point of view, when it was a question of permission for Mr Arenson. Taking on such a thing will always be an act connected with spiritual destiny. I would find it unacceptable to give entitlement for assiduous effort, for knowing a lot; this would soon take us along a wholly superficial, authoritarian road.'

Polzer's attempt had to fail. The new Council asked him to stop his Class work and give back the texts, which he again refused to do.[428] He

---

[426] The Memorandum was withdrawn by its twelve authors in 1949 (H. Poppelbaum in *Nbl.*, 25 Sept. 1949. See also Albert Steffen to Poppelbaum, 31 Aug. 1949, Appendix 34). For the content, see EZ III, p. 45 ff.

[427] Meyer 1994, p. 298 f. Re. 'recall' see Note 475.

[428] Steffen, MSt and Wachsmuth to Polzer, 29 Apr. 1935. Polzer to Council in May 1935. Goetheanum Archives.

then worked only with Ita Wegman, sending applications for membership to her for approval.[429] Conscious of the importance of old-established relationships between Britain and Bohemia, he kept in close touch with George Kaufmann and the London group around Daniel N. Dunlop, who died in May 1935, and organized the Czech School work independently of Dornach.[430] In December 1935 he once more summed up the principles of his way of working for the First Class in a confidential letter to its members.[431] He resigned from the Anthroposophical Society on 30 May 1936.[432]

6.12 Appointments after Rudolf Steiner's death

Finally there were some special arrangements made no longer by Rudolf Steiner himself but still in terms of his original commissioning of the early 'mediators'. The Council in Dornach was inclined to see their work as marginal and provisional (see Chapter 6, introduction), and so it is remarkable that even before the full transcripts were handed on, which started in 1929, there were some commissions to convey the mantras without the lectures, or for study meetings where the mantras were read and free introductions given. The best documented situation we have of this was in Breslau (Silesia). Rudolf Steiner had given two Class Lessons there, on 12 and 13 June 1924, and no transcripts of these exist. In Breslau, school principal Moritz Bartsch (1869–1944) had been working for years with great energy and competence to spread anthroposophy.[433] A letter written in May 1924 in which Bartsch sent applications for membership to Rudolf Steiner shows that people in Dornach considered him a representative of the First Class.[434] Marie Steiner had specially come to know his human qualities and warm commitment to the anthroposophical cause particularly during the agriculture course at neighbouring Koberwitz, where he had played

[429] Meyer 1994, p. 616 f.
[430] Ibid. p. 351.
[431] See Appendix 30.
[432] Meyer 1994, p. 372 and 540.
[433] J. Kiersch in Plato 2003.
[434] M. Bartsch to Rudolf Steiner, 23 May 1924. Goetheanum Archives.

a key role in organizing the event. She had remained in dialogue with him as a friend, and had gone to Breslau in 1926 to read three Class Lessons as given by Rudolf Steiner. Even before this, during the Dornach crisis in February 1926, he had expressed the hope that Marie Steiner and Albert Steffen would take on the readings and that later on others might perhaps also play an active role. He was clearly no longer feeling respect for Ita Wegman and her mission at that time: 'It would probably be good to let these Lessons rest quite generally until you or Mr Steffen will have the time to give them, or until you entrust the task to others, when this will be possible.'[435] One may assume that during her visit to Breslau, Marie Steiner must have talked with Moritz Bartsch about how members' work on the Class subjects might be strengthened by repetition in a suitable form until further Lessons would be given at her next visit. The minutes of the Dornach Council meeting of 2 February 1927 do include the following note: 'Agreed that Mr Bartsch in Breslau work on the Class Lessons as discussed with Marie Steiner in Breslau and letter of 22 Nov. 1926.'[436] A few days after this, Bartsch thanked Wachsmuth for the trust put in him and wrote: 'I think I have understood Marie Steiner rightly to the effect that I repeat the three Class Lessons she has given in Breslau from time to time, speaking freely about the mantras and then reading them aloud.'[437] Some weeks after this, a relieved Moritz Bartsch was able to report: 'I repeated the first Class Lesson on Sunday. Approached the task with considerable awe; considering the magnitude of the subject one feels all too imperfect and unworthy. Now, however, my heart is filled with gratitude; for it was clearly apparent that the spirits of heaven were with us.' He wrote that he intended to 'repeat' the second and third Lessons as well.[438] He was thinking of further repetitions—possibly of further Lessons which Marie Steiner had given in Breslau in the summer of 1927[439]—in early October 1927.[440]

[435] Bartsch to MSt, 14 Feb. 1926. Lit. Estate Archives. One notes that this letter was written at about the same time as one with similar content by Anna Gunnarsson, written on 21 Jan. 1926.

[436] Goetheanum Archives. The letter mentioned has not so far been found.

[437] Bartsch to Wachsmuth, 5 Feb. 1927. Goetheanum Archives.

[438] M. Bartsch to MSt, 3 Mar. 1927. Lit. Estate Archives.

[439] M. Bartsch to MSt, 16 July 1927. Lit. Estate Archives.

[440] M. Bartsch to MSt, 15 Sept. 1927. Lit. Estate Archives.

It may be assumed that Moritz Bartsch also received the complete transcripts of the Class Lessons in about 1931, like several other well-known representatives, with permission to read them out.[441] The undated draft of a letter from Marie Steiner to Bartsch probably also relates to this, in which Adolf Arenson's daughter Auguste Unger was also considered for this work. It is not yet known whether and in what form this letter was actually sent. It does characterize the situation of the Dornach Council in the early 1930s, when increasing the number of 'readers' had become unavoidable (see Appendix 25).

Much like Moritz Bartsch, it appears that Martin Muench was asked to give Class Lessons as early as 1927, again through Marie Steiner, this time for the city of Luebeck.[442] It has not so far been ascertained if Muench worked in a similar way also in Berlin, where he lived. Even before this, Bernard Crompton-Smith had been empowered to convey Class mantras in New Zealand.[443]

We have seen that in 1924 Rudolf Steiner empowered several General Secretaries of Anthroposophical Societies in other countries to convey the Class mantras—Harry Collison, Henry Monges, Johannes Leino, Willem Zeylmans van Emmichoven. It is quite probable that another was the Danish General Secretary, Johannes Hohlenberg (1881–1960), a man of the world whose intelligence was outstanding, writer and lecturer, editor of two anthroposophical journals, committed representative of the social threefolding idea in Scandinavia. His liberal views and uncompromising resistance against German fascism put him in opposition to Marie Steiner and Albert Steffen, and he resigned in

[441] The minutes of the Council Meeting in Dornach on 17 May 1930 say: 'Note taken of a letter from Silesian members concerning Class work mediated by Mr Bartsch.' This was no doubt a similar letter, asking them to permit this well-known mediator of the mantras to read the full texts as well—like the above-mentioned letter from Stuttgart members in the case of Adolf Arenson which had reached Dornach two months earlier.

[442] The minutes of the Council meeting on 12 Oct. 1927 say: 'Agreed that Mr Muench shall work with the Class members in Luebeck (Molwo Branch), as discussed with Marie Steiner.' Goetheanum Archives.

[443] Minutes of Council meeting of 22 Dec. 1926. Goetheanum Archives. Transcripts of the Class lectures only reached there at the end of 1952 (Edna Burbury and Ruth Nelson to Steffen and Council, 15 Sept. 1952. Goetheanum Archives) and were then read by Edna Burbury and Ruth Nelson (I. van Florenstein Mulder to J. Kiersch, 28 Oct. 2004).

1931.[444] Shortly after Rudolf Steiner's death Hohlenberg recommended Knut Moeller as Class representative for Denmark, writing: 'I would especially like to have him in the small group we are now establishing.'[445] So far it has not been possible to discover if the School study group in question did in fact come into existence. It certainly seems perfectly possible that in Denmark, too, such a group was formed at the request of Rudolf Steiner.

In the summer of 1935, Esper Eising (1876–1951), Hohlenberg's successor as General Secretary, was given the task of giving the Class Lessons in Denmark.[446] He was immediately given the transcripts of the early lectures, with the rest following later, and read all nineteen Lessons until 1938.[447] In answer to his question concerning attendance of members who were not known to him personally, Marie Steiner wrote: 'The general procedure is that Class members are admitted to Class Lessons in cities they are visiting on showing their blue and red cards. They have the right to attend in Dornach if they show both cards, and there are now many whom we do not know personally and who have been admitted on the recommendation of a representative. Difficult situations are unfortunately unavoidable.'[448]

Ita Wegman had given the first Class Lesson in Paris. It has not been possible to establish if Class Lessons continued on a regular basis before the Second World War. Simonne Rihouët-Coroze, Chair and General Secretary of the French national Society newly established by the Dor-

[444] T. Christensen in Plato 2003. In June 1934, Hohlenberg wrote a remarkable letter to Albert Steffen asking for clarification as to whether the circular 'For your orientation' sent out by Hermann Poppelbaum and Martin Muench (May 1933), seeking for the sake of the continuance of anthroposophical centres in Germany to show that Steiner's thoughts were compatible with National Socialism, had been written in agreement with the Council in Dornach (Hohlenberg to Steffen, 19 June and 7 Oct. 1934. Goetheanum Archives. For Poppelbaum's defence strategy against the National Socialist regime, see Werner 1999). Steffen did not respond. When the Anthroposophical Society was banned in Germany, Marie Steiner no longer granted Hohlenberg the right to publish lectures by Rudolf Steiner in the journal *Vidar*.

[445] Hohlenberg to Council, 24 Apr. 1925. Goetheanum Archives.

[446] Steffen, MSt, Wachsmuth to Eising, 29 June 1935. Lit. Estates Archives. Re Esper Eising, see M. Eising in Plato 2003.

[447] Eising to MSt, 19 Apr. 1938. Lit. Estates Archives.

[448] MSt to Eising. 27 Apr./11 May 1938. Lit. Estates Archives.

nach Council in 1931, wrote in a letter to French Society members in the summer of 1952 that Class meetings in Paris, discontinued at the outbreak of war, would be continuing at regular intervals from that autumn.[449] It is possible, therefore, that she gave Class Lessons there in the 1930s, empowered to do so by Dornach, as others were at the time. She certainly did from 1952 onwards.

Class representatives were also appointed in Finland and Estonia before the Second World War. Olga von Freymann was appointed for the Swedish-speaking group in Finland; she had managed to organize a first conference for Class members in Helsinki (Helsingfors) in the summer of 1931, with Marie Steiner taking part.[450] Soon after that conference, she was mentioned together with Johannes Leino as Class provider, receiving the Class lecture transcripts for reading in the spring of 1933.[451] In Estonia, Otto Sepp (1884–1932) was Class representative by 1928 at the latest. He was the General Secretary of the Estonian national Society and editor of the journal *Antroposofia*.[452] With Marie Steiner's permission he held Class meetings from 1930 at the latest, 'repeatedly working through' the mantras of the first five Lessons, which probably means they did not yet read the lecture texts.[453] A few months before his death he translated all of Rudolf Steiner's Class Lessons into Estonian. His wife then wrote to ask Marie Steiner 'if Class members were permitted to work on the mantras in smaller groups ... of if we are meant to work only in the official, general Class group and then also individually.'[454]

In the autumn of 1932, Otto Sepp handed leadership of Class work in Reval (Talinn) over to young Valentin Tomberg (1900–1973) for health

---

[449] 'Les réunions de la "Classe" avaient cessé à Paris au moment de la Guerre. Elles pourront, à partir de l'automne prochain, recommencer à des intervalles réguliers' (Societé Anthroposophique—Section française. French newsletter No. 6, Juin 1952). Concerning Rihouët-Coroze, see Gudrun and Jean Cron in Plato 2003.

[450] O. v. Freymann to MSt, 27 May and 22 July 1931. Lit. Estates Archives.

[451] MSt to Freymann and Leino, 2 Feb. 1933. Lit. Estates Archives. Wachsmuth to Steffen and MSt, 27 Apr. 1933. Goetheanum Archives.

[452] U. Trapp-Geromont in Plato 2003. Sepp enquired of MSt on 25 Oct. 1928 if he should send a list of applicants for Class membership to Dornach. He sent it on 8 Nov. 1928, recommending admissions. Lit. Estates Archives.

[453] Sepp to MSt, 1 Nov. 1930. Lit. Estates Archives.

[454] Zinaida Sepp to MSt, 6 Sept. 1932. Lit. Estates Archives.

reasons and with Marie Steiner's consent.[455] Tomberg had attended the 1931 Class conference in Helsinki.[456] Before that he had supported the idea of a Class conference for Russian-speaking members of the School at the Goetheanum, and this did then take place there in August 1931. Marie Steiner evidently gave Class Lessons in the Russian language on that occasion.[457]

Tomberg continued the esoteric work started by Otto Sepp with a small group of about twenty members for the next two years, to everyone's satisfaction. He felt himself to be a devoted pupil of Rudolf Steiner, making the contents of the Class Lessons available to his audience with commitment and warmth of heart. Marie Steiner appreciated his considerable abilities and probably also had great expectations of him. Soon, however, she was to turn away from him in disappointment. Tomberg on his part decided to give no more Class Lessons from 21 January 1934,[458] and resigned as General Secretary after the Dornach AGM in March that year. A year later he applied to Elisabeth Vreede for admission to the 'United Independent Anthroposophical Groups' as an independent member.[459]

This is not the place to go into detail about the conflict behind this. Some things said in the course of it are symptomatic, however, for the way in which ideas about the way of working in the School began to spread within a few years after Rudolf Steiner's death which he, its founder, had never put forward. The evolution of such ideas in the climate of the 1930s is a historiographic problem which has not yet been dealt with. Here we will merely consider how first signs of it may be found in symptomatic statements, and the effect it had, but not how it might be resolved.

As we have seen, Rudolf Steiner had tried again and again to develop the

---

455 M. Hoerschelmann to E. Vreede, 5 Nov. 1936. Goetheanum Archives. See Heckmann 2001, p. 512. Concerning Tomberg, see J. Darvas in Plato 2003, and in detail Heckmann 2001. There also numerous documents on the events that followed in Estonia.

456 He wrote an enthusiastic letter to Marie Steiner, thanking her for the impressions he had received there (Tomberg to MSt, 12 July 1931. Goetheanum Archives). See also Heckmann 2001, p. 96 f.

457 Heckmann 2001, p. 97 ff.

458 Elena Tomberg to MSt, 8 Aug. 1934. In Heckmann 2001, p. 177.

459 Tomberg to Vreede, 5 July 1935. Goetheanum Archives.

School according to the needs of members 'from below' and encourage cooperation between the Dornach centre and the 'periphery' in an 'independent spiritual contract relationship'. In April 1924, when the School was still evolving, he said that the esoteric work of the different separate groups which had existed until then must 'of course' become part of the work of the School. This, he said, was the 'esoteric basis and source of all esoteric work in the anthroposophical movement', and anyone wishing to establish 'anything esoteric' must either 'communicate' with the Council at the Goetheanum or run their affairs completely separate from the School and without being recognized by it.[460] A remark made at a later date went in the same direction: connecting Class members' obligation to be 'representatives' with the need to 'seek coherence' with the leaders of the School for everything one 'does or wants to do' for anthroposophy.[461] Rudolf Steiner never spoke of the leaders of the School having a right to give directions, nor of any form of thought control.[462]

The initiative supported above all by Willem Zeylmans to bring the idea of the World Schools Association (1926) to life again, the World Congress in London (1928) and the Kamp de Stakenberg in Holland (1930), which was the unexpectedly successful first great youth event in the anthroposophical movement, had all given rise to considerable concern, suspicion and mistrust in the centre at Dornach.[463] Could one still be sure of keeping Rudolf Steiner's legacy pure and cultivating it in a serious way if immature young people, not sufficiently clear about things and possibly misled by personal ambition and half-baked passions sought to gain prominence?

---

[460] 18 Apr. 1924, GA 270/1, p. 149 f.

[461] 28 June 1924, GA 270/2, p. 116.

[462] Rudolf Steiner was magnanimous when it came to non-anthroposophical spiritual connections and inclinations of Class members, though he did ask for loyalty where the leadership in Dornach was concerned. This is particularly evident from his statements on reconciling Class membership with membership of certain Masonic orders, which had become a problem, for instance, in Harry Collison's case (Address of 2 Sept. 1923 in London, GA 259; see Villeneuve 2004, p. 1162 and 1215 ff.). The same holds true for his dealings with Roman Catholic cleric Trinchero who was considered a 'representative' after joining the Anthroposophical Society in 1924 (note in members' records at the Goetheanum) and to whom he gave a personal mantra in September 1924 (GA 268, p. 104 f.).

[463] See EZ III and Haid 2001.

When Valentin Tomberg sent out the first instalments of his *Anthroposophical Studies of the Old Testament* in November 1933 it was against this background. He felt himself utterly a devoted pupil of Rudolf Steiner, loyally sharing in the great task of developing anthroposophy further in harmony with the age. He had a personal relationship of trust and confidence with Marie Steiner, and because of this also offered his services in Dornach itself. He was truly astonished to hear that his *Studies* met with distinct resistance at the 'centre'. Gentle criticism of an approach in Dornach that was 'looking back', archival, and his idea that authentic supersensible spiritual research would still be possible and necessary after Rudolf Steiner's death, led to suspicions that he was making excessive claims. Roman Boos, prominent social scientist and lawyer, closely connected with Marie Steiner, argued with his usual acerbity in the newsletter that the anthroposophical movement had no need of new initiates.[464] At the same time, Tomberg's second marriage led to accusations of 'mystical and erotic occultism'.[465] Marie Steiner later summed up her reasons for turning away from Tomberg by saying that 'entirely of his own accord, in publications he titled *Anthroposophical Studies*, he proclaims himself to be the one who is now the bearer of the living stream without which anthroposophy would have to die out. He is therefore denying that the wisdom given by Rudolf Steiner, on which he bases himself, and to which he owes everything, like the air we breathe, has power of life and influence, claiming this instead for what he is now thinking he is giving from direct esoteric sources. In acting like this, he has brought his membership of the Class to an end'.[466]

Tomberg then withdrew completely and worked with his own study group only. That was not the end of the affair, however. Around Easter 1936, when Tomberg had already joined the 'United Independent Anthroposophical Groups' through Elisabeth Vreede, Marie Steiner authorized Linda Kasemets to lead the work of the School in Estonia, provided that members who continued to work with Tomberg were excluded from the Class Lessons. This affected ten people, about half the number of members who had been attending so far. One of them, Maja Hoerschelmann, wrote to Elisabeth Vreede that Marie Steiner had replied

---

[464] *Nbl.* 7 Jan. 1934, p. 2

[465] MSt 1981, p. 325.

[466] MSt to R. v. Dumpff, 25 Mar. 1936. In MSt 1981, p. 322.

to letters about this from Zinaida Sepp and Regina von Dumpff that the members concerned could continue to attend Class Lessons in Dornach and elsewhere, but not in Reval. 'Mr Tomberg has his own esotericism [Marie Steiner wrote] and people who continue to work with him might easily let this esotericism flow into the work of the group.' The enclosed 'extract from the rules for Class members' stated that 'Class pupils are obliged to obey the higher leadership and are not permitted to publish anything without first referring to them. If they do so, that is, allow anthroposophical essays or works to appear or be distributed without permission, they are following their own esotericism and thus excluding themselves from the Class; the same applies also to pupils who support such work.'[467] Marie Steiner's original phrasing in her letter to Regina von Dumpff is much milder.[468] It cannot be denied, however, that Marie Steiner and the Council of Three in Dornach who had responsibility from 1934 onwards, did exclude ten committed Class members from the regular local Class meetings because they attended an anthroposophical study group with—as they said—views of a different kind. What induced Marie Steiner to do such a thing? What made someone like Maja Hoerschelmann, upright and of good will, her arguments absolutely objective, take words of Rudolf Steiner—to which reference was made in the situation—to mean that 'obedience' was demanded towards the 'higher Class leadership' and to believe that members of the School needed 'permission' from that leadership to publish anything, the kind of 'approval' which could still be demanded in the domain of the official Roman Church at that time? The value judgements and moral attitudes behind it all at the time did serious harm to the anthroposophical movement until well into post-war times. Their origin and effects urgently need to be more accurately established. It is certainly quite evident that the need for loyalty towards the School leadership which Rudolf Steiner spoke of at the 1923 Christmas Conference and in Class Lessons, in terms of a 'freely entered into spiritual contract' had here been interpreted in a way that led to an authoritarian relationship of direction and dependence, and those affected felt it to be more of a threat than one would think from the actual words used. In 1933 the School began to fall

[467] M. Hoerschelmann to Vreede, 5 Nov. 1936. Goetheanum Archives. See Heckmann 2001, p. 517.

[468] MSt 1981, p. 321 ff. Also Heckmann 2001, p. 233 f.

back into outdated social forms, and it was only in the second half of the twentieth century that it began to free itself of this after following lengthy further circuitous routes.[469]

There is no point in going into the present controversies concerning the person and destiny of Tomberg here. One voice from among those around Tomberg in the early 1930s may be heard, however, for it comes strangely close to thoughts Ita Wegman had late in life. Valerian Schmaeling, mathematics teacher in Jaunlatgale, a small Latvian town near the border to Soviet Russia, wrote to Elisabeth Vreede in 1938—not long before the outbreak of the Second World War—about the aims of the 'United anthroposophical groups' with which he felt connected: 'Over the past 14 or 13 years, since Rudolf Steiner's teaching work on earth had come to an end, many other subtle things have no doubt also changed; my feeling is that if one had been thinking of further development, further extension of spiritual science, one would also have started differently, from another direction, as it were. Much that is esoteric would still need to be translated into exoteric conceptual forms and life [. . .], uncovering the path of inner development more and more as it changes from something individual and esoteric to something that is moral and social. In short, opening once more the gate of living anthroposophy that has been closed for so long would lead to metamorphosis, renewal of the impulses and also of the *forms*.' Feeling his way, phrasing things so that they remained open, this modest man tried to express what moved him and the 'Renewal' or 'Resurrection Group' in Riga who had gathered around his friend Jablokov to seek renewal of the 'Michaelic esotericism which Rudolf Steiner founded, in the spirit of the 1930s, i.e. in the gentle light of the Nathan Jesus'.[470] Ita Wegman was seeking this at the same time for a renewal of the First Class. We now need to consider her particular destiny in the gaining of insight.

[469] For a comparable situation in Prague, see Ludwig Polzer, Appendix 30.

[470] V. Schmaeling to E. Vreede, 5 Jan. 1938. Goetheanum Archives. The Group had initially been called 'Sunday Group'. The Russian word for Sunday, 'voskresyenye' also means 'resurrection' (Schmaeling to Vreede, Oct./Nov. 1937. Goetheanum Archives).

7 Between free rendering and reading aloud—How can the First Class 'rise again'?

An attempt will now be made to sum up the core ideas of the early 'mediators' given in the last chapter and consider them in relation to statements made by the individual who had originally been appointed by Rudolf Steiner to be his closest collaborator in leading the School of Spiritual Science and who to the end remained true to the mission thus entrusted to her.[471] Strangely opposing trends become apparent. Serious, reliable and committed esotericists whom Rudolf Steiner had entrusted with the task of passing on the mantras of the School and protecting them had—essentially with just one exception—to carry out that difficult task for a greater or lesser number of years without recourse to the lecture transcripts. Many of them had faced the additional challenge of translating the mantras into their mother tongue and thus developing an appropriate terminology and suitable formulations for this. With no fixed text available, they had to do the work over and over again to meet a different human situation. Nor did they have the support of an established official authority. And finally they faced the urgent wish of members to hear the authentic texts, Rudolf Steiner's original words. The result was that in time all of them, some with greater and others with less hesitation, proceeded to read aloud the transcripts which had in the meantime become available.

It was exactly the other way round for Ita Wegman. She would have felt it to be presumptuous to offer spiritual contents entrusted to her by Rudolf Steiner in person in any other way than in the exact original words. She held to this view untiringly for more than ten years. Then a crisis of illness and destiny, where everything she had so far felt to be valid was put in question, led to growing certainty that work with the wisdom given for the First Class needed complete renewal, a 'resurrection', as she ultimately called it. Reading out the transcripts was no longer of prime importance. She did not succeed in bringing the new way she was seeking to full realization. Yet what she had in mind did in many respects relate to the initial experiences of the first 'mediators'.

[471] For references to quotes see chapters 5 and 6 and Appendix.

The first thing to emerge more clearly than has so far been assumed as we attempt to gain an overview is that right until his death Rudolf Steiner firmly refused to pass on the transcripts of his esoteric lessons. He would not permit this, neither for the purpose of their being read out in the Class Lessons he had inaugurated outside Dornach, nor for the personal orientation or preparatory work of the individuals whom he had asked to convey the mantras of the School. The only exceptions we have found were Lili Kolisko in Stuttgart, where special occasion had arisen for this, and the provisional arrangement in Prague which was only for a few months. As far as we know, not even Marie Steiner or Ita Wegman were empowered by him to read out the texts. Marie Steiner had the transcripts because she had been made the administrator of Rudolf Steiner's literary estate in his will. Ita Wegman had been appointed 'co-leader' of the School by him, and presumably received the texts on his written instructions. We do not know whether Rudolf Steiner imposed these restrictions merely because he wanted to ensure accurate historical documentation in case doubt arose after his death, or whether he wanted to keep the possibility of reading the texts aloud open for a later time. The statements made by Marie Steiner, the one person who—as far as we can see—discussed the problems in question more in personal talks with him than did anyone else, leave no doubt, however, that he firmly refused to make the texts available. 'It was a dreadful thing for him that they existed. The life in the typed, printed word had been ahrimanized.'—'If we merely read out the lectures which R. St. gave us in the Class Lessons, we bury the life of the word.'—'... [H]e strongly resisted these transcripts being given to anyone to read, even the most prominent individuals doing the work in other countries when they came to Dornach for a short time & wanted to read them in our home: "They do not exist at all..." he would say very firmly.' Having carefully considered her discussions with Rudolf Steiner, Marie Steiner came to the conclusion: 'It was not the direction he wanted to take, that these lectures should be merely read out.'[472] When she decided after all, after his death, to read the transcripts aloud, the reason she gave was that, following Rudolf Steiner's example, there would be situations where one would not do what was right in principle because there was the greater necessity 'to prevent something worse'. She characterized this as a kind of

[472] See Appendix 7. In the last sentence given in GA 270/1 (p. XII), the word 'not' is missing.

'sacrifice'. There can be no question, therefore, of Marie Steiner considering the spread of the reading-aloud practice desirable or natural when it occurred after Rudolf Steiner's death, going far beyond the exceptional situation in Stuttgart. Her feeling was that she was accepting a regrettable but inevitable necessity.

At the same time, Marie Steiner was clearly aware that in 1924 Rudolf Steiner had asked a number of trustworthy people to convey the School's mantras to groups of members outside Dornach. She was not able to attach the kind of importance to this which we do from our point of view today, and probably considered these arrangements, which at first seemed improvisations, to be of secondary importance and only temporary. Yet she did clearly state Rudolf Steiner's concern in the matter in a few sentences. As 'guideline ... for the work of the group[s] who wished to live through the mantric verses together' she noted: 'The individual who spoke the mantras was meant to work out what he or she wanted to say in connection with them. He therefore wanted a form of independent work on the mantras, based, of course, on the wisdom received. Above all, however, living with the mantras themselves.'[473]

Ita Wegman's report on Rudolf Steiner's advice to Count Polzer points in a similar direction. 'Out of what you have heard, out of the mantras, what you have, out of this you can develop a form of work with people who want to do it with you.... Do what you can, and also as you will, but out of what you yourself know. As you are able and wish to do it on the basis of the mantras, with various members who also wish it, are able to and wish to do it.' Yet even she did not initially take up such indications. When she herself advised Willem Zeylmans in September 1925, she wanted Lessons not given by herself to be limited to a solemn recital of the mantras and the ritual elements, signs and seals, with the possibility of following this with a pause, and then reading some other text from Rudolf Steiner's work or saying something oneself.

The first 'mediators' appointed by Rudolf Steiner were initially aware of the burden of responsibility on them, the inadequacy of their limited individual abilities, and at the same time also the productivity of individual effort. After working with the mantras for five years, Helga Geelmuyden said at a meeting in Dornach: 'This responsibility was much greater than are my abilities to carry it. But I have tried always to work with the

---

[473] Appendix 7.

greatest truthfulness through something which I had to recognize as having come from the processes of initiation, given as such in the mantras.' The situation was aggravated, she said, because the Lessons given by members of Council were taken as the standard, so that individual effort did not weigh much compared to this, 'that recognition is not easily given to anything coming from individual effort, where one does not always adhere exactly to Rudolf Steiner's words'. The wish to receive the transcripts for reading aloud therefore grew stronger also among those whom Rudolf Steiner had appointed. Urged on by requests from the ranks of members they finally did all of them change to reading the texts aloud—with the Dornach Council's consent—though not without reservations. 'We must be infinitely grateful to have permission to receive the texts of the Class Lessons; no fear, then, of personal elements becoming a disruptive influence, though the need to do my own work at that time had proved very helpful for me', Helga Gelmuyden wrote to Marie Steiner soon after the above-mentioned meeting.

The most urgent task at the time, when more detailed arrangements and helpful support could still be hoped for, was to pass on the mantras in a way that was worthy of them, send applications for membership with the necessary recommendations on to Dornach, and see to it that the esoteric material was protected according to the rules Rudolf Steiner had given. The additional request that one should find one's own forms of guiding members to living experience of the contents, even though one had no knowledge of the original Lesson texts and was therefore doing it on the basis of personal meditative work with the mantras and the human situation in the given place, then led to widely different approaches in seeking a way. Ludwig Polzer was probably the one who felt most free, and he would often quote the words: 'Do as you will.' He adhered closely to the mantric words, but when it came to arranging his Class Lessons he explicitly permitted himself every freedom: 'In the Class, I never spoke a mantric word that did not come from Rudolf Steiner. It must however be clear to every esotericist who does not want the Michaelic Mystery to take the route which was taken by the Roman Catholic Church and then led to the disputes in the Councils, that the form we give to Class Lessons should be very much alive and must not be dogmatically laid down from outside.' To preserve 'ritual continuity', he would then again and again use elements from Rudolf Steiner's early esotericism in his Lessons. Reading the original texts aloud, something which he did do later on at the request of members, he considered to be a justifiable but certainly not the most dignified or only possible form. 'It therefore seemed to me that reading the texts was not considered by Rudolf Steiner to be something which he wanted to be considered a special privilege.'—'But it is certainly not in accord with his intentions, nor Michaelic, to make Class Lessons dogmatically a matter of reading aloud.' Polzer was sceptical about the possibility of using scientific text analysis to make the esoteric wisdom of the Lessons accessible. 'In the talks we had on the subject, Rudolf Steiner never spoke of studying the mantras, only of Class Lessons and meditating the mantras. If there can be talk of study in this case, this seemed more justified to me for the texts rather than the mantras.'

Attempts to include elements from early esotericism in Class Lessons were made not only by Polzer but also by Marie Steiner and Anna Gunnarsson, albeit unsuccessfully so in the long run, and possibly also by Adolf Arenson. He was hoping for continual vitalization and renewal in the work of the School with efforts concerning the whole thought-content of Rudolf Steiner's life work, from the original esoteric lecture courses of the early years to the 'Leading Thoughts' (guiding principles) after the Christmas Conference. The 'seed' of the guiding principles must be taken to its 'flowering, and bear fruit for us'. Even more definitely: 'Connecting what was given before the Christmas Conference with the new—that is the solution. Please read the above-mentioned address in the newsletter carefully;[474] you will not fail to see that the guiding principles cannot be fully applied unless one also has the spiritual wisdom given earlier. Might it not be possible for something similar to be found in the field of esotericism?' In this respect, Arenson, too, did not consider merely reading out the texts to be sufficient. The 'revelations of the Class Lessons,' he wrote, clearly referring to Lili Kolisko's activities and those of the three members of Council who had since also begun to read the texts, 'are conveyed to members of the First Class by reading out the original texts; this will give everyone—sooner or later—the opportunity to get to know them. But in future our work relating to them must not be limited to this. They, too, must be a seed of the spirit to which we give soul through our own creative work.'

Particular problems arose for early mediators who had to give Class Lessons outside the German language area. Thus George Kaufmann

[474] *Nbl.*, 10 Aug. 1924. GA 26.

wrote to Ita Wegman: 'It does not work well to read straight from the German text in English. I would therefore either need to read the text through before giving a free rendering (as I do when you read the Class), or I would have to do a written translation beforehand and then read it out.' Willem Zeylmans sometimes helped himself with abridged versions in Dutch which he had produced from the complete German transcripts entrusted to him. These evidently served him as an aide-memoire in giving free renderings. Anna Gunnarsson was even more determined to speak freely in her own language, even when the original versions of the texts were available to her. 'If we were to have the actual transcripts, for example, everyone who knows German will, of course, wish to hear them read in those words / and the others too. / It does, however, seem equally natural to me that those others are given the content in their own language. I would add here that if the task were given to *me*, I would not commit myself to doing a written translation and reading this out, but only to an exact, free rendering of the content. The translation is dead and much more likely to cause misunderstanding than a free rendering of summary content. It is, of course, different for the German text, for this has the occult content of the speech sounds.'

Finally we note that the efforts of the early mediators to gain personal access to the mantric content of the Class Lessons led to the feeling that they shared in the responsibility for the destiny of the whole anthroposophical movement. Anna Gunnarsson thus arrived at the idea of a 'Rudolf Steiner Association' and the suggestion that the Council in Dornach might appoint a larger group of those responsible for the esoteric work. 'The continued existence of our Society depends on maintaining the inner work; there must be a group who will always stay together, never tire or let go.' Helga Geelmuyden wrote in a similar vein: 'If there were to be a meeting again in Dornach to find ways in which the work of Rudolf Steiner may be taken forward in a fruitful way, will the mediators of the Class Lessons also be admitted to the inner circle?' She put it even more clearly at the meeting of General Secretaries and Councils in April 1930: For the esoteric work to be taken forward in a fruitful way after Rudolf Steiner's death, there would have to be 'an understanding among those whom Rudolf Steiner himself asked to do the work'. In view of the problems of a Council which had 'not adhered to Rudolf Steiner's principles' and not adequately perceived its responsibilities, 'the representatives in the different countries would have to be called'.

Setting different accents, the early mediators communicated many different experiences they had gained, and these call in question the image of the School that is still widespread today. This is the image of a hierarchic, centralist institute acting on the principle of a kind of spiritual succession. What today's image should be is an open question. Yet anyone seeking to answer this question will give special consideration to Ita Wegman's views, expressed over the years, as to the form which should be given to Class Lessons.

For her it was at first beyond doubt that after the spiritual teacher's death everything should continue the way he had established it after the Christmas Conference. 'Rudolf Steiner said, repeating it again and again, that the School of Michael had been instituted by the spiritual world and was not a human institution. I therefore felt myself to have been appointed by the spiritual world, and after Rudolf Steiner's death had no justification of any kind to let changes take place.' Personal impulses to give form to Class Lessons were therefore out of the question for her at first. The provisional arrangements Rudolf Steiner had made for conveying the mantras to people outside Dornach could be tolerated for the moment but must not be considered to set the standard. 'It is only possible to read the texts aloud, my dear friends, for in this way the Michaelic words are given to you unchanged, as Rudolf Steiner spoke them.' She followed the same line of argument in firmly insisting on the Council's reading privilege. Only those were called to lead the anthroposophical movement who would unwaveringly continue the foundation work which Rudolf Steiner had inaugurated at the behest of higher powers. For her, such a continuation included that for the time being one held absolutely fast to the original Class texts. Until her 'recall'[475] in Dornach in 1935, she had tirelessly given Class Lessons in Dornach and in many other places in Europe, reading out the transcripts; in the years that followed she did so above all in Arlesheim, England and the Netherlands. In the meantime, however, her inner attitude to her esoteric teaching was to change completely.

There is little documentary evidence of how this happened. Behind the few hints to be found in letters and notes from the last ten years of her life

---

[475] The legal term used in Motion I at the General Anthroposophical Society's AGM on 14 April 1935. It is also a wholly inappropriate euphemism. What was meant was her removal from office (*Nbl.* 17 Mar. 1935).

we can sense that something happened deep down in her soul which is almost wholly beyond our understanding at present. If the key could be found, this might be of considerable importance for everyone who cares about the future of the anthroposophical movement.

In the early 1930s, when disputes among members of the Founding Council and in the Anthroposophical Society as a whole were growing more acerbic, Ita Wegman lived in hope that a new beginning might be brought about from the 'periphery' of the movement, from outside Dornach. At times she was considering concentrating wholly on Britain. The economic and political situation in Central Europe was desolate, and this also suggested the idea of changing the focus of her work. Great Britain was a country open to the world. The friends gathered around Daniel Nicol Dunlop had done much work in the public domain even in Rudolf Steiner's day, and Wegman felt closely connected with this group, and also with the Dutch people around Willem Zeylmans. Would it be possible for a completely new beginning for the anthroposophical movement to come from there?

Deeply concerned, Wegman followed the events that led to the National Socialists coming to power in Germany.[476] A few days after the burning of the Reichstag in February 1933, which brought the first great wave of arrests of potential opponents of the regime, she sent a circular to about thirty friends, among them Eleanor Merry, George Kaufmann and Willem Zeylmans, inviting them to a meeting in Berlin in early April; further meetings were to follow in Stuttgart and Holland or Britain. In the prevailing situation, she wrote, it was important not to let existing connections be severed, and to understand and to help one another.[477] She wrote to Fried Geuter and Michael Wilson in Clent: 'The situation in Germany is bizarre and extremely difficult to judge, for evil intent is cleverly dressed up to sound good, and the illusion is actually created ... of being in the right; people are misled to a degree that is beyond compare.'[478] A few weeks later to Hilma Walter: 'The wave of National Socialism appears to throw almost everyone caught up in it into confusion and lead them astray.... One is blind, and on top of it stupid, but at

[476] Concerning the events referred to below, see the circumspect and well documented work of Peter Selg (2005a).

[477] EZ II, p. 188 f. For details, see Selg 2005a, p. 22 ff.

[478] 24 Mar. 1933. EZ II, p. 189.

present there is nothing much one can do against this stream. People who have still kept good powers of judgement are not permitted to speak unless they want the police suddenly to enter their home one day, and to get put in a concentration camp. Nothing remains, therefore, for many people but to leave Germany, organize themselves again abroad, and perhaps have an influence again in Germany later on; and for those who stay there to continue the work connected with anthroposophy which they have taken up quietly and with caution, so that the thread will not be broken.'[479]

Towards the end of that year she wrote once more about her intentions: 'What I intended and considered to be salvation was that a living ring of awakened individuals would arise which would surround the existing powers that bring death and from which new life should arise. The nature of this ring would be such that fastnesses and, as it were, grail castles would arise with people who live there but are also flexible enough to be able to go from one place to another. Done in the right way, I consider this to be a new Michaelic alliance by means of which we can bring something new into the world, to make the new life that wants to arise possible.' In the same letter she characterized the position in the Hamborn and Gerswalde curative education centres which she had just visited, the energy and courage shown by Franz Loeffler, who voted against the regime with all his staff at the Reichstag elections ('which I consider to be extraordinarily courageous, but perhaps not wise'), the 'soul quality' to be met with in such centres which was now in danger. 'Those in power will do everything they can to drive the soul from the majority of the German people . . .' At the same time she had to admit to herself that her hopes for Britain had probably been premature after all.[480]

As the new year came, Ita Wegman clearly did not know how to go on. But her deep interest in consciously following current events took her forward, also through the disputes in the Anthroposophical Society, which were coming to a critical point in 1934, and a serious health crisis that was probably due to this. In October 1923 she had heard Rudolf Steiner's tremendous lecture on the secrets of cosmic meteoric iron, where he said that human beings '. . . must learn to use the meteorite power of the blood in their conscious mind. They must learn to celebrate

[479] IW to Hilmar Walter, 28 Apr. 1933. In EZ II, p. 189 f.

[480] IW to the curative teachers in Britain, 18 Dec. 1933. EZ II, p. 190 ff.

Michaelmas by making this very festival one where one lets go of anxieties, grows fearless, a festival of inner initiative and inner strength by making Michaelmas a festival for remembering selfless self-awareness.'[481] In September 1924, the thoughts and images of this lecture, which also touched intensely on her medical mission, had been deepened during the lectures on the *Book of Revelation* given for the priests of the Christian Community, which she had attended as a member of Council. Rudolf Steiner spoke of the imminent reappearance of Biela's Comet in form of a meteorite shower in 1933; of 'comet substance' being spiritualized through the earth, and the ambivalent effect on the human astral body which might be either beneficial or harmful; of the connection between this event in the heavens and the coming of the Christ in the etheric. 'There are comets which influence human beings in the way I have just described, therapeutically balancing out their nervousness, and others which unleash wild powers of the astral as they move upwards again after having been absorbed by the earth. . . . Before the etheric Christ can be rightly understood by humanity, they must first deal with the coming of the Beast, which will arise in 1933.'[482] All this may have lived on in Ita Wegman, or indeed have been clearly in her mind when on 9 October 1933 she saw the luminous meteoric shower from the southern terrace of the clinic in Arlesheim that evening.[483] The idea of the 'new Michaelic Alliance' of which she wrote to her friends in December, may have come to her as she thus watched events in the heavens.

From March 1934 until well into the summer, Ita Wegman succumbed to a life-threatening illness. In September, reasonably restored, she went to Palestine with friends. A detour which had not been planned originally but decided on because of her state of health took her to Constantinople. Here she became aware of the superficial nature, the 'maya' of events in Germany. At Michaelmas she was in Jerusalem and talked with the others in the group about the tasks not yet completed in that country.[484] Looking back later on this change of mind she wrote that she had 'received a great impulse . . . not to abandon Germany' when in Con-

---

[481] Lecture of 5 Oct. 1923. GA 229 p. 19. *Four Seasons and the Archangels.*

[482] Lecture of 20 Sept. 1924, GA 346. *The Book of Revelation.*

[483] EZ II, p. 193.

[484] According to diary entries made by Werner Pache. EZ II, p. 208 f. Selg 2005a, p. 111.

stantinople. She had therefore decided to work more intensely in that country, initially at Hamborn and then in Berlin.[485]

The first Christmas after her recovery, when she established the tradition of Christmas meetings at her clinic in Arlesheim that was to continue for a long time, meant a 'new beginning' to her. In the notes for the address she gave to the gathering she wrote that it was a matter of letting the spiritual wisdom which Rudolf Steiner had given 'come alive again in one's heart', to create 'an alliance, without formality' of 'people who honestly wish this'.[486]

We note that after her return from the journey to Palestine, followed by a period of rest and study on Capri and in Rome, Ita Wegman markedly reduced her claim to leadership. According to Willem Zeylmans, she expressed her positive feelings towards the newly founded 'association of independent anthroposophical groups', saying that she nevertheless wanted to 'keep a little distance' from this.[487] She clearly did not want to do anything to aggravate the escalating friction in the Anthroposophical Society. 'She said she wanted to attend our events; she would be delighted, but not always want to have the feeling, as in the past, that she had to do everything herself, that everything had to come from her, etc. She spoke very openly, with genuine self knowledge.' This change in approach then evidently also extended to the work she did for the First Class. Zeylmans continued: 'She started to talk about the Class of her own accord. She would like to consider this the most important work. As she does, however, want to have a quieter life [outwardly] on the whole, she intended to try and stay for 3 weeks each, for example, in the different centres, if we wished this, and give 7–9 Class Lessons during that time. Three weeks in London, three in the Hague (Stuttgart will probably not come into consideration for the time being); then an extended period in Arlesheim, and then again with us.'[488] A meeting in early January with the seven signatories to the 'declaration of will', which had marked the beginning

---

[485] IW to F. Geuter, 21 Feb. 1935. EZ II, p. 207.

[486] Selg 200a, p. 150 ff.

[487] See also Selg 2005a, p. 94 ff. and p. 158 ff.

[488] Zeylmans to Kaufmann, 13 Dec. 1934. London Archives. In 1930, Wegman had still maintained to Willem Zeylmans that every more important initiative should 'come from the medical section', and Zeylmans did not agree with this (IW to Zeylmans, 7 Jan. 1930, Selg 2002, p. 130 ff.).

of the 'Association of independent anthroposophical groups', then led to a distinct aloofness from the intentions of the friends in Britain. As soon as the visitors had departed, Wegman wrote to Walter Johannes Stein to explain her change in approach as being due to concern for the Christmas Conference impulse, and also an intimate supersensible experience she had had during her illness. 'The day after your departure, but while it was still night, I knew exactly that I would still have to wait before going to England. Something so very different lives in me compared to what I met there that I cannot make myself go on as if nothing had happened, as if I had merely been on a short holiday trip. It was given to me to look into the world of the spirit, I met the Christ and Rudolf Steiner, who sent me back to earth and expect of me that I do something different from the way I have done until now.'[489]

The inner experience, only mentioned very briefly to a close friend, was probably the deeper reason why just a few weeks later she gave her first Class Lessons 'in free form'.[490] She probably still also gave Lessons after this where she would read. But it is clear that she was no longer seeking justification for the spiritual work in the School in protecting and preserving the original words, but in the common endeavour of members who were attending to gain immediate, direct *experience in the spirit.* The 'new Michaelic alliance', as she had called it in a kind of premonition in 1933, now took definite shape before her inner eye. She wrote to Alice Wengraf on 31 January: 'I feel great need to keep out of all disputes and to do only the things that are directly connected with Michael and have been the impulses of the Christmas Conference. One cannot talk about this a lot, I want to hold it in my heart and try to feel myself to be in direct connection with the Spirit Association in the spiritual world, for its mirror image, the Anthroposophical Society, can no longer be the vessel for anything which can flow from this

[489] IW to W. J. Stein, 9 Jan. 1935. EZ III, p. 112. See also IW to Gertrud Goyert, 29 Jan. 1935 in Selg 2005a, p. 164 f.

[490] Notebook entry of Werner Pache based on statements Wegman made in a meeting on 27 Jan. 1935. See Selg 2004, p. 174, and Selg 2005a, p. 163. The preceding entry by Pache was: 'Dr Wegman called us together—Deventer, Bockholt, Bort, Kaelin and his wife, Pracht, Eugster, Russ, Marti and Pache. About the Spirit Association and the Christmas Conference, to live this in all faithfulness. She herself wanting this.' Copy in IW Archives.

Spirit Association. One must therefore build things up again slowly, very slowly—and perhaps this can only be done in the heart—to let this vessel be there again in purity.'[491]

At the end of February 1935, she once again described what she had lived through during her illness and afterwards and what her aims now were in an intimate, deeply moving letter to Maria Roeschl who had been appointed the first leader of the Youth Section and was one of the important people in the 'Esoteric Youth Group'.[492] Again she referred to the experience of which she had told Walter Johannes Stein. 'Strangely enough, when things [meaning the friction in the Anthroposophical Society] were taken to absolute extremes, I was taken into illness and was unable to attend any meetings or share in the decision-making. I felt this to be a strange sign, understanding it to mean that I really no longer had anything to do with these earthly things. At the time, when the illness got worse and worse, I thought that I then no longer had to do anything on the earthly plane. An experience lived through in the spiritual world taught me something else, however. It was not in the spiritual world that I was expected, I learned in an encounter I had with Rudolf Steiner, where the Christ spirit was also present; no, it was demanded that I still do something on earth. From that moment onwards I was also given the strength to take my recovery firmly into my own hands.' This, she wrote, was how she took the impulse to come back to the original impulse of the 'Spirit Association' (School of Michael). 'I cannot yet say what will become of it; I am preparing and waiting, and do not wish to put myself forward anywhere, nor to tie myself down.'

Surprisingly decisive, she then gave her image of renewal of the School's work for the future, doing so a few weeks prior to her 'recall' at the AGM in April 1935. 'The First Class, as it was given and now is in the hands of many, is as yet far from exhausted, but it must be handled differently from the way it has been handled until now. I am slowly feeling my way and things become clearer as I do so. All the old forms, even the very last form for anthroposophy [meaning the one given at the Christmas Conference] have been thoroughly ruined, and it now seems to me that we must no longer look for one form for the life of anthroposophy, but that every individual himself is the form with which anthroposophy wants

[491] Selg 2005a, p. 165.
[492] See Haid 2001.

to unite. Where this has happened, people will find one another and unite to become part of the true Spirit Association. The [Anthroposophical] Society is no longer needed, for anthroposophy is now on earth. It all depends on each individual today. They must then out of their development form a higher Association which has its roots in the spiritual world. This preserves all individual development, the freedom of every individual, with each feeling connected with this Spirit Association or School of Michael through his own insight. This is what I heard within me. That I, myself, am in this impulse—this is what matters. The rest will arrange itself.'[493]

After the disastrous AGM in April 1935, where she accepted events calmly, it became more and more clear to Ita Wegman that the School must find its new form independently of the Anthroposophical Society as it then presented itself. In June 1935 she wrote to George Kaufmann: 'The position of the Anthroposophical Society, in which the Class was originally given, is so different now from what it was after the Christmas Conference that I have the feeling that the Class, which has been linked with this Society, is now in a very different situation from before. And as I told you before, I would like to come back to the basic impulse of the School of Michael, which lies in that School itself, not connected with the Anthroposophical Society. I have an inner obligation towards this School of Michael, and also want to act in accord with this obligation and take responsibility. I want to awaken awareness again in people of this Spirit Association which is in the spiritual world. Because of this, this School must be conducted differently now compared to before.'[494]

We must not conclude from statements like these, which have to be seen in the context of the crisis the Society went through in the winter of 1934/35, that Wegman wanted to abandon the established stream of Class work completely. In Britain she continued to maintain her reading privilege and the old membership cards. At the same time she felt concern, wondering if they were not admitting too many new members who were not adequately prepared, or if there was not the danger of a degree of routine in giving Class Lessons. 'It is very nice indeed,' she wrote to Kaufmann in April 1938, 'that you give the Class so much now. Yet I do very much have the feeling that

[493] IW to Roeschl, 22 Feb. 1935. Selg 2005a, p. 261. See also Appendix 26.
[494] IW to Kaufmann, 19 June 1935, after Selg 2005a, page 261.

people can largely only understand the Class if they rightly understand anthroposophy. And I do feel a bit concerned that so many people are admitted to the Class who perhaps do not yet have a really good picture of anthroposophy. . . . Too much of the Class can also evoke something which perhaps is none too good.'[495]

Peter Selg has written an impressive study of the last three years in Ita Wegman's life, when she lived mainly in Ascona.[496] It emerges that she only gave occasional Class Lessons during that time.[497] Wartime events made it impossible to travel outside Switzerland, but there were also inner reasons for her reserve. When her friends in Arlesheim expressed their regret because she would not be giving a Class Lesson there at Christmas, she made them aware that not one of the people concerned had shown the necessary inner activity. 'There is something in me which expects everyone who has done the work in the clinic in recent times and also attended the Class to have resurrection-thoughts, above all in my own case. All repetition, done at the same pace, with no progress made, full of energy, often has a paralysing effect.'[498] The same theme a few weeks later: 'Do you really think that it is so absolutely necessary for Class Lessons to be given again? It all seems so outdated to me, when people have come up with nothing new. The Class must rise anew, be received in a different way now. . . . I would so much like to bring something new; it lives in me, but it is so difficult when all one hears is that people want the Class in the old way. There has to be maturity as well, so that the Class comes to be at a higher level through the efforts people make. I am always working on this and have also made progress in many respects over Christmas.'[499]

What did Ita Wegman have in heart and mind in that last phase of her life, not much more than two years before her death? Was she living with the thought of Rudolf Steiner's deeply moving Easter lecture on 22 April 1924, when he spoke of how after the fire that destroyed the Artemis sanctuary at Ephesus the temple wisdom went into the world ether, and how it came alive again in Aristotle's theory of categories, and with

---

[495] IW to Kaufmann, 11 Apr. 1938. IW Archives.
[496] Selg 2004.
[497] Ibid. p. 174.
[498] IW to Marianne Bischoff, 13 Dec. 1940. IW Archives. Quoted in Selg 2004, p. 103.
[499] IW to Madeleine van Deventer, 20 Jan. 2941. After Selg 2004, p. 103.

reference to this of the fire that destroyed the Goetheanum and the 'resurrection' connected with this?[500]

The end of the Second World War was then in sight. In December 1942, a little more than two months before her death, Wegman had a long talk in Ascona with Werner Pache, her trusted and experienced co-worker at the curative education centre in Arlesheim, about expected developments. If Germany was occupied by the forces of Russian Bolshevism, spiritual work would no longer be possible. In spite of the gloomy prospect she held firmly to her inspiration of September 1934 to visit the friends there, wholly on her own accord, and continue to pursue her therapeutic impulse. According to Pache's diary: 'She would then wish to go to Germany, quite on her own, from friend to friend, and keep them aware of the work of the spiritual world.'[501] How she may have envisaged a rebirth of the First Class at the time must remain an open question.

Surely Ita Wegman's intuitions and thoughts relating to this show a strangely close similarity to the prophetic thoughts which Albert Steffen, the poet, wrote in his diary barely three years after Rudolf Steiner's death? And were they not also close to Marie Steiner's will to have a new beginning, wholly based on individual people's sound common sense concerning the present time? Was it perhaps the case that the schisms and tremors in the anthroposophical movement up to the middle of the twentieth century, which many felt could never be resolved, were unavoidable and necessary so that a new beginning might come out of the strength of the I?

---

[500] *The Easter Festival in Relation to the Mysteries*. Also 4th lecture in *Course for Young Doctors*. GA 233a.

[501] After Selg 2004, p. 85

8 A brief look at developments after the Second World War

Before we take a final brief look at the work of the First Class after the Second World War, let us sum up the different views on School leadership which we have come across in these pages. From its founding to his death, Rudolf Steiner led the School of Spiritual Science together with Ita Wegman. With her, the other four members of the Council of the General Anthroposophical Society, whom he had, like Wegman, also appointed Section leaders, and two further Section leaders, Edith Maryon and Maria Roeschl, he established the Faculty of the School as the organ for leadership. Ita Wegman, always in consultation with him, was responsible for decisions concerning admission to the School and the handling of the mantras. She was the 'guardian of the mantras'. After Rudolf Steiner's death she continued to see herself as the 'co-leader', as he had called her, her idea being that after his death the teacher was continuing to act through the 'esoteric Council' he had appointed, and that her own intentions were identical with those of the other Council members. In this she was mistaken. Marie Steiner and Albert Steffen did not consider Wegman competent to be the leader. Open and clear discussion to reach agreement on this sensitive point did not arise. When Steffen then took office as first chair of the Anthroposophical Society at the end of 1925, he explicitly stated, on the one hand, that he was not at the same time taking on leadership of the School and that this was solely in the hands of the leaders of the individual sections; on the other hand the statement issued in early May 1925 that the Council retained its functions as appointed by Rudolf Steiner was not withdrawn. The lack of clarity arising from the discrepancy between these two views aggravated the disputes, which fed on personal animosity, claims and hopes, in the winter of 1925/26. The final outcome was that Ita Wegman formally acknowledged Albert Steffen, the new first chair of the Society, as leader of the School. She did not give up her responsibilities as 'guardian of the mantras'. At the same time Marie Steiner claimed her normal rights as heir to the literary estate. No open process was entered into to achieve mutual understanding and clarify the views held in this complex situation, views that did not wholly diverge but proved difficult for members of the School to combine in a clear picture. The temporary and superficial solution, which did not go to the heart of the matter, was that Albert Steffen, Marie Steiner and Ita Wegman would together sign new membership cards and give Class Lessons—on an equal footing, as it were. Wegman passed applications for membership on to the Council as a whole for decision, but considered it important that she continued to be taken seriously as 'Secretary'.

Members came to respect this less and less, however. Many people who did not know or care about these agreements considered Albert Steffen and Marie Steiner, office holders and outstanding individuals, to be the people who were competent, had full powers to deal with problems of all kinds, and would both deal with needs as they arose in everyday life, without consulting the other Council members on every detail. Symptomatic examples are the authorization given by Steffen and Marie Steiner at Whitsun 1929 for Anna Gunnarsson to read Class Lessons, and the issue of Class Lesson transcripts in the early 1930s and later.

Following her 'recall' in 1935, Ita Wegman continued to give Class Lessons and accept new Class members on her own responsibility, and was therefore performing leadership functions, but unconnected with the other members of the Founding Council (except for Vreede). At the same time she was looking for new esoteric reasons for thus working independently of the 'broken-down' Anthroposophical Society. She soon also handed on copies of the Class texts to people whom she trusted, in order to keep the esoteric work of excluded members going. Marie Steiner, Steffen and Wachsmuth, empowered by the resolutions of the 1934 AGM, were on their part appointing new Class readers and admitting new members without recourse to Wegman and Vreede.[502] Two separate traditions thus developed—especially in Holland and Britain—and continued to run side by side until well into post-war times when they came together again. Events in Estonia were symptomatic of a trend which could also be observed elsewhere,[503] with the leaders in Dornach claiming the right of central control and exclusiveness after the split in

[502] From 1936 onwards, Guenther Wachsmuth also read Class Lessons (David 1974, p. 24).

[503] See Count Polzer's comments concerning divergent views on attending Class Lessons in Prague, Appendix 30.

1935. Instead of centre and periphery finding each other in free interplay, which had been Rudolf Steiner's wish, the issue had become one of adaptation and subordination. The leadership problem had apparently been solved, though in a questionable way. It was to rear its head again many years later.

In 1942 and 1943, tension grew between Steffen and Wachsmuth on the one hand and Marie Steiner on the other. The Class Lessons in Dornach, their rhythm intensified in 1934 and when war broke out in 1939, faded away and at the 1943 Easter Conference ceased for some time (until 1949).[504] In June 1943, Marie Steiner established the 'Association for the Administration of the literary and artistic estate of Rudolf Steiner, PhD', later called 'Rudolf Steiner Literary Estate Management', without involving Steffen and Wachsmuth in this. As the Second World War came to an end, with not only Central Europe waiting for the vigorous spread of anthroposophical initiative, the next great conflict in the history of the anthroposophical movement arose. This dispute over the rights in the physical legacy of Rudolf Steiner further paralysed activities at the centre. After Marie Steiner's death at the end of 1948, Hermann Poppelbaum and Wilhelm Lewerenz were co-opted to the Council at the Goetheanum. Poppelbaum's initiative started the process of reconciliation with the groups of members who had been excluded in 1935. Following a first consensus between Albert Steffen and Willem Zeylmans van Emmichoven, the problematical 'Memorandum', which had created havoc at the AGM that year, was withdrawn.[505] When national representatives of the Anthroposophical Society met for the first time at Christmas 1949, Zeylmans was invited as a guest and he himself invited a representative of the Anthroposophical Society in Great Britain.[506]

In the meantime, esoteric work had continued steadily in Great Britain, Holland and Scandinavia. In the spring of 1944, Karl Koenig, authorized by George Adams-Kaufmann, started to introduce Class work to the curative education centres of the Camphill Movement.[507] At Whitsun

---

[504] David 1974, p. 24 f.

[505] Steffen to Poppelbaum (attn of Council), 31 Aug. 1949. Goetheanum Archives. Appendix 34.

[506] Poppelbaum to van Dunné, 27 Oct. 1949. Zeylmans to Poppelbaum, 3 and 4 Nov. 1949. Goetheanum Archives.

[507] F. Bock: The work within the School of Spiritual Science in Camphill. Appendix 37.

1949, Class lessons were read again for the first time after the war in Dornach.[508] A number of new Class readers were appointed by the Goetheanum.[509] Guenther Schubert read Class Lessons for some time from November 1949 for the Literary Estate Management.[510]

In Norway, a special development came soon after the war ended. In 1946 a group of Class members came together, with Marie Steiner's consent given following a request from General Secretary Bjarne Eliassen, to study the Class texts. This work continued for many years. Joergen Smit was a member of the group, together with Sissi Tynaes, Nils Gustav Herzberg, Sigen Roll Wikberg and Bjarne Eliassen. Having experienced this shared work on the texts, Joergen Smit took the initiative, once the Society conflict had calmed down by 1970, to bring new life to Class work within the Norwegian national Society and give free renderings of Class Lessons.[511] Called to lead the School of Spiritual Science in Dornach in 1975, Joergen Smit, having achieved competence in this way, encouraged free renderings, a way of working which was then completely new and unfamiliar to many Class members. He also developed new approaches for the metamorphosis and further development of the School in form of a second and third Class that would meet the needs of the time.[512] In December 1960 and then again in November 1965, the first meetings of Class readers from different countries were held at the Goetheanum. Readers' groups developed in some countries—regionally so in Germany.[513] More and more conversation groups developed in conjunction with read and freely ren-

---

[508] Wachsmuth to members, 21 May 1949. Goetheanum Archives.

[509] Charles Gaze in London (Gaze to Poppelbaum, 31 Oct. 1949). Raimar Thetter in Vienna (Council minutes, 14 Oct. 1949). Max Benirschke in Duesseldorf, Paula Dieterich and Julius Solti in Hamburg, Friedrich Husemann in Buchenbach nr. Freiburg i. Br., Helmuth Knauer in Wiesbaden, Martin Muench in Berlin, Adelheid Petersen in Heidelberg, Sophie Porzelt and Erich Schwebsch in Stuttgart, Wolfgang Rudolph in Hanover, Lorenz Woersching in Munich (Council, 10 Jan. 1950, and Council to Ludwig, 18 Jan. 1950, Goetheanum Archives). Giovanni Collazza in Rome (St Pederiva in Plato 2003).

[510] Council minutes, 11 Nov. 1949, Goetheanum Archives.

[511] Oddvar Granly to J. Kiersch, 30 Dec. 2002. Concerning J. Smit, see also O. Granly in Plato 2003.

[512] See Elizabeth Wirsching's report on J. Smit's lectures at the anthroposophical summer 1986 conference in Aarhus. Appendix 35.

[513] Concerning the term 'Class reader' or 'Lector', see footnote 206.

dered Class Lessons, to work with the content or with questions concerning the meditative life.[514] The work of the School started again in many countries around the world, most recently in the parts of Central and Eastern Europe and Asia freed from Soviet dictatorship. The work done in the individual Sections of the School is gaining in volume and broadening year by year, also with regard to work done in the public domain. In the 1990s, regular collaboration developed between Section leaders and Council members on the School's Faculty, with the Dornach Council handing over leadership of the School to this body in 2000. Two years later, the Faculty entrusted leadership of the General Anthroposophical Section to the Council members on the Faculty, this Section also having responsibility for the affairs of the First Class. It is evident that further efforts are being made to achieve the interaction between 'periphery' and 'centre' that had been Rudolf Steiner's aim. At the same time professionals connected with the different fields in the Sections are coming to realize more and more that nothing can grow and develop in anthroposophical life unless new impulses are gained from the source spring of Rudolf Steiner's esotericism.

Can the work of the First Class contribute to this even today? Opinions differ. Let us therefore conclude by taking a brief look at the question, much debated in recent years, as to the consequences of publishing the Class Lesson texts. In Rudolf Steiner's day these were still strictly guarded and protected.

Guenther Wachsmuth and Albert Steffen died in 1963, the one soon after the other. Steffen had still given his consent to Margarete Bockholt joining the Council at Easter 1963. She had been one of the closest collaborators of Ita Wegman, and the future destiny of the esoteric work was dear to her heart.[515] Two years later it was decided, at the request of Hermann Poppelbaum and Rudolf Grosse (member of Council from 1956), and against the wishes of Herbert Witzenmann and his adherents, that the Goetheanum would no longer boycott the publications of the

---

[514] In 1950, when the group work authorized by Marie Steiner was in full progress in Norway, Hermann Poppelbaum, on behalf of the Dornach Council, still replied in the negative to an enquiry relating to this from Nuremberg: 'The view of the Council is that discussing the mantras in *groups* is not the right way, for this creates responsibilities which no one is able to meet today.' (Poppelbaum to Mrs Ludwig, 4 Apr. 1951. Goetheanum Archives. See Appendix 35.)

[515] Concerning M. Kirchner-Bockholt, see G. Wolff-Hoffmann in Plato 2003.

Literary Estate Management.[516] The works of Rudolf Steiner, a respectable number of which had by then been edited and published by the Literary Estate Management, were on sale again also in the Goetheanum bookshop. It was particularly thanks to the initiative taken by Rudolf Grosse, who had at first been very much on the side of Albert Steffen and Guenther Wachsmuth in the disputes over the literary estate, that constructive talks were held with the Rudolf Steiner Literary Estate Management, ultimately to the effect that in 1977, a first printed edition of the Class texts, based on the short-hand records and newly edited, was available as a private edition. For the use of those responsible for Class Lessons, it included such blackboard drawings and Rudolf Steiner's handwritten mantras as had survived.[517] The four volumes carried the notice: 'This copy is the property of the School of Spiritual Science at the Goetheanum, CH-4143 Dornach, and may be used only by the person whose name it bears. It must be returned to the School, if requested, within the period stated.' This did not mean that the Literary Estate Management acknowledged any rights on the part of the School. It continued to hold all rights and also reserved the right for itself to issue the newly published texts on loan to people of its choice.[518]

Officially, the transcripts of Rudolf Steiner's Class Lessons thus still had a degree of protection. Those joining the School according to the traditional rules would only hear the texts 'from mouth to ear', as originally demanded. As in 1924, members were only permitted to copy the mantras from the blackboard and keep them for personal meditation. Now, however, several hundred copies of the books went out into the whole world. With no close contact between the two institutions where this work was concerned, no one could really say any more what was happening to the texts. It was found that the Literary Estate Management had, in consequence of various individual decisions made by Marie Steiner, given stencil copies to trusted individuals even before the books appeared in 1977.[519] In 1965, major parts of the texts had been circulated

[516] 'Declaration' of the Council in *Nbl.*, 2 May 1965. See Kurt Franz David: Kontinuitaet und Entwicklung, *Nbl.*, 23 May 1965.

[517] The Goetheanum was represented among the editors by Hagen Biesantz, Kurt Franz David and Rudolf Grosse, the Literary Estate Management by Guenther Franz, Edwin Froboese, Hella Wiesberger and Hans Werner Zbinden.

[518] Concerning the modalities and their rationale, see Hellmers 1992.

[519] Loc. cit.

by Lothar Arno Wilke (Hamburg) without any protection at all.[520] In the Netherlands, where the texts were already out of copyright, a publisher of occult literature brought out an almost complete, though faulty, edition. In Germany copyright had been extended. The Literary Estate Management and the School of Spiritual Science had to accept the fact, however, that legal means would soon no longer serve to protect the texts. Anyone would have the right to make money out of them. In view of this situation, it was important to edit the whole available material once more with the greatest care and then publish it as part of Rudolf Steiner's Collected Works. This was done. The texts were published in 1992 by 'the Rudolf Steiner Literary Estate Management in collaboration with the leaders of the School of Spiritual Science at the Goetheanum, Dornach/ Switzerland'. As stated in the preliminary remarks, this was to ensure 'their authenticity and connection with the collected works of Rudolf Steiner, as general copyright protection for the work of Rudolf Steiner would cease at the end of 1995'.[521]

It is not the task of this book to offer a final opinion on the problematical issue of publishing the Class texts. As already stated, both Marie Steiner and Albert Steffen were considering something like this soon after Rudolf Steiner's death. Shortly before her death, Marie Steiner was giving thought to making the texts freely available.[522] Joergen Smit presented important aspects for those who to this day are convinced of the fruitfulness of meditating on the contents of the First Class and working together with the Goetheanum in terms of an 'independent spiritual contractual relationship'. He did so in the remarkable address he gave to responsible members of the anthroposophical movement on 7 April 1990 (see Appendix 36).

Unless they had gone into complete oblivion, great esoteric phenomena in human history always became public knowledge after a period of sacred seclusion, developing new ways of working in the process. This also holds true for the wisdom of the School of Spiritual

---

[520] *Mitteilungen fuer die Mitglieder der Anthroposophischen Gesellschaft, Christian-Rosenkreutz-Zweig Hamburg e.V.*, Nos XX (St John's Tide 1965) and XXI (Michaelmas 1965).

[521] GA 270/1, page IX. Editors were Edwin Froboese, Hella Wiesberger and Gian-Andreas Balastèr for the Literary Estate Management, and Manfred Schmidt-Brabant, Hagen Biesantz and Joergen Smit for the School.

[522] MSt to H. Geelmuyden, 21 July 1948. In MSt 1981, p. 351.

Science. To become aware of this may take us further than any logical arguments designed to save a venerable tradition or declare it out of date.

In his seventh Epistle, Plato showed how, in terms of ancient mystery wisdom, we can find truth that brings life—not by holding on to and being held to the word, but by sharing life and practising together. More than two thousand years ago this referred to basic themes in occidental esotericism. Rudolf Steiner was able to connect with these when he established the School of Spiritual Science. This is a direction which is most likely to help all who work together in the School to move forward also in the present time.

APPENDIX

1 Rudolf Steiner
The School of Spiritual Science[523]

This institution cannot come about on the basis of abstract thoughts from 'above'. It must arise from the needs of our members, from 'below'. The Council of the Anthroposophical Society are planning to establish a Youth Section, for this meets the needs of young people today and what they are seeking from the very depths of their being. The Council will arrange this in such a way that those needs can be met to the extent to which they arise.

This is also how it will have to be for the other Sections. It means, however, that the needs which arise among the members must be truly flowing through the whole Society, ultimately coming together in the expectations which members have of the Council. There should be growing awareness that the purpose of the Christmas Conference was not that of establishing a mere 'administrative council'. Administration has to be, of course; we should not forget that it is necessary, and its work needs to be careful and accurate. But the main thing will be an attitude among members which really puts the Council at the Goetheanum at the centre of the Society's spiritual interests. All such spiritual interests should come together at that centre.

This Council should never think of limiting in any way the initiative for one thing or another in individual parts of the Society. Yet people should come more and more to consider it necessary for the Council to be informed of everything that arises in the Society. The Council can then establish harmony between the intentions of a group of people in one place and those arising elsewhere. This Council will not wish to act like an authority 'from above'; they will make it their business to have an open heart and real understanding for everything that seeks to come to realization on the initiative of members. In this respect, they also hope to meet with understanding in that members come to meet them, *actively* meet them, when they want to do something out of their own initiative, based on the aims of the anthroposophical movement. It was in this sense that I said at the Christmas Conference: *this* Council is to be an initiative Council.

If members are willing to see this Council more and more in such a

---

[523] Essays in *Nbl.* of 6 and 20 April 1924.

way, the Council will be able to be true advisers in all the Society's affairs. And they want to be an 'adviser', knowing full well that it would be utterly against the spirit of the Anthroposophical Society if they sought to be a Council which 'decrees'. With the advice given they would appeal to nothing but members' independent insight; but the Council will only be able to be a real adviser if members have the right attitude and bring to them, to the place where the Council is, the aims and endeavours that live among members.

It is far from the minds of the Council at the Goetheanum to establish a connection with the work done in the Society through paragraphs and programmes; the wish is to let the immediately human quality, which is also able to act individually in every detail, come into its own quite generally within the Society. And the aim is above all to achieve this in connection with everything which is to be done for the School of Spiritual Science.

★

The lectures now being given for the generally anthroposophical part of the School are intended to present a view of experiencing the 'threshold' between sense-perceptible and supersensible world. Those who truly seek to have insight into human nature will need to understand that all the beauty, greatness, sublimity which 'nature' has to offer cannot take us to the human being. For the inner life of the human being who is active in the outside world has its source spring *not* in the natural but in the spiritual world. The senses and the rational mind bound to the brain are unable to penetrate to the latter. They must cease to be active if the human being wants to come face to face with the world of his origin. When this activity ceases, the human being first of all finds himself quite unable to perceive anything. He looks at his surroundings and darkness appears to him like a 'nothingness' which exists because he is unable to perceive. This inability can only give way to abilities to see in the spirit when the human being becomes aware of higher powers in himself which create 'senses of the spirit' just as physical powers create the bodily senses. The precondition for this is a complete transformation of the inner human being, from one form of existence to another. The individual must not, however, lose one form of existence before gaining another. The right transformation is the outcome of the right living experience of the 'threshold'. Knowledge of the human being in his true nature is only possible from a point of view that lies beyond the threshold. People who wish to take in with sound commonsense the information given by someone with insight that comes from the field beyond the threshold must also have an idea of what the individual with insight has lived through at the threshold. For they will only be able to judge the supersensible rightly if they also know the conditions under which insight into this supersensible sphere is gained.

It will only be possible to give meaning to the words used to speak of the results of supersensible vision when one understands what the individual with vision went through before he gained the power to coin those words. If one does not understand this, it will seem as if the words meant nothing supersensible but only things perceived through the senses. This, however, causes confusion. The words become deceptive; illusion results rather than insight.

The aim here has been initially to characterize the esoteric work of the School. Members outside Dornach will receive the Class material in a suitable form as soon as the work which needs to be done because of the Christmas Conference at the Goetheanum has developed so far that a step in this direction will be possible.—The words spoken exoterically here will be developed esoterically in the School.

2 Admissions up to March 1925

1924	February	309	(first admission 12 February,
	March	186	first Lesson on 15 February)
	April	314	
	May	232	
	June	248	
	July	121	
	August	89	
	September	262	(last repeat Lesson 20 September)
	October	16	
	November	44	
	December	80	
1925	January	101	
	February	156	
	March	32	
Total admissions		2190[524]	

[524] Source: Goetheanum Archives.

3 Facsimiles of early applications for admission and membership cards[525]

Als Mitglied
der
Ersten Klasse
der Freien Hochschule
für
Geisteswissenschaft
am Goetheanum
wird betrachtet Frl. Catharina Savitch, [illegible]
Die Leitung:
Rudolf Steiner

Als Mitglied
der
Ersten Klasse
der Freien Hochschule
für
Geisteswissenschaft
am Goetheanum
wird betrachtet Fröken Helli Björkroos
Für Die Leitung:
Albert Steffen Dr. I. Wegman Marie Steiner

525 Goetheanum Archives.

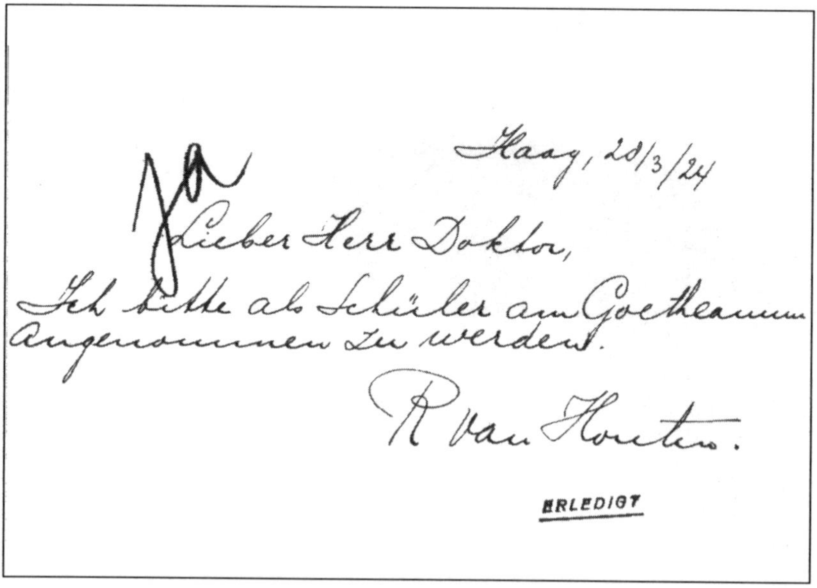

Ja

Haag, 28/3/24

Lieber Herr Doktor,

Ich bitte als Schüler am Goetheanum angenommen zu werden.

R van Houten.

ERLEDIGT

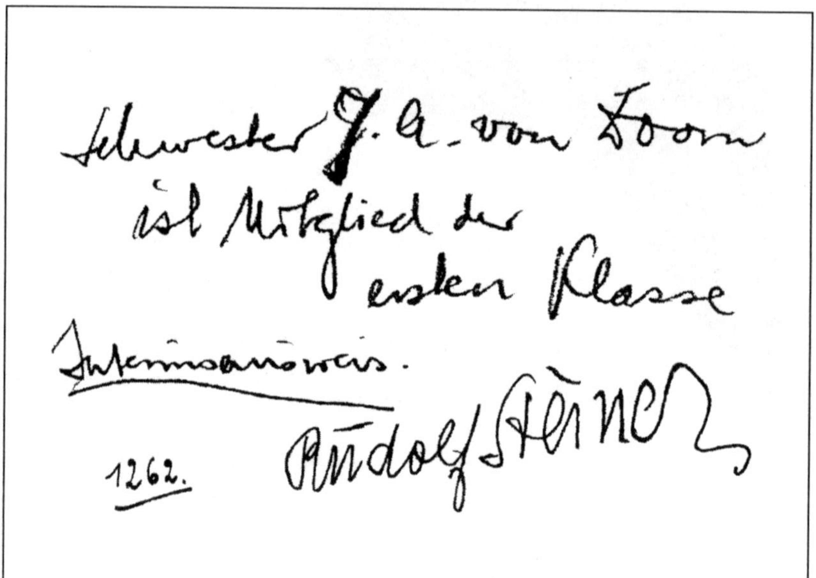

Schwester J. A. von Doorn ist Mitglied der ersten Klasse

Interimsausweis.

1262.

Rudolf Steiner

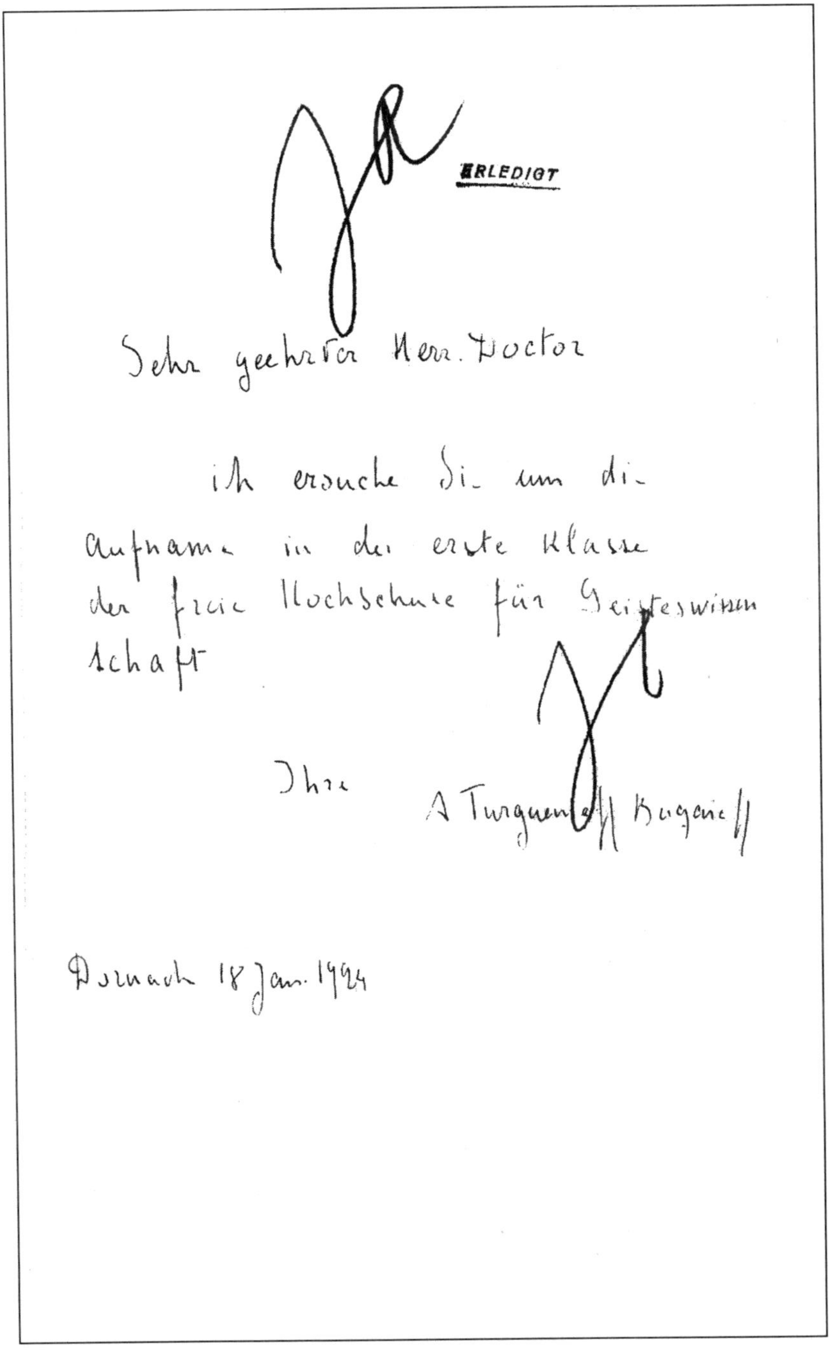

ERLEDIGT

Sehr geehrter Herr. Doctor

ich ersuche Si um di aufname in der erste Klasse der freie Hochschule für Geisteswissenschaft

Ihre

A Turguenieff Bugaieff

Dornach 18 Jan. 1924

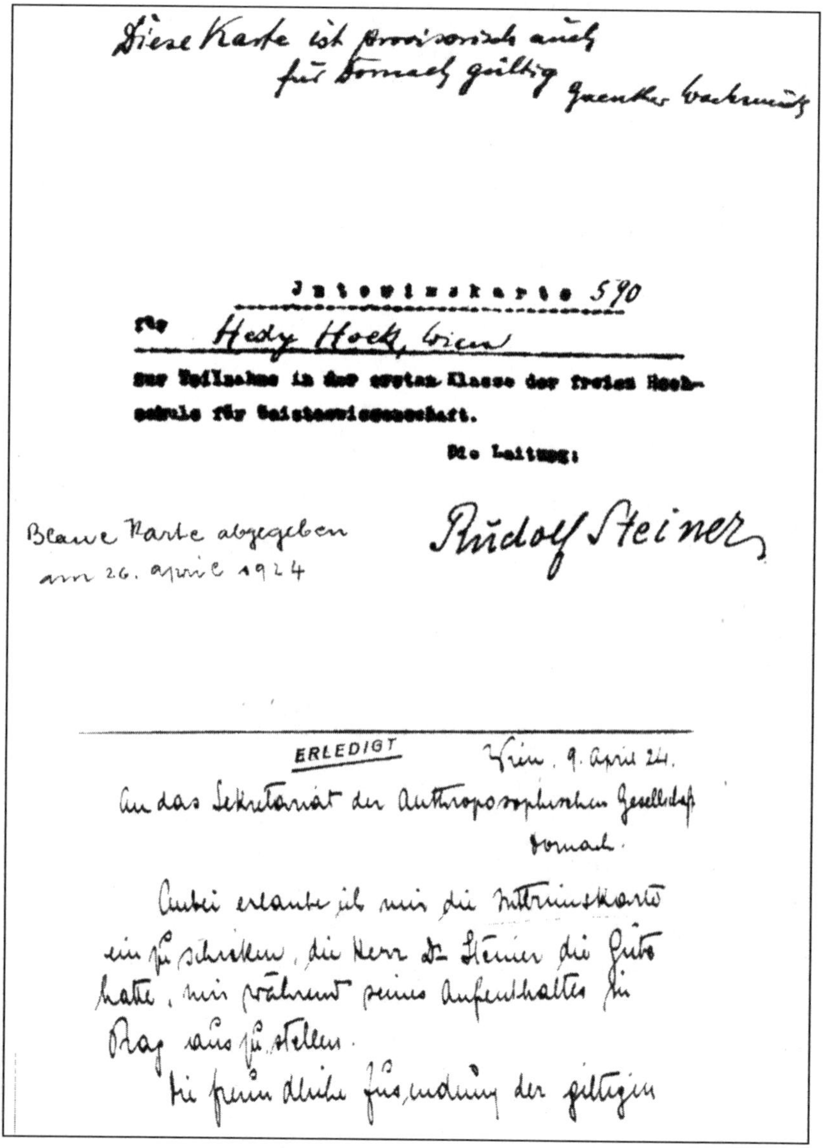

Diese Karte ist provisorisch auch für Dornach gültig Guenther Wachsmuth

Interimskarte 590

für Hedy Hock, Wien

zur Teilnahme in der ersten Klasse der freien Hochschule für Geisteswissenschaft.

Die Leitung:

Rudolf Steiner

Blaue Karte abgegeben am 26. April 1924

ERLEDIGT

Wien, 9. April 24.

An das Sekretariat der Anthroposophischen Gesellschaft Dornach.

Anbei erlaube ich mir die Interimskarte einzuschicken, die Herr Dr. Steiner die Güte hatte, mir während seines Aufenthaltes in Prag auszustellen.

Um freundliche Zusendung der giltigen

4 From Ludwig Polzer's diary, 11 November 1924[526]

Arrived in Dornach today. He [Rudolf Steiner] had heard that I was in D[ornach], and asked me to come and see him. His studio had become a sickroom. He was sitting in an armchair for the first time. We spoke of my father. Then about the matter of the Michaelic School and the Esoteric Group. When I asked how I should give the Class in Vienna and Prague, he said lovingly and with emphasis: 'Do it as you wish.'

I am taking on a great responsibility with this. The continuity of the M[ystica] E[terna] is maintained and changed in accord with the times. After a longish silence I asked R. Steiner if he was also thinking of establishing a master class, as in the old esotericism. His answer was more or less as follows.

'Following the institution [of the master class] the Class for members of the General Anthroposophical Society is to be put in the hands of Dr Ita Wegman. A Class II for Section leaders and lecturers, national leaders, members taking initiative will still need to be established, and I will ask Marie Steiner to lead this. Then as a final class a Class III, which I will establish and lead myself as a kind of master class.'

He then talked about details and the number of members in the classes. Class I, unlimited. The texts will guide people through the year, similar to the Calendar of the Soul, and beyond the rhythm of the seasons speak more directly to the spiritual individual, so that *Practise spirit reflection* can become a living experience in the spirit and shared experience of the human stream of destiny in awareness and responsibility.

Class II, 36. People will be admitted to this who have the relevant experience, in the realm of the spirit, as members of the First Class. Moral qualities will have to be of crucial importance here.

Class III, 12. These would then be the esoteric Council. This Class III, called the 'master class', will be purely ritual in character, celebrating at the three altars at the same time. Having turned to the relevant archangelic spirits in Class II, we will turn directly to the Spirit of the Earth, the Christ Spirit, in Class III.

Rudolf Steiner again kept silence for some time, thinking deeply. Then it was as if his face was suddenly overcast by a dark cloud, and he sighed, breathing heavily. We spoke of the Christmas Conference and the con-

[526] From Meyer 1994, p. 562 f. Concerning authenticity, see Footnote 99 above.

stitution of the School. He also spoke of the tasks of Albert Steffen, Dr Vreede and Dr Wachsmuth, which were purely administrative. 'They hold the position within the Sections which is in accord with their destiny.' We then talked about his brother and sister. He kissed me on the forehead again as I left.

5 Marie Steiner to Eugen Kolisko
Letter of 4 April 1925[527]

Dear Dr Kolisko,

I am writing from deep concern regarding the work of Rudolf Steiner. I have seen clearly that our Council, the way it is now, is an orphan child, a nothing. Above all I worry about Albert Steffen, who would be the salvation for all of us if there were someone at his side who would take on the burdens of being first chair, who would be a speaker, a man of the world, active and experienced, someone who had gone through Rudolf Steiner's school and was both correct and tactful. This man is you and you only.

There never are two people at a critical moment for the most responsible position. And there is only Steffen in whom the spirit flows at its finest now. We must protect him against a brutal outside world.

I have heard that your presence here has been considered once before, and that the intention was to attach the research institute to Dornach. This would also mean that your wife could soon have her work here; and she is the only one who has demonstrated that she can guide the esoteric classes, and would therefore be considered before all others for this. I am writing to you in private for the moment. I would be infinitely grateful if you would come here after the conference to discuss this with Steffen. Thinking things through most carefully during the night I have realized that this is the only way out. I was not able to get up this morning and so could not attend the Council meeting. But I wrote to Mr Steffen in the above sense, asking him to speak to the others about this conviction of mine. I suggested that Dr Roeschl be elected for my position; she will no doubt be glad to accept, and it is good that she will then be working in both societies. There is no possible way in which I can remain on the Council; it would not be a good thing. I can serve best by stepping aside now. And I do have the Performing Arts Section.—You may be surprised. Well, [Walter Johannes] Stein dreamt the truth. And so it probably has its roots in destiny. And if you and Roeschl accept, the work may perhaps be saved and Steffen, too. All of this has been considered in a wholly responsible way.

Yours faithfully,
M. Steiner

---

527 From M. Steiner 1981, p. 92 f. The letter is wrongly dated 4 March.

6 Marie Steiner on her situation following the death of Rudolf Steiner

This text consists in fragmentary notes in a notebook probably written in the spring of 1926 (Notebook No. 20, Literary Estate Archives), some of it difficult to decipher. The notes were written between copies of mantras for the First Class, and several drafts for an address Marie Steiner intended to give as an introduction at the founding of a special form of Class Lesson at the end of March 1926 (see text relating to this in Chapter 5). The sequence of individual notes is not entirely certain. Some connections can be seen with the letters to Eugen Kolisko and Albert Steffen. Illegible parts are marked '. . .[?]'.

At the time K[olisko] said he'd take the chair if the whole Council agreed to this. The Council in their majority had decided that everything was as before, that R. St. would be 1st chair as ever, and that nothing had changed. It was childish, but the majority decided the issue. Dr W[egmann] came to me and asked forgiveness for what had happened. She said demons had influenced the situation. I had to/was able to [written one on top of the other] accept that as the only explanation,—also must not deny in advance that the good will is there for the future. What decided the matter for me was that Albert Steffen decided [?], though with a heavy heart, to stay at his post. I therefore stayed as well.

Our role on the Council was intended to be merely decorative, as became progressively clearer, and soon it also became clear that our name was being misused. The body which I have been calling super-council has been busy; it had its own agenda ... [passage ends].

When soon after R. St.'s death [crossed out: immediately after the cremation] I had to see the way in which the new course was inaugurated by clueless, immature people, I felt I had entered into the world which no longer had anything to do with the spirit of R. St., a world of violence and brutality.

It was a shattering [?] blow that held a dreadful fear of the future. [Crossed out: There was only one thought in my mind] Away, then! Not into this lie about life. Nothing good could come of this. At the time Albert Steffen spoke as if it were impossible for him to be chair. [Crossed out: It was the time when Albert Steffen felt extreme reluctance even to consider being chair.]

Taking all the circumstances into account [in my thoughts] I went through the list of anyone who might best hold the position and could take my place on the Council. Above all I thought that it would have to be someone who had gone through the moral training which R. St. had tried to bring to life for (bestowed on) those who worked with him in Stuttgart [for] that [crossed out: way of life?] inner correctness [?] which R. St. found so indispensable in dealing [?] with people. (—an Austrian, I thought at the time, would have more of a feeling for this),—someone who was not wholly tied up with Stuttg[art], who was able to talk and finally also to communicate with the people on whom he'd have to depend. I thought of Dr Kolisko and wrote to him in those terms.

7 Marie Steiner on forms the Lessons of the First Class might take

The fragmentary material which follows was presumably connected with preparations for an introductory address for the special Class Lesson which Marie Steiner gave in the spring of 1926 (see Chapter 6). (Notebook No. 20, Literary Estate Archives. Some sentences have also appeared in GA 270/1, p. XII.)

I would ask you to consider today's meeting as an introductory session during which I want to speak to you a little about the way in which I envisage our work.—I will only be able to take it on if I can reconcile it with everything I received in years of working with Rudolf Steiner by way of instruction, teaching, insights into his inner life, and expressions of his will.

Above all I have his words in my ear concerning the transcripts of the Class L[essons]—lectures from which people read aloud now: they do not exist at all . . .

It meant that I was to consider them non-existent.—It was dreadful for him that they did exist; the life immanent in the words had been ahrimanized in the typed, printed texts. [Variant in a draft showing close similarity, Notebook No. 20: If we merely read the lectures which R. St. gave us in the Class Lessons, we bury the life of the word.] He let it happen, probably thinking of a more distant future, and because he had already made many such sacrifices (I may say here, however, that he never permitted us to take things down in our earlier esot[eric] Lessons). But he was adamant in resisting anyone being given these transcripts to read, even the most prominent individuals doing the work in other countries when they came on short visits to Dornach and wanted to read them in our home: 'They do not exist at all . . .' those were his firm words.

Getting clear in my mind as to the meaning of those words, it is my conclusion that it was not in accord with his will that these lectures should merely be read out.

He did, however, later make an exception in 2 cases, giving in to the requests made. [Apart from Lili Kolisko this might refer to the group in Prague. See Chapter 6.2.]

He did similar things in some cases where he'd say to himself: Here something worse must be avoided by doing something which I otherwise would not permit, not considering it to be right in itself.

As I have had talks with him on several occasions on just this point, I must think most seriously about it when I want to weigh up in my mind where something which one feels is not right has to be done in order to prevent something worse. Woe if one does such a thing out of inner immaturity, out of wish nature.—It should really only be done when it goes entirely against one's wishes. As firmly against one's wishes as it also was for R. St.

Now I know well that one has not withheld [cannot withhold?] this wisdom from humanity, but we cannot examine and consider long enough how to take care of it in the right way.

And so I also consider the other aspect, something which he himself gave as a guideline for the work of the group who wished to live through the mantric verses together.

The person who spoke the mantras was meant to work out what he or she wanted to say in connection with them. He therefore intended a form of independent work on the mantras, based, of course, on the wisdom received. Above all, however, living with the mantras themselves.

To enter into these mantras in a living way, one cannot hear and speak them often enough. Those who know what Rudolf Steiner thought of speaking in the right way, using objectively configured speech, with a feeling for the sounds, and have been asked to awaken a feeling for this in others, must seek to meet this task in the way he intended.

There was something else which R. St. demanded. He would say so again and again in his esoteric lessons, and this is also laid down in the transcripts of the Class Lessons: One must approach these things in the right mood.

And he expressly stated that this must not be a mood of sentimentality.

He demanded seriousness above all; silence, reverence.

We are therefore meant to approach esotericism in a reverent, receptive mood, suppressing superficial thought life, curiosity, pleasure in being critical, maudlin sentimentality, and learn a mood of reverence, reverent silence.

We learn this best if we endeavour to put aside the everyday garment of our habits and maintain some sense of solemn dignity, dreadful philistines though we may be.

8 Ita Wegman
Memories of the Christmas Conference[528]

Fully conscious, but without a word about the future, leaving no directions or messages for one person or another, the Master left us. And the answer to a direct question with regard to this, consciously given, was No. Why was that so?

The Christmas Conference is still very much with us, a fundamental event for the Anthroposophical Society. There is not one member who attended it who is not wholly convinced that with this Conference the Anthroposophical Society gained depth and a direction that meant a new, independent beginning compared to what had gone before. It was not only the Anthroposophical Society from now on, for the anthroposophical movement was also part of it. With unheard-of élan, with new energy for the work, fired with new impulses, Rudolf Steiner fused the movement with the Anthroposophical Society which before had its own administration and own, separate Council. From that moment—it was on 25 December 1924—a new karma arose for the Anthroposophical Society; something new was added to its old karma, and Rudolf Steiner from then on identified himself with the Society.

Did every member really understand this at the time, understand that from now on he or she would have new, weighty responsibilities? Did members understand the act of sacrifice which had been made? Rudolf Steiner took the karma of the Anthroposophical Society into his own karma. It was an unheard-of risk he took, a deed where one could almost sense and feel the whole cosmos shaking when it was done. It was a historical moment and it would have to be seen if the spiritual powers—which had shown great good will and generosity in giving to the anthroposophical movement, which means Rudolf Steiner himself, the benison of spiritual knowledge, doing it in such a way that it was also permitted to speak of it—would now show the same good will towards the Anthroposophical Society. Leadership of the Anthroposophical Society calls for management. The wishes, thoughts and will of members come to expression in the Society. Can it be that the light from the spiritual world will flow through it with the same power and intensity? That was the anxious question, and one had to wait and see how things would develop.

---

[528] *Nbl.*, 26 Apr. 1925.

Meanwhile the Conference proceeded gloriously. Rudolf Steiner appointed the Council for the Society. He chose this Council with Michaelic impulse and arranged things in the way in which work with this Council was possible for him. The Society did not appoint the Council, Rudolf Steiner did, the reason he gave being that this Council was connected with him, and he therefore called it esoteric.

This was clearly stated, and the Anthroposophical Society, having sent many of its members to the Conference, certainly grasped the implications of the situation, showed enthusiasm and warmth and agreed, with many, indeed most of them, vowing to find their way into this new situation and serve the Master with renewed energy, new feeling and will.

A wave of enthusiasm caught fire, something great had happened; each felt this consciously or unconsciously, the feeling was there. Yet there was still the anxious question as to how the spiritual side would continue. Well, one day the answer came also to this question. It was deeply moving to hear this answer from Rudolf Steiner's own lips.

It was in Paris that he was for the first time able to convey this important message to the members present, only a small number having gathered there. The message was that the flow of spiritual revelations had not ceased, and that the spiritual powers had given the Anthroposophical Society the benison of spiritual knowledge with even greater good will than before. Suddenly the tension had gone, one was inwardly jubilant for sheer happiness. The spiritual powers are well-intentioned towards us because the Christmas Conference had been received by members in the right spirit. The face of the Master was radiant, he was happy himself, and his faithful disciples gathered around him in gratitude in the nice small hall in Paris. And now truths flowed mightily from his lips. He had more and more to give. He repeated the glad tidings which he had uttered for the first time in Paris in Dornach, Torquay, London, in Holland, and important truths were given from the world of the spirit. It was as if the floodgates of the spiritual world were opened to let the spiritual wisdom flow through. Unforgettable days, everyone felt lifted up, each felt in festive mood day by day, it was as if the gods, too, were celebrating.

The time was short, but intense in what it brought about. Everyone who had attended the Christmas Conference, the Michaelmas Conference, in the right spirit could personally experience the inner change in themselves, making them different people, with the spiritual world very close, indeed one found oneself to be within it.

Then the Master fell ill. At first it was just physical exhaustion, and then it became evident that there were deeper causes, karma coming into effect. From January 1925 onwards he would no longer speak of exhaustion but of karmic influences. May members not ignore such things but take them most seriously indeed! He left the physical plane and in addition to what had gone before left us the new thing which had been put into words at the Christmas Conference, had created new situations, making regrouping necessary.

Everything he had intended to regulate, and everything he had said at different meetings after the Christmas Conference, was still done in the last two months of his life. Destiny permitted all administrative business still to be dealt with shortly before his death. And so he was able to leave his physical body without considering it necessary to give further directions as to the guidance of the Anthroposophical Society.

It was clear to us whom he had chosen for the Council that we must not leave the post he had appointed for us; it was clear to us that it is a sacred duty if we are going to be serious about the things the Master had brought us from the world of the spirit, to stay grouped around him, so that, although no longer among us physically, he could work among us and in us. This was the mood which lived in us. And so we still consider Rudolf Steiner to be first chair in the midst of our Council, and all members of Council in the functions to which Rudolf Steiner appointed them.

May the members meet us with the same feelings as those we have for the Society, to take the work forward according to the intentions of our leader Rudolf Steiner, to let the Christmas Conference, his legacy, bear fruit.

9 Albert Steffen
Introduction to the first Class Lesson Dr Wegman gave in Dornach on 4 June 1925[529]

Dear friends,

It is incumbent on me to say a few words here. The esoteric Council, called esoteric by Rudolf Steiner, our teacher and guide, when he appointed it at the Christmas Conference, has asked the members of the First Class to come here tonight in order to resume the Class Lessons. The Council has already informed you via the newsletter that its members will for the time being retain their functions. Rudolf Steiner often said that members of the First Class who wished to pass on the mantras should apply to him or to the Secretary, Dr Wegman. This custom will be retained. With the agreement of the esoteric Council, Dr Wegman now takes on the task of continuing the Class Lessons here, beginning today. It is incumbent on me, the second chair, to reflect on the solemn warning that the School of Michael is the heart of the Society, the heart of the Anthroposophical Society. With the Class Lessons, Rudolf Steiner has given us something that is most sacred. May all hold it sacred.

I would now like to invite our highly esteemed friend Dr Wegman to begin.

---

[529] Goetheanum Archives.

10 Diary entries by Albert Steffen concerning his talk with Eugen Kolisko and Walter Johannes Stein on 5 June 1925

The talk with those two [Kolisko and Stein] had the following result. Dr Wegman knows that they have come here (they answer in the affirmative when I ask them). And they also answer in the affirmative when I ask if they will inform her [Wegman] about the subject of the talk.

(I then exclaim: Why doesn't she talk to me herself?) Adding in my head: and she complains to those two, trying to use them to persuade me? and I look at them. They feel my contempt. 'We did not put ourselves forward', they say. It was Frau Dr Steiner who had Kolisko called. She broke the barrier. It is her fault. And now we must do what we can to restore order. They then explain that it is important to put these things in words and make them known to the Society as they are, and I am to help them with this.

I would not have done so yesterday,[530] for I would not have said that Dr Wegman was the leader appointed by Rudolf Steiner.

Me: Why am I asked to say something which I do not know?

This means that people who are not on the Council are telling me things that go on there and have not been known to me, for instance that the verse was written down [this probably refers to a mantric formula which Rudolf Steiner himself only spoke during the Class Lessons, not writing it on the board to be copied down], that Dr Wegman introduced herself in Paris as co-founder. That a ceremony took place.

I formulate the outcomes of this and then read them out to those two, asking if it is correct and adding that I would submit this to the Council.

There are two fundamental issues.

1) Appointment of the esoteric Council. 2) Establishment of the S[chool] of M[ichael] by Rudolf Steiner and Dr Wegman. Ceremony. One made the promise to be a faithful member. Handshake with Rudolf Steiner and Dr Wegman.

Yesterday's outcome: that it had not been shown clearly enough, [they said,] that Dr Wegman was co-founder of the S[chool] of M[ichael] in person, and that she was leader not as Secretary but the effective esoteric leader (say those two, Kolisko and Stein).

---

[530] See Albert Steffen's Introduction, Appendix 9.

Someone wishing to give Class Lessons must be authorized by Dr Wegman. And not by the Council. The Council cannot, for example, vote against her. (It follows, though this was not actually said yesterday, that she can admit and exclude people. That she is in charge of information given. That her commands simply are autocratic. That she is a dictator, that she is the—heart of the Society.)

And now they ask that I say this, and I am told off for not saying so yesterday, sticking to the facts I know instead.

When I ask if she is the spiritual leader of the Society (because she runs the S[chool] of M[ichael], the answer is 'yes'.

I say it would then be necessary to withdraw the statement that I am this. Who put it in the paper? Not me. But so far it has not been withdrawn. That is how they obey the 2nd chair. Am I just to lend my name, like Hindenburg?[531] I was not told that she introduced herself as leader in Paris and is now going to Stuttgart and Vienna. I always hear of it only from outsiders (and so does Marie Steiner). She [Dr Wegman] does not say in Council the things she said to Stein and Kolisko. I hear from Uehli that she is going to Stuttgart. From Lauer that she is going to Vienna.

All these are reasons why I speak of the facts, that I am on the Council not in real terms but only nominally so, for my name. That must no longer be so. I am resigning. I cannot take responsibility for things of which I do not know anything.[532]

Now comes the meeting....

I do, however, formulate the questions very exactly as to what the Council's view is on the First Class, producing the piece of paper on which I wrote the questions put by Dr Stein and Kolisko:

1) Council and leadership of the School are two things. The latter was autonomous and could not be voted against by the Council.

I say that in my opinion the Council is also involved in the leadership. As Rudolf Steiner's successor, this also meant it had the leadership, and appointed Dr Wegman simply because she was the one with whom Rudolf Steiner had been working.

I ask if Dr Wegman claims the right to exclude members of the Council

[531] Evidently referring to the political role played by Paul von Hindenburg who was elected president of the German Reich on 26 Apr. 1925.

[532] Diary entries of 5 June 1925. Albert Steffen Foundation Archives.

from the Class (for if the Council does not have the leadership and if Council and School are separate, members of Council are just like other members of the Class).

(She says she would not consider it to be right, is being evasive; she does not want to negate the right.)

Marie Steiner says she would ask if it was not required for me to sign the cards,—the three others all stay silent. I say, ironically: General silence.

Then I continue, saying that I would have to have clarity as to my position. According to some people, I am the chair. But only exoterically, with Dr Wegman the leader esoterically. I merely exist to sign cards, etc....

She is afraid of having things taken from her.

I say I do not intend to take anything she has away from her, I merely wanted to be clear about my position.[533]

[533] Diary entries of 20 August 1925. Albert Steffen Foundation Archives.

11 Ita Wegman to Albert Steffen Letter of 21 August 1925[534]

Dear Mr Steffen, Arlesheim, 21 VIII 25

I was unable to come last night because I felt off colour and tired. This was also the reason why I was unable to keep my promise to Felicitas, who had asked me to visit her because she had started to cough again. Over the two nights and days I have tried once more to examine carefully what Rudolf Steiner said to me about the School of Michael, and to examine myself, too, to see if I have been at fault.

To make sure mistakes will not arise or persist, let me put a few things clearly before you once more.

I myself have not done anything to put myself forward with Rudolf Steiner in esoteric matters.

One day he appointed me, and, as you yourself will now have heard from Dr Wachsmuth, I had to stand beside him and also receive the promise to be faithful to the School of Michael, which was affirmed by shaking Rudolf Steiner's hand. This was not right away at the beginning, but only later, when the School of Michael had existed for some months. Before that, Rudolf Steiner gave me various esoteric formulae, and I was taught various esoteric things.

Some rituals were also established. Every afternoon at about 6 p.m. Rudolf Steiner would speak the meditations with me which he felt were suitable, and these were changed on various occasions. This speaking of the meditations continued also during his illness, even on the last afternoon before he died, and he would pray with me. Christian Rosenkreutz played a great role in those meditations.

Even before his illness, Rudolf Steiner gave me a small cross with small rubies set in roses which he used to wear on a red ribbon around his neck. He put it around my neck with his own hands after we had performed a ritual together.

You saw this cross on Rudolf Steiner's body, Mr Steffen, when he was laid out. I put it around his neck once more after his death (with Marie Steiner's agreement). I took it back again the day before the cremation.

Rudolf Steiner said, repeating this again and again, that the School of

[534] EZ III, p. 58–60.

Michael had been *instituted out of the world of the spirit* and was not a *human institution*. I therefore felt that I had been appointed by the world of the spirit and was not justified in letting there be any changes after Rudolf Steiner's death. For me, there was only one question: When the first and main leader is no longer able to guide it directly, can I, as second leader, guard the School as such and continue to guide it in the sense that the wisdom of the School of Michael, given by Rudolf Steiner in the Class Lessons (of the School of Spiritual Science) would be reiterated? I inwardly answered the question with 'yes'.

I asked the Council, spoke in all modesty with Marie Steiner about the things I have now said in this letter, did not want to put myself forward at all, yet also had to *take everything* said to me through Rudolf Steiner *seriously*, taking *my appointment seriously* as well.

I am now absolutely amazed at Frau Dr Steiner's suggestion that Mrs Kolisko be asked to come to Dornach and give Class Lessons. Surely this would be impossible, as you, Mr Steffen, did also admit.

Until now it has not proved possible to give regular Class Lessons here. It has been possible for me to institute the School of Michael everywhere where it is appropriate and give Class Lessons. Here, it seems, it is not possible. I would now ask you to help me, or give advice, dear Mr Steffen, as to how to do it differently.

With kind regards, *Ita Wegman, MD*

12 Ita Wegman to Toni Voelker
Letter of 25 September 1925[535]

Dear Miss Voelker,

I am in receipt of your letter and do, of course, leave it entirely to you to arrange the matter with the gentleman in question. But now I do want to tell you on my part how such a thing could come about. When Rudolf Steiner established the School of Michael, I was referred to by him as the one who was to support him in this. Initially this meant that people were to come to me about passing on the mantras and so on, and very often also about admissions to the Class, and with many of them my opinion was taken into account also as far as their health on admission was concerned. Later Rudolf Steiner wanted me always to be present for admission. Every time that he admitted someone, he would, after asking some questions, address the following words to the individual concerned: Are you going to remain faithful to the School of Michael?—When the individual had said 'yes', Rudolf Steiner would say: Give me your hand, therefore, and also Dr Wegman, who will be guiding the esoteric School of Michael with me.—Generally speaking, only individuals whom Rudolf Steiner did not already know from earlier esoteric functions came to be admitted in this way, for he would deal with applications from older members who were well known to him by post. So it was mostly the younger members who experienced admission in this way. And those admissions were always also in the presence of Dr Wachsmuth whose office it was to bring applicants into the studio.—This has also made it possible for this to be discussed further, for many, many people do of course know about it from personal experience. This is the only explanation I can think of, not knowing of anything else that might have given rise to such gossip.

I hope that this clarifies the situation for you, dear Miss Voelker, and will be only too glad if you can help to create clarity in the unclear situations which now arise quite often, the reason being that Rudolf Steiner left us before everything had been properly consolidated.

With kind regards,

---

535 IW Archives.

13 Ita Wegman to Juergen von Grone Letter of 20 November 1925[536]

Dear Mr von Grone,

This is to inform you that Dr Wachsmuth and I have returned from our travels and therefore have resumed our work here. I am writing to let you know this because things will again be done in the way Rudolf Steiner arranged them, with all correspondence sent to the Secretary. Otherwise the work might be inconsistent if, as now happens so often, letters are addressed now to one member of Council and then to another. It is, of course, always a bit difficult because of the travelling, but in spite of this one ought to try and follow the directions given by Rudolf Steiner as consistently as possible. The journeys are generally also arranged in such a way that there is always opportunity in between to deal with matters here. I am very sure that you will welcome this, with everything going on as before.

Concerning your request for a list of Class members, we will endeavour to send a copy of this to all national societies in the immediate future.—The reason why many of the new applications for the Class, where you were asked for information, have not yet been accepted is that one would wish, i.e. myself or one of the other members of Council, to know the people who have applied. Where that is not the case, or if the people concerned did not have the opportunity to come to a Class Lesson in person, I have so far left those applications open, and the occasion will surely arise at some time also for these people, depending on their karma, to attend a Class Lesson here or in Germany. Admission without at the same time also having the real experience of a Class Lesson surely also cannot count for much with the people concerned.

I am writing to you in some detail so that you may be able to be informed and can answer questions that are asked accordingly.—I hope things are going alright in Germany.

We had very good results for the Goetheanum in our travels.

Yours sincerely,

---

[536] IW Archives.

14 Ita Wegman to Albert Steffen
Letter of 16 March 1926[537]

Dear Mr Steffen,

As the person most involved in the course of events which have arisen around the School of Michael, it is incumbent on me to inform all members truthfully of the things they have a right to know. I therefore take the opportunity, dear Mr Steffen, to do so, asking you to publish this letter if you will agree. (It would be disastrous for the view to arise that I had assumed leadership of the School of Michael without due justification.) It would indeed be a disaster if opinions and reports were to circulate among members that could not be checked. It would then be impossible later on to put such unofficial reports to rights. Perhaps it will be possible for me to give a full picture in this letter of what happened with the School of Michael before the death and after the death of Rudolf Steiner. Do not forget that from beginning to end I was always present at admissions, at the discussions, not only here in Dornach but also abroad.

When Rudolf Steiner was then no longer with us physically, the question as to what should be done about the Class Lessons was discussed with the Council. For me personally, the fact remained, indisputable as far as I am concerned, that the School of Michael is an institution made by the world of the spirit, and that everything which happens through it is spiritual reality. When Rudolf Steiner said to the members in the Class Lessons that members must strictly adhere to specific principles which in the main were to the effect that the mantras given to members could not be passed on unless the individual who wanted to pass these mantras on to another member had obtained permission to do so, be it from him, Rudolf Steiner himself, or from me. With this, I—and Rudolf Steiner gave the reason for this in the following words: It has nothing to do with bureaucracy, but is an act in relation to the world of the spirit—was also appointed the guardian of the mantras by the School of Michael. I took this appointment very seriously, also as instructed by Rudolf Steiner. You'll remember that I referred to this also in another letter to you, (that I, and all this has to be said, was daily asked to go to Rudolf Steiner for a

---

[537] IW Archives. Passages put in curved parentheses are crossed out in the draft. After EZ II, p. 65 ff.

shared hour of meditation, which I had to do with him, and this took place regularly with me present there to the last day of his death [sic]. You also know that I received a gold Rose Cross from him which he had worn himself, and that he put this Cross around my neck himself.) that other important things took place of which I cannot now speak in an open letter, things which bear out my connection with the School of Michael. You also know—I have spoken of this in public and many members who experienced it for themselves know of it—that the members who were admitted in the month of September in 1924 had to shake hands not only with Rudolf Steiner but also with me, and it was declared that I had to guide the School of Michael together with him. The words and the situation were as follows. Admissions took place in the studio. I had to stand next to Rudolf Steiner, the members were brought into the studio by Dr Wachsmuth. Rudolf Steiner put some questions to the individual asking to be admitted, and if he or she could be admitted Rudolf Steiner said the following words: 'If it is your will to remain faithful to the School of Michael, give me your hand, and also do so to Dr Wegman who will guide the School of Michael with me.' This was in the month of September, shortly before Rudolf Steiner fell ill. Before that, admissions did take place in my presence, but did not involve me directly, and without the ceremony of the handshake.

Admissions were no longer done in this way during his illness, but were only done in writing. As to guiding the School of Michael, this was not discussed at first during the illness, until members then asked permission to give Class Lessons in the way in which Mrs Kolisko had given them for the Waldorf school's faculty in Stuttgart and later for members, using her own short-hand records with Rudolf Steiner's special permission. Such permission was, however, never given to anyone but Mrs Kolisko. Rudolf Steiner did give some people who were well known to him permission to speak the mantras before Class members, adding some explanations. He would also always emphasize that the shorthand records of the Class Lessons did not really exist, and if someone were to read aloud from them, this could only be done with the greatest care and responsibility. He asked me to work intensively with the School of Michael again, and when I said that I did not yet have the transcripts of the shorthand records he permitted me to ask Mrs Finck for these transcripts and also signed the letter which I wrote on the subject to Mrs Finck, the official stenographer. (Mrs Finck wrote back to say that she could only let me have part of them, the rest had already been given to Marie Steiner, and one had to wait for these until Marie Steiner would have returned from her tour with the eurythmy group. Rudolf Steiner then left the physical plane. After this, Marie Steiner also let me have the missing Class Lessons.)

After Rudolf Steiner's death, the conviction would not leave me that I was connected with the School of Michael. I felt myself to be the guardian of the mantras and therefore also the guardian of the explanations given in addition to the mantras, being unable to separate the two elements which together make up the content of the Class Lessons.

The Council then decided that I should read the Class Lessons. This is to say that the objection raised against me, that I saw myself as sole leader of the School of Michael and Rudolf Steiner's successor, is not in accord with the facts. I have regarded myself as guardian of the mantras and the contents of the Class Lessons which are connected with them, doing so with love and devotion. Rudolf Steiner always spoke of them as Michaelic words. The best evidence that I did not consider myself to be [the] leader is that I never signed the blue cards as 'leader', but 'for the leadership'.

The reproach that in the various countries and cities where Class Lessons were established I introduced myself in a different way from the one which you, Mr Steffen, had used for me in Dornach, I can meet by saying that it was not possible for me to choose the same words as those which you had used. All you said was that the Council had agreed that I should read the Class Lessons; and I was charmingly invited by you, Mr Steffen, to do so, which I did greatly appreciate. In other countries and cities I would always in addition stress that I felt connected with the School, which was a reference to the admissions in September which I described earlier. I would also stress that I felt it to be my duty to serve the School truly and faithfully. This is something which all those who now know of these things can and must understand, and above all the members who were admitted in September must have realized that I could not help feeling closely connected with the School of Michael. These members cannot have forgotten the mood which prevailed at the admissions ceremony in those days.—I therefore still do not fully understand why objections could be raised concerning my attitude. When I gave you this explanation at the time, you yourself, Mr Steffen, said that you had not known anything about this and that if you had known this, and also that I stressed my devotion to the School of Michael out of that mood, you would not have had any objection, and that you would also have introduced me differently at the time if you had known about these admissions.

It has thus been, and I must stress this, a case of misunderstanding which arose because each of the others thought that you were correctly informed on all points. This is a profoundly tragic situation, and we simply must understand this.

The reproach that I admitted people without the Council's knowledge is something else I'd wish to clarify. At the very beginning [from April 1925] no admissions were made, and if there was an exception made here and there, it was always with older members who had been members of Rudolf Steiner's earlier esoteric school. When we then spoke together about admissions to the Class—you will no doubt remember—you agreed with me that admission could only be considered for people who presented themselves in person. And we then agreed that the Council should be involved in deciding on admission in difficult, unclear situations, with you yourself examining the application where necessary. I have always adhered to this. I have never admitted someone whom I did not know personally or had examined.—The conditions for admission established by Rudolf Steiner were quite simple. Apart from being a member [of the Society] for two years, serious study was demanded for spiritual development and awareness that admission meant taking on a serious responsibility. It was of course also natural for members who wanted to be admitted to the School of Michael to turn to me, above all as we had agreed that admissions could only be on a personal basis. It was not a condition on admission that one had to have particular esoteric abilities, only the will to develop further; and it certainly was possible for me to recognize this will since I am a member of Council and at the same time also working as a physician. Apart from one case where Marie Steiner did not agree, with the individual concerned not to be admitted on account of his youth, I cannot think of any other case where the Council did not agree to the admission. Class Lessons in other cities were always given with the Council's knowledge, for the invitations to those Class Lessons were always submitted to the whole Council. You yourself were also in agreement, for at the last Christmas Conference you also mentioned my travels to give Class Lessons as the work I did, expressing your satisfaction.

I could wholly understand that a large number of people were not happy that only I myself was giving Class Lessons and other members of Council did not. You also know that I always thought you should give Class Lessons at the major conferences, and that I also said this early on. That Marie Steiner would also want to give Class Lessons I took for granted, so I did not expect anything but that members who wanted to have Lessons given by Marie Steiner would also receive these from her one day, as soon as Marie Steiner herself would announce this. There was no resistance to this whatsoever on my part.

I was then very surprised when I saw all the misunderstandings and opinions arise, as though I granted the right to give Class Lessons only to myself. On the other hand I did of course also know that a fairly large number of members were perfectly satisfied with my reading of the Class Lessons. (I know very well that esotericism cannot flourish in a soil where people do not accept what is given. But perhaps esotericism might flourish again if each can do the work in the place where he is accepted. There is no possibility of my transferring the leadership to you, for this could not be as I did not have the leadership, with the School of Michael an institution which only by the spiritual world [*sic*], which was then wrongly understood. I had only [to take on] the guarding of the School of Michael and as [I] was not officially appointed leader of the School, although Rudolf Steiner had spoken of me as co-leader of the School at the admissions, which he did not do with anyone [else], there was after his death [sic]. In my function as a giver of Class Lessons, I can, of course, regard you—as *chair* of the Council which shares in the responsibility for the esoteric knowledge of the Society, so that it will not be lost or lose its power—as the leader of the School of Michael, if as chair of the Council you are willing to take complete responsibility for it, also responsibility towards the spiritual world. If you were to do this, everything would soon be arranged, and something you have said already can come about, which is that because there are many kinds of people, the Class Lessons are arranged so that members are able to choose to whom they want to go, without making the boundaries too definite, and one will not think ill of members if they appear now in one place and then in another, with you then *gathering all* together in the big Class Lessons. Only in this way could esotericism flourish again, with existing measures not overthrown, which cannot be overthrown because they have flowed from the world of the spirit.)

I would also like to say again here, as stressed earlier, that I wholly and entirely acknowledge you, Mr Steffen, to be the first chair of the Society with all rights and full responsibility, and that as chair you can also assume leadership of the School and all responsibility for it. This is something you will have to decide for yourself.

If you were to decide for it, everything would soon be arranged.

And I herewith express my fullest trust and confidence that you will arrange things in the best possible way, to the satisfaction of all members, taking account of all requirements necessary for the School of Michael.

I very much wanted to say this to you once more in explanation.

15 Adolf Arenson
Circular of October 1926[538]

My dear friends,

Considering the whole position of our movement, I have had some thoughts on the internal history of our Society, and I believe these may not be without value to our members. Perhaps not all these things are suitable for putting into print as they might possibly be used for oppositional purposes.

Yet it should be possible to take up the positive ideas arising from this, for they come from actively entering in one's mind into all that has happened in our movement and our Society from the time when our revered leader Rudolf Steiner started his work.

I would ask you to take the thoughts which follow in that sense.
With anthroposophical greetings,
Cannstatt, October 1926 *Adolf Arenson*

Eighteen months have passed since our teacher and guide Rudolf Steiner left us. It is more and more becoming apparent how his death meant for us, whose task it is to keep his work pure and take it forward, that the position changed completely at a stroke. In the early days one would often still hear people say that 'everything will go on as before, for He is still among us,' but those voices have gradually fallen silent. Facts are without mercy—it simply is no longer as it has been. The rich flow of revelations from spiritual worlds has ceased; the wise counsel, the smoothing hand which again and again balanced out disharmony among members are no more. The work of the School, which started with the Class Lessons and was to continue with the establishment of the second Class has come to an abrupt halt.

This is the harsh and naked truth, but it is beneficial, for it can induce us to draw firm lines as we sketch out our task for the future. This task can only mean that we let the growth points contained in every word he spoke, everything he did, come into flower within us. This alone is how in a modest way we can show our gratitude for what was given to us, passing the wisdom he entrusted to us on to the world, so that it is there

[538] After Wiesberger 1997, p. 309 ff.

for the whole of humanity. A precious legacy he left for us are the Leading Thoughts [guiding principles] which appeared week by week in the newsletter. They must not lie fallow; the welling life in them must not grow frozen, it must be taken up in serious endeavour; the seed must be taken forward to flower, to bear fruit for us. Rudolf Steiner himself stated clearly how he thinks about this work in his Address to Members in No. 31 of the newsletter on 10 August 1924 [in GA 26]:

'Taking together the things to be read in different lecture courses, you can find the points of view out of which one has been able to speak with reference to the guiding principles.... Yet another point of view is probably the most important of all. There is no question of anthroposophical contents being heard or read in a superficial way; they must be taken into our living inner soul nature. The essence lies in taking the thoughts and feelings one has received further. With reference to the lecture courses now available in print this should be encouraged specifically through the guiding principles.'

And this is also how it is with the wisdom given in the revelations of the Class Lessons. They are conveyed to the members of the First Class of the School by being read aloud to them. In this way everyone will—sooner or later—have opportunity to familiarize himself with their content. In future times, however, our work relating to them must go beyond this. They, too, must be a spiritual seed to which we give soul quality through our own creative work. The words which the spirit of Benedict speaks to the monk in *The Soul's Probation* very much also apply to us:

> Our brothers see it as their duty
> to bring about the downfall of this spiritual sin,
> And in this purpose they can find support
> in words I spoke on earth.
> They do not realise these words of mine
> can only go on being fertile
> when those who have succeeded to my work
> in the right way develop them.
>
> [Adam Bittleston translation]

As to whether the time is ripe for this today—this I leave open. What is important is to point to it even now, to strengthen initiative in us so that the living stream will not gradually cease to flow. Because of this, it is necessary for us to take a good look at our situation today, clearing away prejudice, correcting erroneous views, in a word trying to live in the truth and in reality 'without which sound esotericism cannot flourish'.

Up to the Christmas Conference, the Anthroposophical Society provided the frame for the anthroposophical movement—and it was the tremendous aspect of the Christmas Conference that from now on the two were to be a whole. To make this possible, Rudolf Steiner placed himself at the head of the Society. Now genuine esotericism flowed directly through him into the Society, now it was assured that the actions of the Council would always be in accord with the aims of the spiritual world, with Rudolf Steiner its representative on earth. Today we are alone, left on our own; today we must work patiently and with dedication to gain the gifts he gave us. Which is the road to take us there?

He himself showed the way. To really comprehend the last thing he gave us—the guiding principles—to develop them further in the right way, he himself pointed to the spiritual wisdom given in the lecture courses from 1906 to 1920.[539] To connect what was given before the Christmas Conference with the new element—that is the solution. If you read the above-mentioned Address in No. 31 of the newsletter [GA 26] you will not be able to avoid the conclusion that it is impossible to understand everything given in the Leading Thoughts [guiding principles] without the spiritual wisdom that was given earlier.

Surely it must be possible to find something similar in the field of esotericism.

Great ignorance of the facts prevails in this respect. To give an example, let me quote a passage published in *Oesterreichische Blaetter fuer Freies Geistesleben* [Austrian publication for independent life in the spirit] and as far as I know not gainsaid to this day. It concerns the institution of the Class Lessons, and says (page 9): 'The character of the "course" of study which Rudolf Steiner developed for this School is such that he has completely separated from his person the teachings he has so far given on a personal basis, making them into an objective, systematic form of inner development which the School can now offer to anyone who joins it as a member.'

Thus it says here that up to the Christmas Conference esoteric teaching

[539] Meaning the lecture courses which had appeared in print in Rudolf Steiner's lifetime.

could only be given to individuals and on a personal basis by Rudolf Steiner. The facts contradict this completely, however. From 1904 onwards there have always been groups that were educated specifically for esotericism by Rudolf Steiner, representing such a 'systematic form of inner development'. Rudolf Steiner spoke of this on different occasions, and it is also made clear in his words at a discussion of the Class Lessons: 'The three Classes did originally exist in the Anthroposophical Society until 1914, though in a different form.'[540] There is also clear reference to one of these 'schools' in chapter 36 of *Rudolf Steiner: An Autobiography* [or *The Story of My Life*]. A few things may be said to characterize this institution which played a significant role in the development towards esotericism within the Anthroposophical Society.

It was an institution in which there were different degrees, with members advancing through them depending on how far their souls had developed through karma to prepare them for the content of those degrees. Promotion to a higher degree would be in forms similar to those practised in occult societies (e.g. in Freemasonry)—not in imitation of those orders, however, but as a result of spiritual investigation. Rudolf Steiner was at the head as leader of the school and mediator of spiritual realities; his companion and co-worker was Marie von Sivers.

Let me also briefly refer to an experience I had; in view of my advanced age I consider it my duty to speak of it, with only few witnesses of the scene still surviving.

During a ceremonial in a higher degree, which only a small number of people were permitted to attend, Rudolf Steiner himself made it known that the collaboration of Marie von Sivers must be seen to have full justification—not being symbolic as with the rest of us. And this in such a way that *a reality* was implied *that goes beyond death and birth.*

It is easy to see that on rising to higher degrees, the esoteric impulses would flow in ever greater abundance, and that in the almost ten years of that school's existence—up to the outbreak of war—those lessons were something of profound significance for members' inner development.

This is what can be said in this context about an institution which under Rudolf Steiner's guidance offered members the opportunity to rise to progressively higher levels of esoteric life. These communities no longer exist. They had to stop when war broke out. But the knowledge

[540] See Chapter 2, Footnote 25.

and deepening which souls gained during ten years of serious esoteric work are part of the spiritual substance of our Society.

'Tests for the maturity of humanity', as Rudolf Steiner called them, have existed in all times. One of them was the stream which came upon European humanity at the end of the eighteenth century. It degenerated during the French Revolution with its grotesque adoration of the 'Goddess of Reason'. Another is the emergence of spiritual science. Future developments will show how humanity relates to this.

Tests for maturity came also for the Anthroposophical Society. Hence first attempts to show karma in its real form which go back as far as 1904. It is only today that we can speak openly of karma.

One serious test was the founding of the independent Anthroposophical Society in 1912. Then the attempt to introduce the threefold nature of the social organism—this was a test for the maturity of the Society *and* of humanity. Then the great test that came with the Christmas Conference, made acute to the point of sheer infinity by the physical death of our teacher and guide.

We are now in the midst of this test, and it will depend on how we relate to it if we will gain the strength we will need for the greatest and most decisive test which will have its beginning at the end of the century: to help and support the work of Michael.

Michael expects such help from us. May we succeed in not disappointing him.

16 Harry Collison to Adolf Arenson Letter of 7 November 1926[541]

My dear Herr Arenson,

Thank you very much for your letter of 3rd November and with it the Rundschreiben [circular]. I think I have received all the Sendungen [mail] so far.

The only reason for my not writing is the difficulty I have to express myself properly in German.

Now, you ask for my opinion on the Rundschreiben. I think it is excellent and an honourable and sensible statement of facts. I hope it will do good. It *will* do good to those not already perverted by ambition and prejudice and the love of personality. But the love—the craving—of personality is so strong in some of our members that I am sceptical as to any power of conversion. And the sad part of vanity and personality is this—that the possessor of vanity and personal feeling is prevented from being conscious that he or she possesses them. Vanity & personal feeling is a cruel mirror distorting all the truth.

I have had great trouble here lately. It is as follows:—some of the members think that at the opening of the Rudolf Steiner Hall I did not pay enough attention to Frau Dr Wegman & Zeylmanns. It is quite true; for in my opinion the persons who naturally would open a Rudolf Steiner Hall should be the President of the Society (Steffen) and the lady who bears the honoured name of Steiner!. So some of the members have agitated for the presence of Frau Wegmann, that she should continue her First Class lectures. I accepted a compromise viz:—that the Vorstand [Council] should be asked to send Frau Wegman.

But the Vorstand in Dornach never meet, I received no answer to my letters, except a bare acknowledgement from Wachsmuth. Wheeler, Kaufmann & Dunlop then wrote without my knowledge to Frau Wegman asking her direct without reference to the Vorstand. They sent me a copy of the letter after it had gone. I had no alternative but to demand the resignation of Wheeler & Kaufmann. Fortunately an answer came from Steffen, just in time; it was an answer to my own letters to the Vorstand. Meanwhile Wheeler, Kaufmann & Dunlop had made a

[541] Original English, uncorrected. Literary Estate Archives.

sufficient excuse and the matter is for the moment at rest. Frau Wegman is coming next week to hold the First Class. She is coming with her attendant spirits:—Kolisko and Zeylmanns. But I am determined that she shall just hold the First Class meetings as allowed by the Vorstand. But is all this suspicion & intrigue the right atmosphere for a First Class?

There are two existing facts that make things very difficult: (1)—A Vorstand that should be the head of the Society, but it never meets. (2) The attitude of false personal sentimentality that is making a Sect of the Anthroposophical Movement. And this brings me to a question that I keep on asking myself and would like your opinion.

Remember that Christianity was not a Sect to begin with, but there was a struggle between Peter & Paul as to whether it should be a sect or not. Am I right in my historic facts?. It became a sect, & more & more narrow & dogmatic by every century it grew. Should we—anthroposophists—not be above Sects and Sectarianism?. It seems inconsistent for me as an Official to say what follows. It is this:—Would not Dr. Steiner's work flourish much more if there was no Society at all but only a Union of Souls, a Federation so to speak.

You may answer that there is a great deal of business detail & for this we must have officials. My answer is that we have none, now. Our Vorstand does nothing. In England, we are making no progress with the Society, but we have many students outside the Society. Dr. Steiner's last gift was to present his cycles free to all the world. Is that not an indication of his wish? People who are interested will subscribe the funds required, whether or no they belong to the Society.

I am tempted to resign, & I know that my health is bound to force my resignation at no distant date. I am doing all I can to prevent sectarianism & hold the banner high in the sense of your excellent & helpful Rundschreiben. I must try & so shape the movement here that when I retire it shall not become a Dutch Sect or English Sect, with the deceiving name of 'International'.

Again thanking you most sincerely for your timely & helpful Rundschreiben, I remain, as always,

Your affectionate friend & may I say colleague

H. Collison

Please show this to Dr. Unger and Frau Dr. Steiner and anyone who will understand it with discretion & sympathy, even if not agreeing with it.

17 Adolf Arenson to Albert Steffen
Letter of 24 December 1926[542]

Dear Mr Steffen,

My October circular has yielded consequences that were neither foreseen nor intended, though in the interest of truth I must consider them favourable. There is no reason for me to go into the individual opinions that have arisen; I said what I felt it was my duty to say, and have no need to retract any of it. I would, however, like to add something on the point of esotericism which I touched on in the circular. I did not feel it necessary to add it to the circular but it may well be of interest to you, dear Mr Steffen.

With regard to the view, so often voiced, that the Christmas Conference made everything that had gone before invalid, I have, I believe, fully demonstrated that with his Leading Thoughts [guiding principles] Rudolf Steiner did himself refer to spiritual wisdom given in the earlier lecture courses. For there can be no argument about Rudolf Steiner's own words in No. 31 of the 1924 newsletter which I quoted in my circular. I followed this with the words: 'Surely it must be possible to find something similar in the field of esotericism.' And by simply reporting the facts I gave members the opportunity to form their own opinion. I did not go beyond this, exactly so as not to touch on the freedom of the others.

I would, however, like to add the following for you. Before the war, two laws were spoken of again and again in the esoteric communities. One referred to the absolute truthfulness without which all esoteric striving is pointless, the other to continuity, i.e. picking up the threads from earlier elements in existence.

Rudolf Steiner opened the Christmas Conference not with words but with symbolic strokes, and with this brought the law of continuity into play. To anyone who belonged to the institution which Rudolf Steiner described in the 36th chapter in his autobiography, those strokes said: 'With this I connect the new element I want to give to you with what exists from before, true to the law of esotericism.' Again there can be no argument about this for those who know these opening strokes.

---

542 Copy after Wiesberger 1997, p. 316 f.

There is scarcely any need to stress that picking up the threads from what went before implies the possibility of bringing in something completely new, indeed something of a sudden leap, just as the flower follows on from leaf development in a plant and yet is something entirely new.

My reference to continuity with regard to the work which it is incumbent on us to do in future on the Leading Thoughts [guiding principles] and the esoteric wisdom of the Class Lessons was thus wholly in accord with what had been given to us through Rudolf Steiner.

Although those communities had to cease to exist with the outbreak of war, these two fundamental laws of all esotericism—truthfulness and continuity—shall live on in our souls, and it is our sacred duty to care for Rudolf Steiner's legacy in the terms of these laws.

I considered it important to tell you this, merely adding that I leave it to you to make whatever use you wish of the content of and the actual words used in this letter.

I enclose a copy of my letter, with which you are familiar, in its final version and am

with warm anthroposophical greetings
signed Adolf Arenson

18 Eleanor Merry to Ita Wegman
Letter of 6 October 1927[543]

Dear Dr Wegman,

Many thanks for your letter—after our 'Human Freedom Group' meeting Mr Dunlop, Mr Kaufmann and I talked about it until 2.30 in the morning! The situation is now like this:—that Kaufmann, Wheeler and Dunlop will discuss the whole matter with Collison; and if Kaufmann develops a powerful impulse to write directly to the Vorstand (Dornach) himself, he will do so. Very, very much depends on Kaufmann's karma . . . deeply connected with his individual nature . . . for he was given the task of translating the mantras by Rudolf Steiner and with this to enter deeply into them . . . and other things as well, of course.

Wheeler is the weak link . . . and it may be that he does not want to come to full agreement with Mr Dunlop . . . Mr Dunlop has, however, a particular (I cannot describe it!)—but a peculiar strength—a 'weight'—better than I have ever seen it in him before.

So today I really have nothing to report. I would therefore like to say a few words about myself.—

I see in amazement how the things I have seen in the spiritual world are now so clearly taking their course . . . especially how many people among us suddenly find themselves in a place where all is 'darkness' and where they have to make big decisions *absolutely* without any help from earlier experience, and where those who are right beside them cannot offer advice—For always when you would like to give advice or receive it, countless other points of view become visible. The shadow—which also moves actively within—is everywhere, and still the great hand points forward, into the darkness. This image now shows itself in every detail.

On waking up yesterday I saw a kind of summing up of different earlier 'visions'—. This became a marvellous explanation of the different major steps to initiation, how they connect with the different hierarchies in two ways—as a *principle* with which the initiate unites, and as *deeds* which arise from this—from the earthly and from the cosmic aspect. This has been shown to me in a wonderful way.

Then it showed itself like this . . . that Rudolf Steiner, in bringing

[543] IW Archives. Second half in original English, uncorrected.

anthroposophy into the world as something that was physically and psychically truly *creating form* for a new stage of humanity, was working from the region of the Spirits of Form; that he is *now* working from the region of the Spirits of Movement for the earth ... and like a kind of reflection of the war in heaven ... truly lets a kind of duality arise in the Society. (It is *very* difficult to describe, especially in German!) It is like that—because great flexibility is truly necessary ... The *form* for the new is given ... now the matter must continue on. I must now continue in English: [remaining text is original English] 'The Spirits of Motion act as *distributors* of force or movement over the whole world, assembling these different parts of the new type. The 'threefold' idea *is* really in essence this distribution because the threefold idea must eventually come into being through its forces being not centralised, but distributed as a kind of ferment everywhere in the world. Then—when the *distribution* and the *form* are *both* accomplished, the Spirits of Wisdom begin their work.— When the new 'form' is thus in 'movement' they guide the whole 'weight' of the spiritual movement to a new geographical position in the earth (beginning of 6th postatlantean great epoch) and this alters the *planetary position of the earth*. It's orientation to the Sun is changed.—& so on .—

Now this general idea seems to show that the first beginnings of the work from the sphere of the Spirits of Motion *can only come about through strife & division*. If therefore an action is taken which tends to break the centre, to cause a 'split'—what is *behind* the action is really something that is leading to a larger unity in the future.

The danger is that the 'split' should be only one-sided. When, in the opinion of the 'Frau Doctorites', (!) Frau Dr. Steiner was being attacked (1926) they rose up & fought for her. That made the *first* split. If *we* rise up & fight in the same way for *you*, we may get a kind of *balance of two opposites* which seems to be a necessary factor for the creation of true *movement*.

Of course there is the other aspect also—namely the working of the 'Eastern' & 'Western' occultism. But if 'split no. 1' works *without a counterbalance* it will mean the ultimate supremacy of the 'Eastern' stream. If 'split no 2' takes place, the very weight of the 'Western' stream will start the time movement & flow of the spiritual currents which the Spirits of Wisdom will ultimately require for their work. The 'Western' is so infinitely stronger in reality for the very reason that it is in harmony with the Spirit of the Age & the development of the Consciousness Soul [Spiritual Soul].

Therefore—it seems to me that we should not fear any action which may seem at this time to destroy unity.

I do not know what you will think of all this ... I merely tell you because it may possibly have some points about it which may help. On the other hand it may be of no use for the present moment. Please—if you can't understand my English,—ask Mrs. Dank to translate it. There is a great deal more, but I cannot write details in a letter. The whole thing seems to me a message of courage & hope in the face of difficulties—& contained many beautiful pictures explaining certain aspects of the long ladder of ascent through initiations & the principles & actions involved in it.

The *difficulties* lie all in the immediate personal decisions that have to be made ... where no ordinary earthly advice or help avails. The Spiritual Beings are ready, & waiting for *our* actions—and if we can find the *wise* way to act we shall not be acting destructively.

With love

Yrs

Eleanor C. Merry

Please, if possible, write some sort of answer to this letter!

19 Daniel Nicol Dunlop to the Council Letter of 19 December 1927[544]

Dear Friends,

For some time I have been very much concerned over the condition of the Anthroposophical Society in this country. Indications of this have been increasing in number lately and are having marked effect on the work of the Society, and will inevitably,—if something is not done to check them—injure the Movement and create difficulties of a serious nature, which ultimately might lead to a division in the work of the Society although an outward appearance of unity in Membership might be maintained.

I do not desire to enter at this moment into a detailed description of the external evidences of this state of affairs. I feel convinced, after due reflection, that these tendencies to disruption must be checked, if possible. Broadly speaking, an attempt is being made to drive a wedge between the work of the First Class and the general work of the Society—referred to colloquially as the 'Esoteric Section' and the 'Exoteric Section' of the Movement.

If the influences at work to increase this division continue, it may ultimately lead to multiplicity of Group activities without coordination of any kind. Already those who regard Mr. Collison as the Leader of the Esoteric Section, are, by their attitude towards the work of the Society and the Headquarters, having a retardative effect on the whole of our activities.

Mr. Collison announced in the English News Sheet some time ago that he was Leader of the First Class in England. I do not think it was Mr. Collison's intention to mislead members in this matter, but the significance of this announcement at the time it was made has been considerably exaggerated, especially as since then Mr. Collison has very seldom visited Headquarters or attended meetings of the Executive. Certain members have been more and more inclined to regard this as clear evidence of a division that exists between the First Class and the work of the Society in general; and Mr. Collison has clearly stated that the real reason for his lack of interest in the work of the Executive and of

[544] Original English, uncorrected. Goetheanum Archives.

Headquarters is due to the situation that has arisen between himself and Mr. Kaufmann as persons of confidence in the First Class.

The letter from Herr Steffen on behalf of the Vorstand [Council], dated Oct. 14th 1926, in which he stated: 'Mr. Collison as *Secretary General of the English Society* and as a man of confidence in esoteric matters occupies the first position. He is to be regarded as steward of the Meditations. Mr. Kaufmann in his capacity as translator is to be regarded as a person of confidence in the School. In accordance with Dr. Rudolf Steiner's instructions the Class Lessons cannot for the present be placed at anyone's disposal.'; . . . and the authority which Mr. Collison has had authorising him to hold First Class Lessons and give the Mantrams and Signs, he claims establish him as *Leader* without need of consulting Mr. Kaufmann whom Dr. Steiner made responsible with Mr. Collison for the care of the Archives and Meditations.

Neither Mr. Kaufmann or Mr. Collison's colleagues on the Executive have seen *Mr. Collison's* letter to the Vorstand, to which this letter of Herr Steffen's was a reply. This is a statement of fact, and not intended as a complaint against Mr. Collison.

This condition of affairs has resulted in a conflict of opinion between Mr. Collison and Mr. Kaufmann about First Class matters and responsibilities. Various efforts have been made to overcome this disagreement between Mr. Kaufmann and Mr. Collison, but so far without success.

I have come to the conclusion that as Secretary General of the Society, it is my duty to ask that these matters should be brought before the Vorstand as a whole, and to ask them to consider appointing additional persons of confidence in the First Class, under the Leadership of the Vorstand.

On Friday last at a meeting of the Executive at which Mr. Collison was present, I stated that some action of this kind appeared to me to be absolutely necessary; and I asked Mr. Collison if he had any objection to my writing and making this suggestion, and he said that he had no objection. My other colleagues on the Executive also considered that some action was necessary if the present spirit of disruption was to be crushed in the germ; otherwise they felt it might grow to considerable dimensions and seriously endanger the Movement in England. In *assenting* to my writing to the Vorstand, Mr. Collison did not necessarily commit himself to *agreement* with it; but he raised no objection to my writing. It was agreed by all members of the Executive that the situation was serious and was likely to become more serious if matters were allowed to go on as they are. It was agreed, also, that it was the desire of all, in the interest of the development of the Movement in England, if possible to reach a *real* basis of cooperation, regarding the Anthroposophical Movement, Exoteric and Esoteric as *one spiritual Movement*—indivisible.

My suggestion to the Vorstand is as follows:—

That two additional members should be appointed as persons of Confidence in the First Class, under the authority of the Vorstand, in order to unite the Esoteric and Exoteric parts of the work together in unity, and overcome the present difficulties. I think the persons appointed in addition to Mr. Kaufmann and Mr. Collison should be appointed by the Vorstand from among the members of the English Executive, as they are members elected by the Society to administer its affairs and carry out its work in detail, and are therefore persons of responsibility in the Society. The present members of the Executive are:—H. Collison (President, ex. officio), D. N. Dunlop (Secretary General), M. Wheeler (Treasurer), George Kaufmann (Secretary),—all these elected by the annual General Meeting; and two additional members elected by the Council: Mrs. Larkins, and Miss Beverley (Manager of the Book Department).

I therefore suggest that Mr. Wheeler (Treasurer) and myself (Secretary General) should be appointed persons of confidence in the First Class, in addition to Mr. Collison and Mr. Kaufmann. Mr. Collison would still remain the person of confidence in the first position. But the care of the Mantrams and the necessary arrangements for conducting the affairs and meetings of the First Class, would be in the hands of the four persons of confidence, under the Chairmanship of Mr. Collison, and under the leadership of the Vorstand. No individual, however prominent, can lead the Society either exoterically or esoterically, without the cooperation of his colleagues. This way of conducting the affairs of the First Class unitedly would do away with the idea that there was any division between it and the external work of the Society; and would no doubt in time remove the differences which have arisen between Mr. Collison and Mr. Kaufmann.

The annual General Meeting of the Society in England will be held at the end of January, and in my judgement it is necessary that a reply should be received from the Vorstand before this Meeting, stating whether they approve of this suggestion.

I hope the Vorstand will realise the importance of this matter, and accept my assurance that it is only put forward in the interests of the Movement as a whole. I look forward to a reply at an early date.

Very sincerely yours
D. N. Dunlop
Secretary General.
Anthroposophical Society in Great Britain.

20 Harry Collison to Marie Steiner
Letter of 4 September 1928[545]

Dear Frau Doktor,

I shall be arriving at Basle on the 24th or 25th September and shall stay there until I come to the Wachsmuths for the festival. I am coming early for a particular reason and also for that reason staying at Basle, quietly and privately.

Miss Pethick told me very privately that you would consent to my taking a few notes of the 1st Class lectures so that I may not always have to ask Mr. Kaufmann's favours. It seems strange that I should be deprived of a privilege that is enjoyed by Kaufmann and Mrs. Wedgewood who both have the translations of the whole lectures in full. Frau Wegman is always requesting me to give the lectures of the First Class 'in my own way'; but how can I do it when I am not allowed to take notes?—!! I have had Kaufmann's notes of Lectures 1, 2, 3.

At any rate, the First Class no longer possesses the sacredness of the time when Dr. Steiner held it. Many strangers—to my knowledge—have had access to the mantrams;—and two at least are now definitely opposed to Anthroposophy.

You will probably be too busy to see me, so would you kindly leave them in an envelope with Fraulein Lehmann or some other trusty person, & I shall call for them on Tuesday, 25th. I can let you have them back in a very few days. I shall only take rough notes, & of course shall keep it all very strictly secret.

I hope you are well & not working harder than your strength will allow.

Yours very sincerely, *Harry Collison*

[545] Original English, uncorrected. Literary Estate Archives.

21 Ludwig Polzer to the Council Letter of 27 February 1930[546]

To the Council of the General Anthroposophical Society

In reply to your letter of 20 February 1930 I am able to give the following information:

In the autumn of 1924, Rudolf Steiner granted me the right to give Class Lessons. When I asked him how I was to do it, he told me: 'Do it as you wish.' At the time, the Class Lessons Rudolf Steiner gave in Prague were taken down in shorthand there, with his permission, with the transcripts left in Prague. Dr Eiselt and others would then read the texts aloud for Class members.

It therefore seemed to me that Rudolf Steiner did not consider reading the texts to be something which he intended to convey a special privilege. In the talks we had on the subject, Rudolf Steiner never spoke of studying the mantras, only of Class Lessons and meditating the mantras. If there can be talk of study in this case, this seemed more justified to me for the texts rather than the mantras. Initially I gave the Class Lessons without reading out the texts, and I only did so later at the request of some members, also considering it to be more modest.

In the autumn of 1923, when Rudolf Steiner gave an esoteric lesson in Vienna at my request, he also permitted me to take this further and to extend the es[oteric] group. He also knew that I continued to do so after the Christmas Conference.

The request you make of me I must consider a disruption in almost six years of es[oteric] work which has had a unifying and harmonizing influence when difficulties arose between members speaking different languages, especially in Prague.—Doing this work, I have assumed es[oteric] responsibilities towards a number of people and established a continuity, the discontinuation of which I consider it to be an impossibility in es[oteric] life. It has also become clear that in the esoteric sphere it is not all the same to people who is giving the Class Lessons, which has also been evident in Dornach. I do not feel in any way dependent on permission from the Council in Dornach in this work I do

[546] Goetheanum Archives.

in the old Austria-Hungary and neighbouring places, not being subordinate to the Council. I acted as a disciple of Rudolf Steiner, empowered by him in person, can see only him as leader in my work, and am es[oterically] responsible only to him.—I therefore cannot allow formal intervention to disrupt this work.

I felt it incumbent on me to discuss this matter with the members of the Austrian Council, for such a profound change would not be inconspicuous, and the Council in Austria feels itself in the interest of the anthrop[osophical] cause to be not only administrative but also initiative.

All members of the Council consider your request to be such as to go against the spirit of the es[oteric] work. I have been asked to continue giving the Class Lessons as before.

Mr van Leer, who will shortly be going to Dornach, is prepared to take this letter with him and represent my own and the Austrian Council's stance.

Yours sincerely,
Ludwig Count Polzer-Hoditz

22 Lili Kolisko to Guenther Wachsmuth Letter of 23 March 1930[547]

Dear Mr Wachsmuth,

Please forgive me for only replying to your letter today, but I suffered some hesitation, being unable to understand that you cannot gain clarity in Dornach itself. Nor does the point seem that important to me. It is after all not really a question as to whether or not I informed Dr Wegman of my intention to read Class Lessons again. As far as I can understand the problem, it is a question as to whether even more people are in future to be empowered by the Council to read Class Lessons, or if, on the other hand, everything that exists is to be Council privilege.

As you wish to be informed by me merely in order to form a personal opinion, I am, of course, happy to tell you what I have also been saying at the Council meeting. On the occasion of my lecture at the agricultural conference in January I communicated to Dr Wegman in person that I intended 'soon' to continue again to read the Class Lessons, as many members are urging me to do so and I can no longer close my ears to their pleas. I did not mention a particular date at the time. I then decided to start again on 27 February, Rudolf Steiner's birthday, and made this known two weeks in advance, as always. I did this by informing the German national council, which then had to inform the individual branches, the Independent Anthr. Soc. and some members who live in the Stuttgart area. As the interval had been somewhat longer this time, I also sent the information to Dr Wegman, and this must have reached Dornach on about 15 February. The words were more or less these (I have not kept a copy of the letter): Dear Dr W, I would like to inform you that I have decided to continue reading the Class Lessons again after a relatively long interval. The next Class Lesson will be on Thursday, 27 February.

This was an independent decision, made on the basis of the existing situation in Stuttgart. I did not discuss it with Dr Wegman beforehand, though I also had not heard from her in January that difficulties were likely to arise.

I felt this form of providing the information to be adequate, for I was

[547] Goetheanum Archives.

not thinking of asking permission but merely wanted to let her know that I would be continuing again now, after a relatively long interval, with something which I did already do at Rudolf Steiner's request when he was still alive.

I hope that you will now have a clear picture and would ask you truly to consider these explanations to have been given merely to inform you personally.

Yours sincerely,
L. Kolisko

23 Ludwig Polzer to the Council Letter of 9 May 1930[548]

To the Council of the General Anthroposophical Society in Dornach

When I came to Prague today for Class Lessons, Dr Eiselt felt it incumbent upon himself to give me a report on the meeting of General Secretaries in Dornach and particularly the matter of the Class, as it was discussed there.

With regard to this, I have to say the following:

Rudolf Steiner empowered me to give the Class Lessons during a private talk I had with him in mid-September 1924, with no one else present.—I gave my first Class Lesson at Michaelmas 1924.—When I visited Rudolf Steiner in his sickroom on 11 November 1924, I asked his permission to take up Class work also in Prague. Dr Wegman was present in the room during this talk, but some distance away. There was *never* any reference to a small group to whom I would explain the mantras. We did speak, however, about the relationship between the Class and the small esoteric group for whom Rudolf Steiner had given an es[oteric] lesson in the autumn of 1923 in Vienna, giving me permission to continue with this.

I must stress once again that I asked Rudolf Steiner how I was to give the Class Lessons, and that he replied literally, unambiguously and with clear precision: 'Do it as you wish.' Otherwise I could never have taken on the responsibility of doing the Class work in the way I did. At that time in November, I wanted then to go to Mrs Finckh, so that following those words of Rudolf Steiner she would give me the texts of the Cl[ass] L[essons]; Marie Steiner was away, however, and so I did not do this but turned to Mrs Kolisko. She then asked Dr Wegman if she might give me the texts, and was given permission by her.—I then went repeatedly to Stuttgart, gradually making my own copies of the texts there.

When Dr Wegman was in Prague in the autumn of 1925, a document was drawn up because pretensions had arisen from the Czech side, and signed by her and Dr Wachsmuth. This acknowledged, in the name of the Dornach Council, that I would do the Class work in Czechoslovakia. The document also says that I am entitled to appoint functionaries for the Class work. I am in possession of this document.

[548] Goetheanum Archives.

After Rudolf Steiner's death someone came to me in Dornach (I no longer know today who it was), asking me to stop the Class work for the time being, in the interests of Dr Wegman, adding that Dr Wegman would re-appoint me again.—My answer was that I had been empowered by Rudolf Steiner and did not need any other form of appointment. I also informed Mr Steffen of this, and he said: You were absolutely right in what you did.

Please let my declaration be added as an appendix to the minutes of the meeting of General Secretaries on 25 April 1930.

I regret to say that my state of health is such that I cannot attend prolonged and stressful meetings, yet have been continuing the Class work as before, without interruption.—

With kind regards,
Ludwig Polzer-Hoditz.

24 George Kaufmann
Class Lessons at 46 Gloucester Place (1930)[549]

The following things have to be seen to:—

1. To make sure that Mr. and Mrs. Jones, or other suitable caretaker, are in on the evening of the Lesson. Instruct them not to go up and down the stairs during the Lesson; and not to put through any telephone calls or in any way disturb the Meeting.

2. To see Mrs. Parsons and make sure that on that evening there is no disturbance or coming and going on the part of her relatives.

3. To provide that a responsible member—if possible *not* a member of the Class—sits in the front room downstairs (arriving not later than a quarter of an hour before the Meeting commences) throughout the Lesson. This member must see to it that no late-comers, members or others, go up the stairs once the Lesson has begun.

4. From the experience of last time, I also hold it essential that a member of the Class sits immediately outside the door of the room on the 1st floor while the Class is in progress.

5. To see to it that the Group room (front and back on the 1st floor, thrown together) is properly and tidily arranged, with a maximum number of chairs put out in proper order; the Office furniture removed as far as practicable; Dr. Wegman's chair, table, water, reading-desk (raised about two inches above the level of the lectern desk) and reading-lamp suitably arranged; room aired beforehand and properly warmed; *all* windows and shutters closed and curtains drawn, and everything in proper order. All this must be done in very good time. We ask members to be in their seats a quarter of an hour before the Meeting, and many of them live at a distance. The first members generally come 30–40 minutes before the commencement of the Lesson.
The room should be ready by then, so that they can sit in peace and quiet.

6. To see to it that there is a competent and tactful member to inspect the blue cards at the door. He should be there three quarters of an hour before

[549] Original English, uncorrected. London Archives.

the commencement of the Lesson. Our practice is, as at Dornach, to look at the inside of every card. Members who have left their cards behind should be asked to wait downstairs until Dr Wegman's arrival.

7. To provide for a quiet room, adequately warmed, where Dr. Wegman can go as soon as she arrives in the house, for quiet and for any necessary interviews. Mr. Curtis will always place his Office at her disposal, and it is the best situated room, in my judgment.

G. K.

25 Marie Steiner to Moritz Bartsch
Undated draft (c. 1931)[550]

Dear Mr Bartsch,

We are much concerned over the way the Class work is done, and on the other hand serious problems also beset us which arise from all kinds of deep-down human reasons as we increase the number of people reading the texts. We must therefore be extremely cautious and increase numbers slowly. We have first of all decided to appoint two individuals in Germany who, as we assume, will meet with the fewest problems—in Stuttg[art] Mrs A[uguste] Unger instead of her father who has fallen ill[?] [i.e. Adolf Arenson]; you, Mr B[artsch], for places you are able to visit. We assume that you will be happy to take on this task. We are, of course, unable to send you the texts by post, and would like to hand them to you in person. Until then it will probably be best if you do not talk about the matter, as it is a Class and not a Soc[iety] matter.

Yours sincerely,

[550] Lit. Estate Archives.

26 Ita Wegman to Maria Roeschl Letter of 22 February 1935[551]

Dear Dr Roeschl,

I would have liked to write to you earlier, but was prevented, firstly because of having to go to Holland on account of my mother's serious illness and then death, and secondly because of all the work waiting for me here.

It was a great pity that we could not meet when you were here, but, as you also said, 20 minutes was a bit on the short side for this. I was delighted to hear from you that the small conference in Tuebingen went so well. I do think that this way of working with small groups of people is the kind of work that is most fruitful these days.

The feelings you expressed in your last letter to me have moved me deeply. Just like you, I have a great desire to talk to you, and I will certainly make this possible as soon as I can see that the work here, which I had been setting aside for a long time, has been set in train again in the right way. Nevertheless I would like to tell you some things now, in this letter, concerning my stance towards the Society.

I have given much thought to the position I should hold within this Anthroposophical Society, which Rudolf Steiner forged into a whole once again at the Christmas Conference. It has not been possible to do what Rudolf Steiner intended with the Christmas Conference, as you are no doubt aware. Opposition was marked from the beginning, and he knew this immediately after performing the act at the Christmas Conference. We then fought for 10 years to have the principles of the Christmas Conference win through after all. Unfortunately, however, opposition was so powerful that one could not win through, and now it has in fact happened that a split has developed in the Anthroposophical Society. Oddly enough, I was taken into an illness when things were coming to a climax, and was unable to participate in all the meetings and the decisions made. I felt this to be a peculiar sign, understanding it to mean that I really no longer had anything to do with these earthly things. At the time, when the illness got worse and worse, I thought that I then no longer had anything to do on the earthly plane. An experience in the

[551] IW Archives. Also in Selg 2005a, p. 199 ff.

spiritual world taught me something different, however. In an encounter I had with Rudolf Steiner, with the Christ spirit also present, I found I was not expected in the spiritual world but was required still to do something on earth. From that moment I also found the strength to take my return to health firmly into my own hands. As to what my tasks are, this was not made known to me. I also understand that I must discover this by my own effort. During the time when I was far away from Dornach, I always had the feeling and also the certainty that I must unwaveringly remain true to the intentions Rudolf Steiner wanted to bring into the world with the Christmas Conference, but must not, of course, give way to the illusion of hankering after something which was not possible, continue to bemoan it and do nothing further myself. No, it was also necessary for me to come to a decision, one that would make work possible.

One day it therefore became perfectly clear to me that I had to go back to Rudolf Steiner's fundamental impulse which he wanted to give to the new Society, bringing Michael's teachings down from the Spirit Association (Michaelic School), more so now than ever before. I have heard many things about this School through Rudolf Steiner, and also my own and his relationships to it. This is the impulse I want to come back to as the essence of what happened during the Christmas Conference, connecting with it strongly and acting out of it. I cannot yet say what it will turn out to be; I am preparing and waiting to see, and do not wish to put myself forward anywhere, nor to tie myself down. If there is something good in this impulse and there are people who can warm to it, something will come of it. It holds a seed for the future and was the last thing which Rudolf Steiner entrusted to human beings on earth. The First Class, as it was given and now is in the hands of many, is as yet far from exhausted, but it must be handled differently from the way it has been handled until now. I am slowly feeling my way and things become clearer as I do so. All the old forms, even the very last form for anthroposophy [meaning the one given at the Christmas Conference] have been thoroughly ruined, and it now seems to me that we must no longer look for one form for the life of anthroposophy, but that every individual himself is the form with which anthroposophy wants to unite. Where this has happened, people will find one another and unite to become part of the true Spirit Association. The [Anthroposophical] Society is no longer needed, for anthroposophy is now on earth. It all depends on individuals today. They must then out of their development form a higher Association which has its roots in the spiritual world. This preserves all individual development, the freedom of every individual, with each feeling connected with this Spirit Association or School of Michael through his own insight. This is what I heard within me. That I, myself, am in this impulse—this is what matters. The rest will arrange itself.

As to the group with which you are connected, dear Dr Roeschl, I would have liked to have said some things to you about it as well, before the new admissions had been made. As destiny took another direction in this, I will now continue to keep silent about it, and perhaps later on, when we meet in person, some things may be said.

I have heard that you are going to England and will be in Clent for a time. These visits to England seem to me like the Greeks being brought to Rome by the Romans. May they have the right effect for both parties! Something which has happened once before in world history can then arise again at a higher level.

With kind regards,
I am your,

27 Polzer's speech at the AGM on 14 April 1935[552]

If I intervene actively in the strife and the things that are going on in the Society at this time, this is because I feel not merely justified but obliged to do so because of many years of experience and my own observations. I know that I am facing a majority which over some years has arrived at a particular view, especially in Dornach, a view which has been presented in the *Denkschrift* (memorandum). I am therefore aware of the difficulties I am facing in presenting my view as against that view and must therefore say 'No' to the action which a majority in the Society now intends to take in Dornach. I trust in the power of the facts that have guided me, facts I have come to know over many years, for I always faced up to them with neither sympathy nor antipathy, remaining open and upright in relation to the two warring parties.

I am therefore going to take an actively neutral position in saying some of the things which I feel obliged to say at this very moment in time and in this situation. First of all, I have to reject the idea, presented over and over again, that one has to decide for one side or the other. This is also why I refuse to be connected with any particular party. I have to speak out against the frivolous term 'matter of taste' used in the memorandum and also against people saying that people did with 'ill intent' refuse to be convinced of much that the authors say in the memorandum. I thus have to declare on my part that it is not ill intent where I am concerned; my method, *too*, is to seek the truth.

With such a voluminous book as the memorandum before us as a work to prepare and bring about the will, the necessity arises for those who reject it to speak at greater length than is customary at AGMs.

My position is generally neutral, but this cannot prevent me from helping and giving support where I consider this to be necessary and humanly fair, and where I believe myself to be acting in the spirit of Rudolf Steiner.

For me, the individuals whom Rudolf Steiner appointed for the Council and for Section leadership, each in his or her own way, are still wholly right in the positions which Rudolf Steiner gave them. They all have virtues and their faults, and have made mistakes, but this cannot change my view. Mistakes have been made on the one part and the other,

[552] After Meyer 1994, p. 596 ff. Also in EZ III, p. 333 ff.

as is evident in events over the last ten years. The fact that these individuals could not find a way of working together also showed me that after Rudolf Steiner's death the esoteric strength of the whole Council was not great enough, on the one hand, properly to overcome disruptive outside influences, and on the other that there was no one on the Council who was able to bridge the differences. Little was learned from Rudolf Steiner's death that might have brought unity of insight. Instead, impossible pretensions emerged first on one side and then, somewhat less markedly, on the other, especially with regard to leadership of the School. So there was no rational thinking leading to a more open and liberal basis for the Society, with the absence of a universal spiritual leader taken into account. As the need which arose with Rudolf Steiner's death could not be met on the basis of rational thought, this had to lead to highly disastrous consequences, disasters capable of destroying the basis for our Society which could exist only under Rudolf Steiner, but not the spirit and essence of anthroposophy. Whatever happens, this does not release those individuals from the duty to stay at their posts.

Soon after Rudolf Steiner's death I realized, in direct perception, that there was no real will to communicate, to work with Dr Wegman, and that neither Marie Steiner nor Mr Steffen seriously considered such collaboration possible. When I asked Mr Steffen to take on the position of first chair in 1925, he told me: 'I could only work with Marie Steiner, and never with Dr Wegman.' I saw then that right from the beginning there had been no honest will to communicate but only the will to depose, and this was then also particularly evident in the attitude and behaviour of many people in Dornach. This atmosphere, not openly addressed but yet prevailing among people, inevitably had to lead to all the conflict and misunderstanding which arose initially among Council members and in Dornach. And this soon spread from Dornach to the periphery, disrupting the work everywhere.

There are many profound reasons why communication was difficult, and these certainly cannot be wholly put at the door of Drs Wegman and Vreede. The Society, appointed to serve esotericism, was progressively losing its esoteric character with those disputes. It threatened to become more and more a society in merely outer terms, in spite of the emphasis on and development of a completely new dogmatic concept of esotericism.

The memorandum stresses, quite rightly, that to understand the schisms we must go back to the past. I will therefore also go back, but a bit further than just Rudolf Steiner's death, for the rancour and enmity against Dr Wegman do go back further than Rudolf Steiner's death. Opposition existed even before the Christmas Conference, but it was more hidden. I have come across it myself and been able to observe many things with regard to this, for at that time I was very often in Dornach, often for long periods, as Rudolf Steiner would then talk to me about all the individuals who were later to be members of Council, and about many other things. Some of you who are present here today may have heard Rudolf Steiner speak even then of a witch-hunt against Dr Wegman and her work as a physician. He said at the time that this would one day destroy the Society. Yet he would again and again single her out, stressing the need for her collaboration. I was also able to see that certain individuals (I won't mention names) whom he had definitely rejected have come to the fore in recent years and taken the place, or tried to take the place, of others whom he had preferred for some areas of work.

As I am against the motions, I must in giving the reasons for this go specifically into the deeper reasons for those difficulties and enter also into the sphere of esotericism. The memorandum is quite open in its treatment of this sphere, even if in a somewhat primitive way. And so I think I may also speak quite openly about this. I actually consider this to be highly necessary, for many things are not stated clearly and accurately in the memorandum, and I did hear and learn many things from Rudolf Steiner particularly in this area, which means that after his death I have always been able to be consistent and sure in everything I did.

First of all concerning the view which I had to develop over the years regarding leadership of the School. For me, Rudolf Steiner is still the only leader of the School where this still has its esoteric character. The Section for General Anthroposophy surely cannot be taken on by anyone with serious and genuine responsibility. Because of this, it still does not seem illusory to me today to think it possible for the Section leaders to find a way of working together, unless one of them claims leadership on the basis of some kind of succession, which simply does not exist in this case. That this did happen following Rudolf Steiner's death, I have always considered to be a mistake, and I also said so at the time.

Following Rudolf Steiner's death, I believe the affairs of the Class can only be regulated by someone who is prepared to take responsibility towards the spiritual world and Rudolf Steiner and is supported by the will of a number of people, makes this known to the Section Leaders and discusses it with them. I think this would maintain continuity with Rudolf Steiner, which is the condition. I also spoke of this at a much later time with Mr Steffen, when permission for Mr Arenson was being considered. Taking this on will, however, always be an act involving spiritual destiny. Licence granted for 'having done good work', for knowing a lot, would not be acceptable to me, and this would very soon get us into a superficial and authoritarian way.

I must now speak about the situation, as I see it, of Dr Wegman as Rudolf Steiner's collaborator in the Class. For Rudolf Steiner did definitely call her such. I consider it wrong to identify the collaborator in the Class simply as Secretary on the Council. Such identification does seem to me to be an insult in this case. Insults have not been lacking. It is not unclear to me what Rudolf Steiner meant by 'collaborator'. The appointment of the collaborator, that is, assistant for establishing and sharing in the work of a mystery such as the School of Michael in this case, could only be based on a profound destiny connection which Rudolf Steiner perceived in full awareness, emphasized, and to which he wanted to do justice. I am in no doubt that that was the case. Rudolf Steiner literally said to Dr Wegman with this that she was part of a great destiny. Not only Marie Steiner, but Dr Wegman, too, is part of a great destiny with Rudolf Steiner, and this must be borne with all its burdens and pain. Yet the collaborator and assistant is never also deputy or successor, cannot be this, being a woman. Humanly one can understand, however, how Dr Wegman mistook her mission after Rudolf Steiner's death. I do not find that one should bring in condemnatory judgements and persecution on this account, using this error to make what formerly was a hidden witch-hunt into a downright execution, a moral dismemberment. I have to stress that I never talked with Dr Wegman about her incarnations and that no one has ever said anything to me about them. The Alexander business would be openly discussed, above all by her opponents. I did once have a talk with Rudolf Steiner as to under which preconditions and in what situation one might discuss personal aspects of incarnations. This was in Berlin in 1917.

The initiative for the esoteric School of Michael came from Dr Wegman, as Rudolf Steiner said. Taking up this initiative then established the necessary esoteric destiny union between himself and her, the mystery precondition of more recent times.

Before the war, Marie Steiner collaborated in all esoteric, ritual events.

The one was as necessary as the other, like *everything* in Rudolf Steiner's life.

When Rudolf Steiner returned from Britain in 1924, he indicated in various ways that he gradually wanted to give the Class a ritual setting. The ritual element evolving in the Michaelic Mystery then made him speak during admissions of the handshake and the promise that should also be given to Dr Wegman. It was an indication that this destiny union had significance exactly for the Michaelic Mystery. In the memorandum it says that Marie Steiner held a position of not merely symbolic but real significance—this was, of course, known to me—and this is evidently so, for it simply could not be otherwise for someone collaborating with Rudolf Steiner in the mystery school. To establish the beginnings of a mystery school does demand the reality of a collaborator playing a significant role, and Rudolf Steiner documented this by his deed. With both Marie Steiner and Dr Wegman.

Now I must also speak out against talk of old and new esotericism. The experience of death has always been presented in different ways in the mysteries. Death—the tomb—resurrection—being with the divine spirits. Initially in a most primitive form and finally the most magnificent that was given to us in the Class. Rudolf Steiner never had anything to do with an esotericism divided into new and old. On the contrary, from the beginning, even before the war, he devoted his energies to the mysteries, which had to return of necessity, the way they have to be in the present and future. He gave them a content of spiritual awareness and the character they needed for the present time by giving humanity the wisdom of anthroposophy which has equal meaning for the male and the female mind. This meant that it was necessary to give expression to this duality in the ritual presentation of anthroposophy, and the female collaborator thus had that role also because of her gender. A Class Lesson is not just the reading of an instructive lecture but an act which can connect us with the mystery stream of all times. If we fail to maintain conscious awareness of this and do not call it to mind again and again, we abandon the heavenly institution which Rudolf Steiner brought to the earth.

I know that errors were made, on both sides. Everyone is subject to them. But for me that is no reason not to acknowledge something which can never be erased and will continue on. Quite apart from external 'achievements' which for me do not differ so much in significance for humanity in the individual Sections, tendentious criticism of which I must reject. The unheard-of instances of moral defamation, particularly against Dr Wegman in public meetings and printed brochures, I must reject as being against Rudolf Steiner's will. Sometimes it almost seems, if one has indeed known many other things that happened even before the Christmas Conference and feels their continuing influence, as if a hidden, generally no doubt unconscious, grudge is making itself felt against the last years in Rudolf Steiner's life, with Dr Wegman in particular the victim of this. Such a grudge against Rudolf Steiner was also apparent in earlier times.

It is perfectly clear to me that Marie Steiner, having worked for so long with Rudolf Steiner, is the one who is spiritually advanced. Yet the honest, friendly will to come to an understanding has been lacking. This has nothing to do with outer 'achievements', and the term 'achievements' is altogether somewhat philistine, highly unsuitable for the inner affairs of the soul, *inner* achievements. These do, however, play a very big role in esotericism, lest *the head alone were to be active in esotericism.* Constant criticism and enquiries into methods might bring it about that one goes no further with the methods than in an intellectualistic way, is afraid of their results, and wimpishly or in a philistine way seeks to avoid issues in life and destiny.

Let me mention another fact which will show how much was going on in this area. When I met Dr Unger a number of times at the opening of Rudolf Steiner Hall in London, he asked my help in making it possible for the mystery events to be continued to which Rudolf Steiner had given a new form before the war. He actually discussed this with me in detail, considering it to be absolutely essential for the Society. I had to be evasive at the time, for shortly before that Marie Steiner had told me at a meeting that great difficulties existed with regard to this, especially in Dornach.

What I have said so far means that I feel it is necessary to reject the motions put by the community of people working together at the Goetheanum. It is impossible for me to give part of the disintegrated Council the right to make the other part responsible for everything, and again and again, on the basis of terms which have long since become slogans—method—non-method—forming opinions—achievements and arrogantly assert: 'We are the only ones who are justified and capable of taking Rudolf Steiner's work forward, we are the ones with the right method, the others have a non-method; those who are not with us are against us; you must decide if you want to go with us or perish with the others.' This is what one hears all the time. It is not possible to divide anthroposophists authoritatively into whites and blacks, and then withdraw the power to be representative from those who are said to be black, as Dr Vreede put it. This would more and more take the mystery mood out of and away from the second Goetheanum building. And the Council would also be more and more responsible for so much damage caused by the Council dispute itself, harming the health, soul and body of many old, faithful anthroposophists; this would however apply not only to the part of the Council which the memorandum is blaming.

From the time on 1 January 1927, when Dr Boos violently disrupted the Class Lesson, indeed almost pushing Dr Wegman off the rostrum, I have known that if this cannot be made up for again by the whole Council on the soil of the Class itself, the General Anthroposophical Society must fall into decay, grow shallow in an intellectualistic way, in spite of growing numbers attending conferences; that it will progressively lose its original character.

The *memorandum* was intended to point the way in forming opinion at the AGM, and that was the actual reason why it was written. It is, however, written in a combative spirit, for it says in the introduction itself that there is no intention of being impartial, and this makes it destructive, inciting fanaticism and influencing the will. At best I can say that it is a *fable convenue*. It also shows how since Rudolf Steiner's death the very thing which he spoke of especially in his last years is lacking and systematically ignored—to study history not merely from existing sources but to cultivate a history that can be read in the spirit, on the basis of repeated lives on earth. In spite of the dangers and errors each of us will have to go through, and which no one should dare today to condemn authoritatively, this history will nevertheless be written.

Let us consider what has been going on in the Society's history for the last ten years. It started with a war by correspondence, with the letters gaining in volume and growing into brochures and finally books. If this were to continue with either side claiming to be right in external terms, the shelves of libraries and archives must fill up. It would merely prove, however, that Rudolf Steiner was not understood, the Society has lost its way, the centre remains empty, and people make one another sick with literature of this kind. Does anyone truly believe that we are on the right road when such literature increases in volume; does anyone believe that by filling archives in this way we will enter into the next century in the right way; does anyone truly believe that the printed word will still play such a great role at the turn of the century? Does anyone believe that calm can be established for the real work with such fighting words, voting in a fighting spirit? That is indeed the great illusion. The voting done at the 1923 Christmas Conference was only apparently such, in reality it was the expression of a unanimous will. Rudolf Steiner did say *beforehand*, however, what would happen with the Sections, who would lead them, and which individuals would be members of Council. Today it seems as if trust is asked in advance, without saying anything important first as to what will then happen.

The first Goetheanum was built as a mystery centre, it was taken from us because we spoke in purely intellectualistic ways in it. There was no one there who might have protected it. Rudolf Steiner was not allowed to protect it, for he had given it to humanity as a touchstone for their maturity. Rudolf Steiner then laid the Foundation Stone in human hearts. Foundation stones resting in strong hearts are no longer bound to one place, nor to a single building. They must become foundation stones for the mystery centres of the future in different places. The people who will sow the seeds for those mystery centres can only be called to do so by the spiritual world directly and through their destiny. This needs above all esoteric courage, not leading strings and narrow confines.

The second Goetheanum has been built wholly to be open to the world, for the 'little book' to take effect from outside, as with the fourth seal [*Revelation* 5: 1, 7, 9 and 10: 9–10]. The continuation of the mysteries will, however, come from the 'little book' which acts from inside. The most important demand for the anthroposophical movement and Society is therefore trust in human beings, not a grudge against them. Trust, which would have to be given to us first from Dornach, not trust first demanded by Dornach. It will meet the case if it is first given and if Rudolf Steiner can speak through the five Section leaders, but not if you get to read moral sermons in almost every newsletter, taking no account of the changed situation, and if pretensions to leadership can be read between the lines, something which must be hurtful to many souls who are closely connected with Rudolf Steiner. He will not speak if Dr Wegman and Dr Vreede are set aside.

Rudolf Steiner alone can connect all anthroposophists of past, present and future; stricter statutes and anathema against independent actions when destinies collide and one finds it difficult to reach understanding will not do so. The motions and the memorandum are a sign of weakness and will trigger violent responses.

If it proves impossible to get the Council to agree with each other, the only possibility will be for the Sections at the Goetheanum to be open to all, and the General Anthroposophical Society to constitute itself on a completely independent basis, with no central membership admission. After ten years of strife in Council and Society, the setting aside of such a large proportion of members, among them old members esteemed by Rudolf Steiner, will not serve anthroposophy.

The trust given freely and as a matter of course to the spiritual, universal guide and teacher would now, at this time without a guide, need to be given to the power of anthroposophy itself and to individuals of whom anthroposophy has taken or will take hold. This should come to expression in the statutes by trusting group leaders and leaving the establishment of groups and admission of members to them. Not only to those who say 'yes' to everything and subscribe to conditions.

Legal dexterity can formally lead to a different decision; but this is then no longer in the spirit of Rudolf Steiner. Esoteric pretensions, such as the dismissal and appointment of Section leaders, cannot arise under the umbrella of a majority in a vote taken in fighting mood.

I think that financial disaster also cannot be prevented at the Goetheanum unless the demand for greater freedom is met from common sense.

28 George Kaufmann to Montague Wheeler Letter of 26 August 1935[553]

Dear Mr Wheeler,

You will be glad to hear of the outcome of our meetings with Dr. Wegman here during the week-end, of which I told you over the phone in London on Friday night.

The following friends have been present at these meetings:—Dr Wegman, Dr Vreede, Dr Roeschl, Dr Zeylmans, Dr Kolisko, Herr von Grone, Dr Hahn, Mr Geuter, Michael Wilson and myself. At the beginning I gave your message of greeting, regretting your inability to be present.

We have had five fairly prolonged sessions, on Saturday morning and afternoon, Sunday morning and afternoon, and this morning.

We were greatly helped by Dr Wegman reading to us, during these meetings, the first four Lessons of the First Class. These readings alternated with conversations in which we reviewed in the most varied aspects the position of the world and of ourselves today, and the needs and conditions of the esoteric work in the Groups of the Anthroposophical Society in which we have responsibility.

We put before Dr Wegman our feeling of the urgent need for a resumption and more regular and frequent continuation of the esoteric work in our Groups, notably in England and in Holland, and our resolve, as a group of friends from different countries, to assume responsibility in this connection and to assist one-another in so doing.

Out of her special position and responsibility in the School of Michael, Dr Wegman spoke to us of how she was seeking to find the right spiritual guidance for the true continuation of the School after the recent events, which had broken, within the physical world, the basis which was provided for this School in the Anthroposophical Society by the Christmas Foundation Meeting.

After prolonged consultation we came to the following unanimous conclusions with regard to the resumption and continuation of the work in the immediate future.

Dr Wegman will be invited as heretofore to come to our various

---

[553] Original English, uncorrected. Goetheanum Archives.

centres as frequently as is possible for her to do, and read the Class Lessons as given by Rudolf Steiner.

In addition to this, Dr Vreede in England, and Dr Zeylmans, Dr Hahn and Dr Vreede in Holland, will be prepared to conduct meetings of the Class, communicating the Mantrams, and giving such explanations in their own words as appears right to them. This will enable more frequent meetings of the Class, and a more regular communication of the mantrams to the members, than would be possible through Dr Wegman's visits alone. This arrangement is also in keeping with what Dr Wegman herself recommended during the years that followed Rudolf Steiner's passing.

The following arrangements are agreed upon for the admission of new members to the meetings of the Class.

First: The blue certificates of membership, which presume the continued existence of the School of Spiritual Science at the Goetheanum as an united institution, will no longer be used as a basis for admission to the esoteric meetings in our Groups. The confusions resulting from the exclusion of members and groups by the recent General Meeting at Dornach—an exclusion to which the Vorstand-of-Three are powerless to give effect as regards the esoteric School—afford very obvious reasons for our discontinuing, for the present at any rate, the use of these cards of membership, of which a further supply, for the admission of new members, is in any case denied to us.

Secondly: In order not to pre-judge or prematurely fix the deeper issue of the continuance and eventual form of the School of Michael, for which Dr Wegman in conjunction with Dr Steiner and the esoteric Vorstand assumed responsibility in face of the spiritual world alone, we shall use a more provisional form of certificate, simply stating the fact that such and such member has the right of admission to meetings in which the contents given by Dr Steiner in the School of Spiritual Science are communicated. Such a certificate will be issued to the members of our Groups who are already in possession of a blue certificate, and also to any new applicants who are accepted for the esoteric Class. The possession of this certificate will give the holder the right to possess the Mantrams, just as the blue certificate did until now, and the solemn responsibilities involved will be explained to new members as heretofore. The certificate will be issued in conjunction with our Groups of the Anthroposophical Society, which, in the spirit of the arrangements made by Dr Steiner at the Foundation

Meeting, will continue to provide the outer framework of support and protection, within which the work of the esoteric School proceeds. For our own country, the certificate would therefore read somewhat as follows:—

Anthroposophical Society in Great Britain

It is hereby confirmed that .......M........N........... is entitled to take part in the Meetings, wherein the esoteric contents given by Rudolf Steiner in the School of Spiritual Science are communicated.

Date .... (Signed by a person of confidence for the esoteric work in our Society, and by Dr Wegman.)

In pursuance of these arrangements, Dr Wegman has kindly consented to come to London early in October (the exact date has yet to be settled in relation to her other engagements), when she will be able to hold one or two Lessons of the Class, and to introduce Dr Vreede for the work which she will do henceforth in this connection as above explained, which Dr Vreede will then be able to take up during her visit in October and early November. In Holland, Dr Wegman will similarly initiate the resumption of the esoteric work during her visit there in November.

Owing to present conditions in Germany, the holding of closed esoteric meetings there is scarcely possible. Nevertheless, as Herr von Grone explained to us, members of the Arbeitsgemeinschaft [joint association] are deeply concerned as to the continuance of the esoteric work in our Groups, and they will feel strengthened by the knowledge that clear and proper arrangements to this end have been made by agreement among us all.

I am sure you will agree that the above should be communicated to and considered by the Executive, and I take it you will do this at the next Executive meeting, so that the necessary arrangements may be made for Dr Wegman's visit and for the subsequent Class meetings to be held by Dr Vreede.

Sincerely Yours,

29 Ita Wegman to Class members in England (1935)[554]

After a considerable interval of time, we are now beginning again with the esoteric Lessons. Esoteric life is above party divisions and has nothing whatever to do with party. It is however important that human beings who are about to hear esoteric truths should belong together. There should be among them that harmony of feeling which can lift them, during the time of hearing, into a higher community and brotherhood. This is the inner mood that is needed.

When Rudolf Steiner instituted the School of Michael, which in its outer form was known as the First Class, I was the one whom he instructed to guard the Meditations belonging to this School. It was also in conjunction with me that he received new members into the School. A year after his death, the arrangements of the School were modified inasmuch as other individual members of the Vorstand [Council] also undertook the responsibility for the Meditations and for the receiving of new members.—Through the changes that have taken place in the General Anthroposophical Society, the continuity of esoteric life can not be allowed to be impaired. Spiritual tasks are above the criticisms and resolutions of General Meetings.

Therefore, my dear friends, I am now beginning to communicate to you once more the content of the Michael School. In this work Dr. Vreede will henceforth be helping me. She will now stay here for some weeks longer and will work with you in deepening the esoteric life, giving such explanations as are called for, and going through with you the Meditations which are given by the Michael School. The esoteric life will gain by this working together, and I believe that we shall thereby all of us make progress. May blessing rest upon this, which in all sincerity and with the feeling of deep union with Rudolf Steiner we will now begin anew.

[554] Original English, uncorrected. London Archives.

30 Ludwig Polzer
'Personal communication' of 1 December 1935[555]

The Goetheanum exists wherever es[oteric] work is done in the spirit of Rudolf Steiner.[556]

For members of the School of Michael only.

In the interests of the School it seems necessary to me nowadays to state a few things, to render the agitation in Class affairs by individuals at least to some degree ineffective.

Younger Class members who are not very familiar with the beginnings of the School and with Rudolf Steiner's esoteric work are understandably easily made uncertain with inappropriate sham arguments. This gives rise to all kinds of erroneous views which disrupt the work in the Class, being irreconcilable with the spiritual substance of the Class and the conditions for attending the Class.

One main argument brought against the Class—which I have been giving for more than 11 years now—in order to disrupt it, is more or less this: 'Someone wishing to have the Class the way Rudolf Steiner gave it should attend it in the national society; those who go to the independent groups cannot be admitted to the national society's Class. Count Polzer does not give the Class the way Rudolf Steiner did.'

In response one has to say that Rudolf Steiner did not always give the Class in the same way. From February to 2 August 1924 he used neither the sign of Michael nor the seal before and after the Lesson, and also did not speak in a mantric way about the seal marking the connection with the Rosicrucian Mystery. He only did this following his return from England in September, when he gave the Repeat Lessons.

At that time, in September, he also started to ask new members who were joining to give himself and Dr Wegman the promise to be faithful, thus showing that [he] wanted to give an increasingly ritual character to the Class, which he also announced in the last Lesson he gave on 2 August, before he went to England.

He also documented the fact that the School of Michael had been a uniform whole together with the esotericism he gave even before the

---

[555] Archives of Perseus Verlag (Thomas Meyer).

[556] Handwritten addition by Polzer.

war, in that on Sunday, 30 September 1923, before there even was a Class, he did for the first time say the mantra which he would speak before and after every Class at the beginning of a Rosicrucian esoteric Lesson in Vienna. Also connecting the seal of Michael with the verse *rosae et crucis* and the words that went with this clearly showed the oneness of the esotericism and mystery training he presented.

I never said a mantric word in the Class that did not come from Rudolf Steiner. It should, however, be clear to every esotericist who does not want the Mystery of Michael to follow the road taken by the Roman Catholic Church, a road leading to disputes on dogma at the Councils, that the Class needs to be as alive as possible in the way it is given and must not be laid down in an external, dogmatic fashion.

An absolute indication for me that the above is correct are the words which Rudolf Steiner said to me when I asked him on 11 November 1924 how I should give the Class. He said emphatically: 'Do it as you wish.' In Michaelic terms, and I came to see this more and more clearly, this is the only possible answer. Rudolf Steiner agreed that I should take on the task. Some people do, however, deliberately close their ears to what I have been saying a number of times already.

I am sure that following Rudolf Steiner's death the mysteries cannot be further revealed in the present time, but we must continue to cultivate a living, not only rational but also ritual continuity of the mystery contents he has given, also passing them on to people who did not know Rudolf Steiner and yet seek to connect with him esoterically and not only intellectually.

Calling on the brothers, speaking individual mantras which Rudolf Steiner gave on such occasions, are not acts that deviate from the spirit of his actions. But I am sure it is not in his spirit nor is it Michaelic simply to be dogmatic and make Class Lessons a business of reading aloud.

It happens again and again that the objection is raised that I do not give the Class the way Rudolf Steiner did; spiritually this is untrue, though in formal terms it is partly right. This formal correctness is wholly in accord with the majority decision, wholly in line with formal, legal conditions made at the last AGM in Dornach at Easter, when people were put out of office and excluded. This made the General Anthroposophical Society something other than the one founded by Rudolf Steiner.

It also has to be stressed once again that in terms of Rudolf Steiner's work there is no 'Class of the Zemska' and 'Class of the Jednota' in Prague but only the Class given by Dr Eiselt and the Class given by myself. The School of Michael can never be laid claim to exclusively by a group in society at large. I am therefore unable to identify with the statement that people attending the Class in the Jednota cannot also attend the one in the Zemska and vice versa. I on my part have to leave it entirely to the conscience of older Class members how they relate to this individually. Regulations that have not come directly from Rudolf Steiner have no justification in my eyes.

I herewith declare that I have been giving the Class for 11 years, with the knowledge and consent of Rudolf Steiner, and thus carry on in absolute direct continuity. I also believe that it is impossible to pass Dr Wegman over in Class matters, for this goes against the will of Rudolf Steiner who explicitly declared: 'Dr Wegman will lead the Class with me.' Leaving her aside we leave the stream of continuous mystery work to which Rudolf Steiner alone was able to introduce us.

If exoteric 'opinions' determine things concerning the Class, the esoteric mystery content must soon be lost in such a community. The School of Michael as an affair of the spiritual world on earth can never have anything to do with intellectual opinions in the style of external associations.

31 Hans Peter van Manen
Talk with F. W. Zeylmans van Emmichoven in 1958[557]

Personal notes, starting point and beginning

I knew Willem Zeylmans well in the last twelve years of his life. As a student, I was often able to talk to him, among other things about issues of inner development. I have a lively recollection of the important talk concerning my admission to the first Class. This must have been in September 1958. I was still struggling with certain theoretical doubts, culminating in the question as to whether the 'Class' still had the right to exist. What follows is based on memory and wholly or largely comes from that talk. It is possible that after more than 40 years elements from other talks touching on esoteric matters have merged with that talk in my memory. It took place in his study at home.

My initial question was something like this: 'Does the School, and especially the first Class, still have significance today? Does meditating on the Class mantras still have an effect?' Willem Zeylmans answered in the affirmative, although, he said, everything had happened with the mantras that should not have happened. Members of the Class converted to Roman Catholicism and handed the mantras over to their confessor; people in closed psychiatric units shouted the mantras at the walls; in countries like the Soviet Union and Nazi Germany the secret police confiscated Class notebooks, etc. All this will have affected their efficacy, but in his experience the Class mantras definitely still had power—thus Willem Zeylmans in 1958. (Later on he specifically referred to the frequent influence during Lessons of particular individuals who had died, an influence that gave direct inspiration.)

'Speaking freely on the mantras'

I no longer remember how we came to speak of the way in which people were called to be Class readers, it may have been because of questions I interjected. Willem Zeylmans told me among other things that Rudolf Steiner had empowered Lily Kolisko and a number of people 'in the periphery of Europe' to communicate Class Lessons in their particular country or area. He gave several names which I cannot now remember. It may well be that Count Polzer-Hoditz's name was mentioned, but I do

[557] Goetheanum Archives.

not recall. Scandinavia was well represented, I think. Zeylmans emphasized that strictly speaking none of the original members of Council was expressly appointed to this by Rudolf Steiner, although we can say that Ita Wegman had implicitly been given the right. He reminded me that in a Repeat Lesson in September 1924 Rudolf Steiner spoke of 'Dr Wegman, who leads the Class with me', and that he suggested to several new members 'also to have a talk with Dr Wegman'. The following goes in the same direction. During his illness, the shorthand records had been transcribed and submitted to him (R. S.). He then put the finished manuscript into her hands, and according to Zeylmans this confirmed her position as co-leader of the Class. I did not specially ask if he had heard this from her in person, but I assume this to have been the case.

I am not exactly sure when and where Willem Zeylmans was appointed. Some time during the first six months of 1924 or, more exactly, between the Christmas Conference and the Arnhem conference (July 1924). After the Christmas Conference Zeylmans stayed on in Dornach until 9 January. From what he told me, it was clear that he went to Dornach at least once more during those six months, and there spoke with Rudolf Steiner. A third possible date would have been during the Arnhem conference, but the conference programme included two Class Lessons, and the talk that led to his appointment will probably have been some time before that.

In that key talk, in private, Rudolf Steiner told 30-year-old Zeylmans that he would also have to give Class Lessons in the near future, 'speaking freely on the mantras'. This came as a shock to Zeylmans. He felt himself to be too young and inexperienced. Rudolf Steiner listened to this with understanding but would not dream of taking it back. Zeylmans knew that some older Dutch members had as yet little confidence in him, a young General Secretary. He was afraid that the response to his sudden role as representative of the School of Michael would be a serious mood of rejection. He did not reject the proposal, however, but thought long and hard about the When and How.

He found a good intermediate solution by first of all asking Ita Wegman to give the Class Lessons during her regular visits to the Netherlands, and this she did for some years. (I do not know where or how frequently.) Some members found this one-sided and said they would also like to hear Marie Steiner as a Class reader. Zeylmans went to Marie Steiner with this request the next time he was in Dornach, but she rejected it immediately, saying that she saw Holland as a sphere of work for Dr Wegman. Finally, in the late 1930s, when Ita Wegman's health had grown less robust, Willem Zeylmans took on the task himself. Initially he would make extracts of the Lessons which followed the line of the shorthand records exactly. He would not read the text out, but have his open notebook before him as he spoke freely. This appeared to be a satisfactory solution. After some time, however, older members who meant well by him and some of whom had still attended Class Lessons given by Rudolf Steiner himself in 1924, asked if it would not be possible to hear the 'Lessons' twice, a free rendering by Zeylmans himself and the second time read out in Rudolf Steiner's own words. Zeylmans then decided to simplify matters. He stopped his free renderings altogether. Class Lessons were read from then on.

In spite of this, the original request 'to speak freely on the mantras' was not forgotten. During the Second World War, when all anthroposophical activities except for the *Oberufer Christmas Plays* had been stopped under the German occupation, and it was only possible to work illegally, in small private gatherings, Zeylmans gave fairly regular Class Lessons in small groups, possibly in free renderings, though that is only a guess. When the independent Anthroposophical Society in the Netherlands was re-established after the war, Class Lessons were also read again, initially by Zeylmans and in different places. At his request, Pieter de Haan took over the Lessons in Zeist and some other cities. During the 1950s, Zeylmans increased the number of Class readers by asking Henri van Goudoever, Bernard Lievegoed, Elisabeth Mulder and others. Lievegoed introduced a new custom, which was to precede every Lesson with a brief introductory talk. This was at the same time an attempt aimed at a possible transition to free renderings, and over the years this came to happen more and more.

Mention should be made of an episode in the late 1950s. At that time, Zeylmans established the Centrum voor Vrij Geestesleven, an institute designed to take anthroposophy as such into cultural life. He based himself on the configuration of the School of Spiritual Science as Rudolf Steiner had outlined it at the Christmas Conference. He gave Class Lessons in a free style for the staff at the Centre, all of them Class members, on several occasions.

One can do no other

I have not taken note of the exact line followed in the talk of September 1958. Dr Zeylmans certainly went in detail into the problem which arises for the Class reader when he feels doubt with regard to an application as to whether the individual concerned had sufficient inner balance to cope safely with the content of the Class Lessons. Zeylmans, a psychiatrist by profession, gave two examples of decisions made in this regard by Rudolf Steiner that had surprised him. The first was when he, Zeylmans, was visiting Dornach, probably at Easter 1924. He did, of course, attend Class Lessons given whilst he was there. During one Lesson he recognized someone he knew, an individual with mental problems. This could only mean that Rudolf Steiner, fully familiar with the individual and his mental illness, had seen no danger in admitting him to the Class.

The other case was even more striking, if possible. It was in Arnhem. Two Class Lessons were to be given during the three-day members' conference. Before this it was necessary to see a considerable number of Dutch Society members who had applied for admission to the Class. Applicants were received one after the other. Rudolf Steiner sat behind a table, with Willem Zeylmans beside him at Rudolf Steiner's request. (History does not record if Ita Wegman was also present.) Rudolf Steiner instructed Zeylmans to let him know beforehand and in confidence if there was any one among the applicants whom he considered unsuitable. The interviews started and proceeded in good order. Then, however, came the turn of a lady about whom Zeylmans had serious doubts. He knew her to be a scheming woman who caused much disruption around her. He had cautiously hinted to Rudolf Steiner that he had reservations about her. She came in and was utterly charming and pleasant. Rudolf Steiner spoke most kindly to her, with no reserve whatsoever, filled in the blue certificate, signed it, handed it to her and shook hands. Zeylmans felt he had been taught a real lesson. But when the lady had left the room Rudolf Steiner said calmly: 'You are perfectly right. She is a terribly difficult person, but one can do no other.'

Dr Zeylmans told the story to show how immediate and certain the initiate's knowledge of human nature can be, and that his abilities to judge things are very different. He added the following to show what happened afterwards. Fears that the lady would cause further problems did not come true. It soon emerged that she did not have much longer to live. In the light of this, what happened made sense, Zeylmans said. For it can have been of highly positive significance that shortly before the end of life the woman's soul was still able to receive this content (of the Class Lessons) as an impulse for her future. Zeylmans was unable to say if Rudolf Steiner knew or perhaps suspected this.

Something for humanity

The long talk finally returned to the initial question as to whether meditation on the Class mantras still had an effect. Zeylmans said that the cultivation of a meditative subject had its most unclouded effect in privacy, but the destination of 'our' meditations was, after all, to be 'something for humanity' one day, either immediately (like the *Foundation Stone Meditation*) or after a time. Zeylmans gave the Prologue to the Gospel of John as another example. Originally this was a strictly esoteric mantra, accessible only to few individuals—yet within a century it had become something for humanity. This also indicates the future for the wisdom given in the School of Michael. (See also Hella Wiesberger's introduction to the booklet on the publication of the Class texts in 1991 [in German].)

32 Invitation to the first 'meditation session' in the Netherlands

STRENG VERTROUWELYK.

Den Haag, 2. IX. '25.

Aan de leden der 1ste Klasse der "Freie Hochschule für Geisteswissenschaft", in Nederland.

Waarde Vrienden,

Zooals U allen bekend is heeft Frau Dr. Wegman op zich genomen de klasse-uren, voor zoover mogelyk, overal persoonlyk voort te zetten.

De pauzen die b.v. in ons land tusschen twee opeenvolgende uren ontstaan moeten daardoor vry groot zyn. Om nu toch een enge band te houden tusschen de klasse-leden, - en we weten van welke beteekenis dit juist in dit geval is, - heeft Frau Dr. Wegman aangeraden op geregelde tyden uren te houden waarop de klasse-meditaties gezamelyk aangehoord en doorleefd worden.

Het eerste meditatieuur, waartoe alle klasseleden dus uitgenoodigd worden, is bepaald op ZONDAG 13 September a.s., te 's Gravenhage, Ieplaan 85.

Het zal gehouden worden op de volgende wyze:

half drie ontvangst, bovenzaal Ieplaan
drie uur inleiding door Dr.F.W.Zeylmans v.Emmichoven
half vier klasse-meditaties " " "

Met hartelyke groeten
Dr.F.W.Zeylmans v.Emmichoven.

33 Harry Collison to Marie Steiner
Letter of 25 April 1944[558]

Dear Frau Dr. Steiner,

Thank you for yours of the 24th February which I received a few days ago. I am now writing my reply and have sent you a telegram to show that I entirely share your views. This is the only reason for remaining at my post. This also has been getting more and more difficult in face of the intrigue of certain members. This sort of thing is not new and must be expected, and can easily be faced by both of us. But we have to reckon as you say that truth and one's own conscience are more important than the external success of any Society.

Of course you are in a much more difficult position than I am, you are in the very midst of the intrigues and you are physically surrounded by some friends who always wish you well and are very fond of you.

You use the word 'unanimity', it can be a blessing or a curse. I have exposed this craze of unanimity and condemned it when used as a threat to get one's own way or a means of persuasion. A person quick of tongue, but not necessarily good or wise, if he is determined to get his own way, can force his hearers to silence or fatigue, and even deceive himself that they have agreed. Or he uses threats and exaggerates the dangers which will ensue if there is disagreement. 'Peace at any price' is the cry, but it is just a political or diplomatic trick. Dr. Steiner's great word was not unanimity but *Mut* or courage, even to standing alone. Perhaps you and I must prove it. But I am not going to make sickness the excuse, it would not be true. In spite of the tale of evil-wishers, my mind is perfectly clear and my energy also. My trouble is that I cannot move about very much and my eyes grow tired. But I cannot work in the atmosphere of constant quarrelling and personal ambition. I have better work to do.

I have not yet seen your letter to Miss Compton-Burnett, I am writing to ask her if she has it.

I know that correspondence goes on at Dornach, and it is said that I am old, past work and very difficult to deal with. Then why do these same people ask me to continue in my position?

The reason for my not writing to you personally has been that I seem to

---

558 Original English [some typing errors corrected]. Literary Estate Archives.

write only when things are complicated, and I wanted to spare you trouble. And so once in a case of urgency about a year ago I wrote or telegraphed Dr. Wachsmuth, and I expected he would bring any such matters before the Vorstand [Council]. I am now wondering if he did so. Over a year ago I sent a long letter, giving a detailed account of the troubles over here and I offered my resignation. He answered that I must not resign. About the same time I wrote and telegraphed about the First Class and asked if I might admit certain well-known and highly respected members and mentioned their names. I have had no answer. Miss Armour has also written but he studiously avoids this subject. Meanwhile Kaufmann holds First Class meetings, and Heywood-Smith has for some years declared that none should be held anywhere until Rudolf Steiner re-incarnates.

Over a year ago an attempt by a few members was made to interfere with my work in the First Class; the attempt fell through, and the class was very successful and well attended until my illness in the Summer.

I hope soon to start again. But I dare say you have often seen how this question of the First Class can be very dangerous, and can be used in all sorts of ways if the lessons are exclusively in the hands of a few people. Could you give copies and so open it out in some way? Wegman spoilt it by giving it out too widely and this mischief cannot be repaired. But she carefully kept the written lessons in the hands of her friends.

You ask if I hear anything about you. I have not heard a word; people know too well what my views are. But I honestly wanted a word from you and therefore telegraphed.

I hear vaguely of trouble at Dornach but do not know where the troubles are. In U.S.A. and England also there are intrigues and personal attacks between people, and the claiming by certain persons of powers they don't possess. Over here Pethick and Gordon-Jones and Gaze also hold that they have permanent powers given them by you as a sort of sacred mantle, and Pethick says you personally gave it to her 'for many incarnations'.

Whence comes this discord? Is there any nationalistic or personal leanings? Meebold certainly has the knack of annoying those who do not agree with him, and those who agree seem to get obsessed under his control. Many years ago you and Dr. Steiner in Sweden scolded me for taking his part, and said that wherever he goes he creates mischief. Dr. Steiner was right.

Miss Baker is his supporter and with her is Gaze and many others over here. We all know his political views and some people believe anything he says. Others are getting the opinion that we are a quarrelsome lot with a strong political colouring.

Some people seem to forget Dr. Steiner. It is feared [?] we are about to have the autocratic dominance of an Adyar at Dornach and elsewhere. To counteract this I suggest the following rule:—The President shall be elected for three years and then shall automatically retire and not be eligible for election till after another year. The members shall be called together over a year to elect extra members to the Vorstand. This rule as to the President shall apply to each member of the Vorstand.

Then comes the question of Park Road. A few months before the war Harwood came to see me, and in answer to his question I said, if they want re-union they must go to Dornach and ask for it. I could do nothing but I would not object if it was the wish of Dornach, but I would not take office.

Miss C. Burnett says Stein is now very active, but some of the Park Road people are getting tired of his adventures.

I have seen Miss C. Burnett who assures me she has never had your letter; she tells me she telegraphed to you last week to say so.

Last week I sent you copy of my letter to Steffen with notes of the above.

Your affectionate old friend,
Harry Collison

34 Albert Steffen to Hermann Poppelbaum Letter of 31 August 1949[559]

Dear Dr Poppelbaum,

Dr Zeylmans has just been to see me. He referred to the memorandum which was printed in 1935 for members of the Anthroposophical Society only and presented to them by Dr Bessenich, Paul Buehler, Dr Eckstein, C. Englert-Faye, Dr Fraenkl, Dr E. Grosheintz, E. Pfeiffer, Dr Poppelbaum, P. E. Schiller, G. Schubert, Richard Schubert and Jan Stuten. Dr Zeylmans considers it right to inform readers of the newsletter that this memorandum has been withdrawn with the consent of such former signatories as are still alive today (in accord with Dr Poppelbaum's remark at the end of the AGM in the spring of 1949). The letter in which Mr Buehler, known to Dr Zeylmans, states his reservations, a letter which I do not remember, should be added if Mr Buehler has no objection to this (you would need to ask him in any case).

To prevent misunderstanding, I must repeat on this occasion what I have said many times before, which is that I myself had no part in setting up the memorandum and did not read it before it went to print and only partly afterwards.

Marie Steiner provided many handwritten statements for the memorandum, something which was made known by Mr Guenther Schubert, and these were included in the printed text. As to whether these, too, can be withdrawn in the name of the individuals still alive today who are withdrawing the memorandum, will be a logical question for many readers of the newsletter.

The relevant notice may, of course, appear as soon as it is sent to me.

Yours sincerely,
Albert Steffen

559 Goetheanum Archives.

35 Elizabeth Wirsching
Joergen Smit on the three Classes in the School of Spiritual Science

Notes made at the Scandinavian summer conference in Aarhus in 1986

At the anthroposophical summer conference in Aarhus on 27 July to 2 August 1986, Joergen Smit gave a sequence of seven morning lectures. I no longer recall the exact theme of the conference, but according to my notes it was the Anthroposophical Society, the School of Spiritual Science and its relationship to the public domain. I was 30 at the time, and my notes do show some gaps, but they will convey something of some central ideas Smit had concerning the School. It was a conference for members of the Anthroposophical Society, not a Class conference, and it will no doubt be of interest to know the thoughts which Joergen Smit put forward in that very situation. My report follows the themes day by day.

1 *In how far is anthroposophy rejected in the public domain?* It is widely thought today that morality is something given from outside and has nothing to do with the individual's powers of perception. A gulf is said to exist between external morality and the inner world of the individual. It is on the basis of this that anthroposophy is rejected. Yet the public image appears to be variable, at least in Scandinavia. Waldorf schools and published books are recognized to a degree; at the same time there is growing criticism. First steps to self-knowledge tend to prove unsettling. One feels that moral decisions have something to do with one's own self. A next step, and thinking begins to come alive. This is strengthened by regular meditation. One comes to think in images, to *Imagination*. A further step empties the conscious mind so that spiritual elements may stream in by way of *Inspiration*. Finally the seeker for insight connects with spiritual entities through *Intuition*. The gulf between morality given from outside and the I, the self, is overcome in these three steps. Moral qualities live in the element of warmth in human beings, and through warmth the spirit. It is one thing to follow this road oneself, and another, equally important, to know something about the steps that still lie before one.

2 *The three qualities of soul.* In the public domain, the School of Spiritual Science should be a university which is part of the Anthroposophical Society. For the first time in human history, a mystery school is gaining visibility in the public domain. A courageous step taken by Rudolf Steiner, to work with a society of thousands rather than a small core group. The reason for this decision was that humanity had unconsciously crossed the threshold to the spiritual world. Social thinking without awareness of the spirit became an impossibility from then on. Today, the initiation process comes about as an impulse that gives life. Modern people find themselves in the situation of a new beginning, though they have not yet wholly found themselves. They are no longer supported by their culture, as in earlier times, by their profession, by the family. Each is on his own, and meets the Lesser Guardian of the Threshold day by day. There is great urgency. In the encounter with the Lesser Guardian, subjective meets objective; small and personal meets great and cosmic. Cosmic thoughts enter into limited human thinking. A conscious encounter takes place with the three powers of soul. One becomes an organ for something greater. To penetrate to truths in our thinking, we must go more deeply into spiritual truths. New feelings arise, objective feelings which one did not know before—feelings towards sprouting and fading life, the sunset—a completely new range of feelings. There are moments when one's own feelings fall silent and cosmic thoughts enter the arena. The will grows 'great' if we manage to look in a focused way on destiny and life situations, to understand our destiny by considering the life situations in which we are. To enter the First Class means to work with these three qualities, on the large scale and the small. This makes one a representative of the Anthroposophical Society. Rudolf Steiner spoke of an 'experimental method in general humanity' [GA 259, p. 174].

3 *The evolving human being and the School of Spiritual Science.* Our attitude to the world must show itself in human qualities and not in fixed ideas. This is a golden rule for representatives, also in relation to people who have never heard of anthroposophy. To listen, show interest, discover what lives in the other person without judging him. In this way, the School becomes a task for the future. In the public domain, a university

of three 'classes' should be apparent, in all countries around the world. This university lives in the inner human being and can show itself when the necessary qualities are there. Spiritual-soul structure within the School—it must be a quality present in every truth-seeking individual. If that is not the case, one goes back to authoritarian forms. The School's social structure depends on quality, on developing organs, and not on external positions.

The three qualities

—having awareness of the other representatives,
which is collaboration at a higher level.

—encounter with the other as an individual,
with qualities in the other.

—being on the move with anthroposophy.

These three stages or qualities lie outside the personal and small.

1) World thoughts. Living thinking that flows within and from the human being. That is the angel. It longs to intervene. Waits for personal initiative. Connects the thinking of the individual with cosmic thinking. *The individual.*

2) Pure feelings. Strengthened by what comes from above. The archangel. Every time it proves possible for everyone to do his share in the social sphere, the archangel is able to intervene. *The community.* Preparing for the next period of civilization.

3) The will. Organ for the burning issues in the world. *Humanity.* Archai. Preparing for the seventh period of civilization.

4 *The double.* When we read something, go deeply into anthroposophy, we are on our own if we do not understand what we are reading. If we do understand it, we live inwardly with what we have read, and human intelligence meets cosmic intelligence. We are no longer alone but together with Rudolf Steiner. Something higher is present, essence in essence. If the Guardian of the Threshold rejects us we are shown what we still need to work on in ourselves. The Guardian of the Threshold is behind such an experience of the double. You see 'a figure which has everything from the past within it', and at the same time this is the higher I of the human being. The double is a form in which the Guardian shows itself.

An example of how we can have insight into the way the double works:
a) In small groups. Everyone is working on the same subject, and with the evolving human being recognized in the other, it is possible to overcome the double's influence.
b) In anthroposophical groups. The greater the difference between individuals the more powerfully is the double able to work, paralysing the impulse where a void arises in consciousness, a field one does not want to cultivate on an individual basis. (J. Smit often spoke of 'provinces in the soul'.) If one goes on in spite of this, endures, working on oneself, the double is overcome and something higher can enter into the community. A cosmic intelligence is then present, in essence.

Qualities in waking up to the double:
a) A new, as yet uncultivated field opens up for me.
b) The material which has not been worked on begins to change.
c) Do I stay with that material or can I offer it up to the context as a whole?
d) Communion with the light that shines up in this work—'true communion'.

5 *The School of Spiritual Science and its three classes.* A major challenge in our time—solidarity with the whole of humanity. We may be informed on something far away but are unable to change it. A gulf arises. How can it be overcome? At a personal level we can say: Is whatever you say and do covered? That is the situation of the School impulse.
First Class: Each goes his own way towards the threshold and beyond, bearing the other in mind at the same time.
Second Class: Awareness of the higher self develops among these people. The Second Class can arise if one is able to work together out of the higher self. Such a working relationship is still at the level of sleep-consciousness today. It depends on four times twelve people, with all points of the compass represented. Starting to build the temple for the future. We practise the social aspect every day in overcoming anything in us that is one-sided.
Third Class. The centre is found in the world of the spirit. Death is experienced beforehand. The higher self is thus able to act directly on

the will through the physical body. We experience the very first beginnings of the Third Class as we wake up each morning. What are you doing with your life-substance? Conscious awareness enters into the spiritual, away from the physical plane. Anything artistic is preparatory school for the Third Class.

36 Joergen Smit on the publication of the Class texts (1990)[560]

Dear friends,

I will try and clarify some important aspects in the situation of work done in the School of Spiritual Science that concern the publication of the 'Class texts', as they are called, that is, Rudolf Steiner's words taken down in shorthand when he gave the Class Lessons in 1924, including all the mantras.

First of all I would like to try and encourage everyone that we reflect on the basic spiritual aims of the School of Michael, the School of Spiritual Science, the esoteric school of our time which is led by Michael himself. This came in a new way directly at the Christmas Conference, or following it, as a potential given through the Christmas Conference in the year that followed. The School of Michael had been fully active for centuries in the spiritual world between death and new birth in all souls in the spiritual world, those which had died or those not yet incarnated anew, and found their way to Michael. Then, however, the Michaelic age began from 1879, and the School of Michael was not only to exist in the spiritual world between death and new birth, but also to be active in human hearts on earth. That is an absolute necessity for human existence in this Michaelic age. For at the end of the nineteenth century the whole of humanity subconsciously crossed the threshold to the spiritual world. Since then the whole situation of humanity is one that cannot be coped with in human dignity unless there is conscious awareness of the spiritual world, one that is sufficiently clear, with a sufficiently clear awareness of the spiritual world.

This is initially the very general task of anthroposophy, wholly and completely in the public domain: *Philosophy of Spiritual Activity, Theosophy, Knowledge of the Higher Worlds, Occult Science* and all the work Rudolf Steiner did in the public domain, placed in the open cultural world of our time, to encourage this awareness which makes human dignity possible in our time. First of all strength has to be gained for this, however, by people coming together in groups, in branches, in the

---

[560] G & C, 7 Apr. 1990, p. 36 ff. Goetheanum Archives. [A somewhat faulty (? shorthand) record of a talk, not always coherent, so that the speaker's intentions had to be guessed at. Translator.]

Anthroposophical Society, where this general awareness which can and must shine out into the whole cultural world can be strengthened, deepened, intensified by people working directly together within the Anthroposophical Society.

This developed through two decades and a bit more, until by the spring of 1923 it had turned into an absolute disaster. The First Goetheanum—destroyed by arson, and that spring Rudolf Steiner had to say: The Goetheanum has been destroyed by arson and lies in ruins, and the whole Anthroposophical Society is also in ruins;—spring 1923!

But what should one do in such a situation? Withdraw in pessimism and melancholy and say it won't work? No! Quite the contrary! In such a situation of utter darkness it is spiritually right to take a new, big step forward. The Christmas Conference opened the door for the spiritual world, so that Michael and his spiritual cohorts now had a possibility of achieving their will, which was to establish a fully valid esoteric school on earth as the core of this General Anthroposophical Society.

It is important to realize that this esoteric school comes from Michael himself through the will of the spiritual world, and that the whole content of the school first existed and still exists in occult language in the spiritual world; all mantras in occult language, not in German. Rudolf Steiner's great deed has been the mediation, the translation from those spiritual contents, pouring them into the German language, into the verses which then only *become* mantras in the true sense of the word in the activity of meditation. Without meditation the mantras are *verses*, verses in German.

The progress of this School in its first major period was one of gaining real insight into self and world, approaching the threshold to the spiritual world in stages. Crossing the threshold after meeting the Guardian, experiences in the spiritual world, and returning again and again to the initial starting point, the modern person's quest for insight, now by bringing together two qualities: power of thought developed in wholly human ways, where in full consciousness, in the spiritual soul, this approach to the threshold can be found and achieved, the crossing of the threshold, experiences in the spiritual world, and going back again and again.

That is one side. The other, coming to us from Michael himself as sublime spirit, in occult language in the power which through the mantras takes effect in the human being who is then able to ascend to the place whence this comes.

For it does not come as far as the physical world, but only to the etheric world. Because of this it is necessary to ascend one level higher from the everyday conscious mind, to the place where one can receive help from the spiritual world. For it is not present in the everyday conscious mind.

This called for the strictest discipline. And here we see three stages. First, quite generally cultural, anthroposophy through published books, lectures and other activities. Then, intensifying, practising, densifying, preliminary stages in work done together in the branches of the Anthroposophical Society as preparatory school for a true school for initiates. Then, this esoteric School, now with strict spiritual conditions.

One condition. Everything must now arise directly in the School, both individually and in the Lessons, where one is together, with immediate presence in mind and spirit, through activity. And the mantras, initially verses, are doors to this spiritual fact, world of facts, that is, spirits one comes to know in this way. This means that the people who want to gather together there must not do this, for that is not the will of Michael, nor what Rudolf Steiner intended, that one would do something merely to gain greater depth oneself. That depth must be gained, but it is a matter of *wanting to be a representative* of the anthroposophical cause in the whole civilized world of today. Those who did not wish this were not invited. And it is part of this wanting to be a representative in the present time in our civilization that we cultivate conscious awareness of the other representatives. This will create an unbreakable spiritual chalice into which the Michaelic powers can then enter in strengthening this activity. Steadfast in staying together—a basic condition.

Faithful guardianship of this, and then the activity of individual meditation in going back again through these stages to the threshold, across the threshold, to experiences in the spirit, recreating what is already there in every present-day human being in so far as humanity has subconsciously crossed the threshold already; it is a matter of doing it again, a service to future humanity.

Rudolf Steiner's words were taken down in shorthand, with his permission and knowledge. When some people working for the Class then wanted to look at them, as a help and support, he said: They don't exist! The shorthand records were clearly just there for security, in case things were wrongly reported; but they were not at all intended for general use. Rudolf Steiner had never intended those words to be read in any way, either individually or in Class Lessons; instead the aim was to develop something new in every Class Lesson as people go through these stages which can be brought to realization in every group of mantras and in what follows from the groups of mantras. In every Lesson a new endeavour in being thus active in the spirit, active for the future.

The conditions were most strict. Enormous demands made on Class workers. After Rudolf Steiner's death it was soon, or rather immediately, evident that the members were not ripe, in a sense, to achieve this in a fully valid form. I am not saying that they were bad; I am not saying that they failed completely. But they were not sufficiently mature to do this in fully valid form. It was found that, due partly to failure, partly to attacks from outside, and partly by accident, mantras fell into other hands. A rupture, indeed, a decisive rupture, which came almost immediately. After some years it was evident, however, that this life in the School, where it continues regularly—work leading to something new in every Lesson—probably left something to be desired. For people began to ask for the shorthand records in Dornach. At first the request was refused; people were not permitted to have them; and then it was done after all. Carbon copies were made for reading in Class Lessons—not envisaged by Rudolf Steiner!

I am sure much has come of this that is good, with inward, spiritual activity in those Class Lesson readings; I do not want to say anything bad about this. Yet I am quite sure that it has such great significance because great spiritual strength lives in the way Rudolf Steiner formed the words, that this becomes immediate presence when we hear it. But it was not intended. And not only not intended, but the first step towards publication. For by now copies had been made of the texts. In numbers one could still account for, but in a number that could no longer be controlled. And this became evident. For some copies went wildly astray. In the early 1960s we found that 1,000 copies . . . i.e. a printed, somehow a badly printed edition, had been sent out at random all of a sudden to people who had not asked for them, to members of the School, members of the Society, and people who were not members of the Society. Random publication and sending out of Class texts, including almost all mantras.

That was only *one* stage, however. Later there was another wild publication, and exactly as much in this not unbreakable chalice, and now publication and sale has been going on for several years already and copying here and there, in this case simply putting the Class texts in print.

None of this was, of course, considered desirable by Class workers who know about the School, being quite clear that it is not spiritually in accord with the basic intention of the School of Michael. It should never have happened. It was not envisaged. Rudolf Steiner's words: The texts don't exist!—What does one do when a situation arises that goes utterly against the inner spiritual substance, the inner spiritual direction, the spiritual aim of the esoteric school, which then—as we can say in this case—comes as an attack from outside and projects into it? One thing is not in accord with the spirit in any case, which is to let it be, as if it does not exist!—It must be looked at! We must not put our heads in the sand and let be, as if there was nothing there.

The next question is—you cannot get rid of it, for it cannot be forbidden—and now the question is: Is it possible to find a way for a new activity, where this element, which should not have been, is taken on board in a new way?—We may say that we have reached a situation where this undesirable publication, which goes against the spiritual intention of the School of Michael, has become unavoidable, even though it is undesirable and spiritually not necessary, and the question is what do we do with the unavoidable?

The Council at the Goetheanum has had many talks over the last two years to consider what is to be done in this situation so that it will be spiritually right? Then talks with the Board of the Rudolf Steiner Literary Estate. What is possible? Are the paths so divergent that all one can do is look and see what will happen? And over these two years, the situation clearly changed in those talks, so that it became possible to agree to produce a publication with a preface from both the Council at the Goetheanum and the Board of the Rudolf Steiner Literary Estate. It means that publication will not be set aside but made part of things, and it will be the task of this preface to present the situation, in this difficult and undesirable situation, but pointing to what can be done out of it for the work of the School to serve humanity.

The whole text of the preface has been produced and agreed upon, by both Council and Board. Publication is thus planned, but it will be a while yet before it can be implemented. This cannot be done quickly, and along the road from this first point, where the preface has been agreed on, steps still have to be taken with regard to practical consensus on procedure that needs to be carefully considered. It will be some time, therefore, before it is implemented.

This is only one aspect of the matter, however, and in my view not the most important. It is a matter of consciously bringing it in, and not sufficient in itself. For we must then consider, in this situation: How will we now do the work of the School of Spiritual Science in the service of humanity? And then the original impulse comes up, and that is this very service of humanity. Humanity has crossed the threshold in the unconscious. It is an existential necessity for humanity that enough people now follow this road consciously and with insight.

And there we have the three spheres I mentioned—culturally to stimulate conscious awareness of the spiritual in the whole of humanity; within the General Anthroposophical Society to densify, strengthen, practise, working together in a living, human way. Part of this is that a core comes together which not only wants to do what is fully justifiable for personal development, but also wants to devote itself wholly to the cause, be representative of anthroposophy in all situations in life, in thinking, feeling and doing, in our way of life. Those were, after all, the basic conditions Rudolf Steiner gave for being a member of the First Class in the School of Spiritual Science. This now comes up again. Can it be implemented much more strongly than before? And this not only individually, though it must always start with the individual, but in that representatives cultivate, practise awareness of the other representatives, working together to develop this common chalice on the road to the spiritual facts and entities on this road to self-knowledge and knowledge of the world, to the threshold of the spiritual world, the Guardian of the Threshold, experiences in the spiritual world after crossing the threshold, returning to the starting point of the initial question and where this then grows into spiritual reality.

And this is possible. If we say that the mantras are not effective, that is a generalization which misses the point. It is possible that the great effectiveness, which Rudolf Steiner had seen from the point of view of the School of Michael, might have been much greater and also deeper. But the way to the threshold, to the Guardian, is alive in every anthroposophist, unconsciously so in every modern person, and can be brought to conscious awareness. Then we have Spiritual Reality. And if it proves possible to take that step up from everyday conscious awareness through the thought configurations to this etheric element in the work of gaining insight, Michael comes to meet us, and meditative work makes the verses into *mantras*, and the road opens up in all reality to the threshold of the spiritual world, to the Guardian, to crossing the threshold and gaining experiences in the spiritual world.

The condition for this is reference to one's way of life. This alone will give strength. And it is part of this way of life that we relate to others involved in the work. If this is neglected, a paralysing quality arises, all strength is lost, and all one has is theory.

The point is that this road must become spiritual reality for a sufficient number of people at the core of the Anthroposophical Society. It is also permitted to be a member of the Society long before one is prepared to take this difficult road. You can get to know anthroposophy, enjoy meeting the other friends in the Society—this enriches life. Then, however, a stage comes in one's membership of the General Anthroposophical Society when it may be time to take things further. Anthroposophy has then reached the inner human being; I can honestly seek to be a representative of anthroposophy in our way of life, but immediately also *socially*, otherwise it is not true. And this is where we can test every situation in our own life and in other activities within the Anthroposophical Society and its institutions, where there may be a bit of a problem, and look at this and see that it saps the strength of the School of Michael and impedes the whole of humanity.

It is a spiritual battle, a great spiritual battle at the end of the twentieth century. In the next ten years there will be two major attacks among many others—no doubt they number legion. One of them, the most massive, materialism, where everything is only done superficially, when one clings to objects, to superficial, middle-class existence, and sticks to this alone. Materialism wipes out spiritual awareness, preventing people from taking the road to insight and the threshold of the spiritual world in a real way. That is the tremendous ahrimanic attack, and there is so much open to it, not only when it comes to the philosophical content but also in the materialistic way of life.

All activity in the School of Spiritual Science is under pressure from this ahrimanic attack. Only spiritual initiative, spiritual activity from within, can overcome it.

The other danger which has been growing steadily in recent years are the numerous occultist streams close to and around the Anthroposophical Society and also extending into it. A few dozen already, not even working together, but all seeking to arrive as quickly as possible at experiences in the spirit and spiritual influences without taking the difficult road of gaining insight, insight into self and world, to the Guardian of the Threshold, crossing the threshold, and doing so by rising to immediate experience in the spirit through configuring thinking in the spiritual soul. Glad to avoid this hard, difficult work, coming to spiritual experience without such effort, guided by some guru or other, nowadays in several occultist movements close to the Anthroposophical Society, through female figures who take leading roles.

With occultist experiences outside the spiritual soul so attractive to people, ignoring the serious, strenuous and difficult road to insight, realization of the School of Michael on earth faces opposition of one kind. The School of Michael in the spiritual world is not threatened by this. It is sovereign, secure in the face of both luciferic and ahrimanic powers. But on earth, in human hearts, this is a battlefield. And so we must also consider the undesirable publication a move on the part of the ahrimanic powers, seeking superficiality. What shall we do? Certainly not simply ignore this. Consciously include it in our considerations as a first stage, and then, the most important part of the work, the deed, spiritual activity in the School of Spiritual Science that may grow so strong that this other aspect, loss of the outer secret, is wholly made up for by the spiritual substance of the inner secret. For this can never be published, can never be printed; it lives in human beings who seek insight, who want to work together.

I have tried to indicate and clarify some important aspects of this. I would like to emphasize particularly what each of us can do in any situation in life where you do not wish things to be as they are, where you say: bad! Not only undesirable but: *It's not right*; I am threatened by this situation. If you then just go pessimistic, melancholic, and say: Pity! Lost it! that goes against the whole human spirit, paralysing it. We can see any such undesirable situation as a challenge. What shall I do now? New spiritual initiative that goes beyond! I do not go away and leave it, as though it does not exist. I take it on board, but go beyond it to new activity. That is the Council's intention. Not to say, perhaps, that one would recommend publication anyway. Far from it! Not desirable! Not necessary in terms of the thing itself. But unavoidable in the present situation, and it is possible to take it on board, as a starting point for new deeds along our road. Then the new deeds are the most important thing. Moving ahead to what is growing and evolving in the human being, beyond anything grown hard and fixed.

I am sure that there will be many questions on what I have been saying and that these will be objective and justifiable. These questions have lived in each of us for two years and continue to exist to this day. It is not, somehow, an easy solution, like saying now you have dealt with this, it's finished. No, we cannot have it so in this field. Urgent questions that stay with us. But one can try to see them in a wider context and also connect them with the whole difficult destiny of the Anthroposophical Society. For that shows itself in the situation in which we now are. But you cannot throw away your own destiny. It is our destiny that the powers in our present civilization have forced their way in and wield the threat of superficiality, of losing this inmost spiritual substance, and where the question then is if we take this on board as an opportunity for a new awakening to the full reality of the School of Michael's mission for humanity, without which humanity cannot move forward. It is the spiritual battle at the end of this [twentieth] century.

37 Friedwart Bock
The work within the School of Spiritual Science in Camphill—a history (2004)[561]

Karl König had been excluded from the General Anthroposophical Society in 1935 while he worked at Pilgramshain, Silesia. When he came to Britain as a refugee from Vienna in 1939 he took up Anthroposophical work immediately, the work that had been forbidden by the Nazis in Germany and Austria.

Karl König became a member of the Anthroposophical Society in Great Britain (A.S. in G.B.). The work of Curative Education was established, the community building at Camphill began and Karl König made contact with the principal anthroposophists in the country. This took a special turn through the internment on the Isle of Man in 1940, where many anthroposophists met and worked together as refugees. Among these were Dr. Ernst Lehrs and Maria Roeschl-Lehrs.

Back in Aberdeen the work in the School of Spiritual Science could not begin. Karl König records—on 15 July 1943—from a conversation with Maria Roeschl-Lehrs: 'Aus allem was sie sagt geht hervor, dass sie die Klasse nicht halten darf. Bin erstaunt.' (From all this arises the following, that she says, that she is not permitted to hold the Class. I am astonished.)

The work with the Class had to wait.

On Monday 15 November 1943 Karl König met George Adams in London who was responsible for the School of Spiritual Science in Britain. Karl König notes, 'Gespräch mit Mr. Adams über die Klasse, die nun in Camphill von mir übermittelt werden soll'. (Conversation with George Adams about the Class which shall be conveyed by myself in Camphill.)[562]

The next step taken was the establishing of the Ita Wegman Group as a Branch of the Anthroposophical Society.

Then Karl König took the first steps to begin the work with the First Class. Conversation took place with some prospective members in December 1943. But it is only on Sunday 26 March 1944 that Karl König speaks to all the applicants about 'Individual work on the Class and the life

---

[561] Original English, uncorrected, including translation given in parentheses of German passages. Camphill, June–July 2004.

[562] Notebook Karl Koenig, Camphill.

of Rudolf Steiner'. He then read the constitution and admitted twelve members to the First Class.

On Friday 31 March 1944 the first lesson is read.[563] After the lesson the members remain behind for a conversation about the lesson.

Other members apply, among them Mr. Duffy who had established a Bio-Dynamic Centre in the area.

The first lesson is repeated twice and the second lesson is read on Thursday 4 May 1944.

The first seven lessons were all read three times before the next ones were taken. A membership card was issued for each member of the Class.

In consultation with George Adams, Alix Roth was asked to be a Class Holder in 1955. This was shared with the Vorstand at the Goetheanum.

Later on Janet McGavin, Carlo Pietzner, Anke Weihs and Thomas Weihs were appointed. For a time membership of the Class could be applied for by members of the Camphill Community after two years. This was not maintained and applicants were expected to be or to become members of the A.S. in G.B.

Henning Hansmann and Friedwart Bock were appointed as Class Holders at Camphill in October 1975 and at Newton Dee Paul Allan put forward Margarete v. Freeden and Jens Holbek. In Central Scotland Johannes Surkamp and Georg Schad were appointed. Marianne Sander, who joined at the same time, had been a Class Holder in Austria already. The Class in Aberdeen had been held for many years by Mildred Kirkcaldy who asked Camphill readers to help after her retirement and move to Perthshire. Jens Holbek took this on.

When Charles Kovacz retired in Edinburgh, Anke Weihs was asked to hold the lessons there. Karla Kiniger and Tony Fuller were appointed and latterly also Shirley Noakes and Christian Maclean. Following the death of Thomas and Anke Weihs, Astrid Radysh, Vincent D'Agostino and Angelika Monteux were appointed; latterly also John Ralph.

Apart from three meetings every year the Class Holders in Scotland also attend the London meetings and the annual meeting at the Goetheanum.

The active participation of members was called upon in conversation meetings following or preceding each lesson. Beginning in 1979 members conferences are held twice a year at Camphill. A lesson is held, work on the theme of the year is done and an artistic activity deepens the content.

[563] Notebook Karl Koenig, Camphill.

Abbreviations used in the footnotes

IW	Ita Wegman
EZ I, II and III	J. E. Zeylmans van Emmichoven. *Wer war Ita Wegman? Eine Dokumentation*. Heidelberg: Edition Georgenberg. Bd 1 1990, Bde 2 & 3 1992.
GA	Rudolf Steiner Gesamtausgabe (collected works of Rudolf Steiner). Dornach: Rudolf Steiner Verlag.
G&C	Meeting in Dornach of General Secretaries and Councils of national anthroposophical societies
MSt	Marie Steiner-von Sivers
Nbl.	*Was in der Anthroposophischen Gesellschaft vorgeht. Nachrichten fuer deren Mitglieder*. Newsletter publ. by General Anthroposophical Society, Dornach, Switzerland.

Bibliography

(Any page numbers given refer to the German texts.)

1 Works by Rudolf Steiner arranged in sequence of volume numbers in GA

GA 6	*Goethe's Conception of the World*
GA 14	*The Four Mystery Plays*. No. 2. The Soul's Probation. Tr. A. Bittleston. London: Rudolf Steiner Press 1982.
GA 21	Part in *The Case for Anthroposophy*. Tr. O. Barfield. London: Rudolf Steiner Press 1970.
GA 26	*Anthroposophical Leading Thoughts*. Tr. G. & M. Adams. London: Rudolf Steiner Press 1973.
GA 28	*The Course of My Life*. Tr. O. D. Wannamaker. New York: Anthroposophic Press 1970. Other title: *Rudolf Steiner, An Autobiography*.
GA 30	Parts in *Goethe as the Founder of a New Science of Aesthetics* *Three Essays on Haeckel and Karma* *Individualism in Philosophy* *Nature and Our Ideals*
GA 34	Parts in *Reincarnation and Immortality* *Education of the Child* *Rhythms of Learning* *The Education of Children* *Anthroposophy and the Social Question* *Spiritual Research: Methods and Results* *Destiny or Karma* *Three Essays on Haeckel and Karma*
GA 35	Parts in *Philosophy and Anthroposophy* *Psychological Foundations of Anthroposophy* *Spiritual Science* *Spiritual Scientific Basis of Goethe's Work* *Approaches to Anthroposophy* *Christian Rosenkreutz* *Esoteric and Meditative*

Transactions 1905
Transactions 1906
Esoteric Development
Human Life in the Light of Anthroposophy
Mission of Spiritual Science
Seeing with the Soul

GA 36 Parts in *Psychologic aphorisms*
Speech and the Spirit of Speech
On the Life of the Soul
Oswald Spengler
Atomism and its Refutation

GA 39 *Briefe Band II: 1890–1925* (not tr.)

GA 40 *Truth-Wrought Words*
Parts in *Verses and Meditations*
Calendar of the Soul (various editions)
The Year Participated

GA 93 *The Temple Legend*. Tr. J. M. Wood. London: Rudolf Steiner Press 1985.

GA 104 *The Apocalypse of St John* (= The Book of Revelation). Tr. J. Collis. London: Rudolf Steiner Press 1977.

GA 167 *Gegenwaertiges und Vergangenes im Menschengeiste* (not tr.)

GA 181 Parts in *Earthly Death*
Life beyond Death

GA 227 Parts in *Evolution of Consciousness*. Tr. V. E. Watkin, C. Davy. Sussex: Rudolf Steiner Press 1991.

GA 229 Parts in *The Festivals and their Meaning*

GA 233a *Rosicrucianism and Modern Initiation*. Tr. M. Adams. London: Rudolf Steiner Press 1965.

GA 237 *Karmic Relationships 3*. Tr. G. Adams. London: Rudolf Steiner Press 1977.

GA 238 Parts in *Karmic Relationships 4*
Last Address

GA 240 *Cosmic Christianity and the Impulse of Michael*. Tr. D. S. Osmond. London: Anthroposophical Publishing Co. 1953.

GA 243 *True and False Paths in Spiritual Investigation*. Tr. A. H. Parker. London: Anthroposophical Publishing Co. 1927.

GA 259 Part(s) in *Rudolf Steiner Speaks to the British*

GA 260 *The Christmas Conference.* Tr. J. Collis. New York: Anthroposophic Press 1990.

GA 260a *To the Members.* Tr. not known. London & New York: Rudolf Steiner Publishing Co. & Anthroposophic Press n.d. Reprinted as Anthroposophical Leading Thoughts (= guiding principles).

GA 262 *Correspondence and Documents 1901–1925.* Tr. C. & I. von Arnim. London & New York: Rudolf Steiner Press & Anthroposophic Press 1988.

GA 264 *From the History & Contents of the First Section of the Esoteric School 1904–1914.* Tr. J. Wood. Hudson: Anthroposophic Press 1998.

GA 265 *Zur Geschichte und aus den Inhalten der erkenntniskultischen Abteilung der esoterischen Schule* (not tr.)

GA 266/1–3 Part in *The Secret Stream. C. Rosenkreutz & Rosicrucianism*

GA 267 Parts in *The Christian Mystery*
The Secret Stream

GA 268 *Mantrische Sprueche. Seelenuebungen Band II, 1903–1925.*

GA 270/1–3 *Esoterische Unterweisungen fuer die erste Klasse* (not tr.)

GA 300/3 *Faculty Meetings with Rudolf Steiner.* Tr. R. Lathe, N. P. Whittaker. Hudson: Anthroposophic Press 1998.

GA 318 *Pastoral Medicine.* Tr. G. Hahn. Hudson: Anthroposophic Press 1987.

GA 346 *The Book of Revelation and the Work of the Priest.* Tr. J. Collis. London: Rudolf Steiner Press 1998.

2 Works by other authors

Barnes, H.: *Into the Heart's Land. A Century of Rudolf Steiner's Work in North America.* Great Barrington, MA: Steiner Books, 2005.

Bock, E.: Von der Vorbereitung besonderer esoterischer Kreise in den Jahren 1904–1906. In: *Mitteilungen aus der anthroposophischen Arbeit in Deutschland,* Nr. 43, Ostern 1958, S. 2–14.

David, K. F.: Die Einrichtung der Ersten Klasse durch Rudolf Steiner und deren Schicksale bis zur Gegenwart. Hektographiertes Manuskript, 1974. Archiv am Goetheanum.

Faivre, A. / Zimmermann, R. Ch. (Hrsg.): *Epochen der Naturmystik.*

Hermetische Tradition im wissenschaftlichen Fortschritt. Berlin: Erich Schmidt, 1979.

Faivre, A. *Theosophy, Imagination, Tradition: Studies in Western Esotericism.* New York: State University Press, 2000.

Ferguson, N. (Hrsg.): *Virtual History: Alternatives and Counterfactuals. London 1997.*

–: *The Pity of War.* New York: Basic Books, 1999.

Gädeke, W.: *Anthroposophie und die Fortbildung der Religion.* Flensburg: Flensburger Hefte Verlag, 1990.

Glasl, F.: *Konfliktmanagement.* Bern: Paul Haupt, Stuttgart: Verlag Freies Geistesleben, ²1990.

Haid, Ch.: *Auf der Suche nach dem Menschen. Die anthroposophische Jugend- und Studentenarbeit in den Jahren 1920–1931 mit einem skizzenhaften Ausblick bis in die Gegenwart.* Dornach: Verlag am Goetheanum, 2001.

Heckmann, L.: *Valentin Tomberg. Leben–Werk–Wirkung.* Bd. I. 1. Schaffhausen: Novalis Verlag, 2001.

Hellmers, I.: Fehlende Übereinstimmung im Umgang mit der Veröffentlichung von Hochschul-Inhalten. Aus der Geschichte der Veröffentlichung der Inhalte der Klasse I der Freien Hochschule für Geisteswissenschaft. In: *Mitteilungen aus der Anthroposophischen Arbeit in Deutschland,* Nr. 182, IV / 1992, S. 269–276.

Huizinga, J.: *Herbst des Mittelalters.* Stuttgart: Kröner, ¹¹1975.

Husemann, G.: Lili Kolisko. Werk und Wesen. In: *Beiträge zur Erweiterung der Heilkunst nach geisteswissenschaftlichen Erkenntnissen,* 1978, Heft 2, S. 37–53.

Kaltenbrunner, G.-K.: *Dionysius vom Areopag.* Zug/Schweiz: Die Graue Edition, 1996.

Kolisko, L.: Eugen Kolisko. Ein Lebensbild. Manuskriptdruck 1961.

Liedtke, R.: *Die Hermetik. Traditionelle Philosophie der Differenz.* Paderborn: Schöningh, 1996.

Lindenberg, Ch.: *Rudolf Steiner. Eine Chronik 1861–1925.* Stuttgart: Verlag Freies Geistesleben, 1988.

– : Fehler, Erfindungen und Fälschungen. Zur Memoirenliteratur über Rudolf Steiner. In: *Mitteilungen aus der Anthroposophischen Arbeit in Deutschland,* Nr. 174, Weihnachten IV/1990, S. 261–267.

– : *Individualismus und offenbare Religion. Rudolf Steiners Zugang zum Christentum*. Erweiterte Neuausgabe. Stuttgart: Verlag Freies Geistesleben, 1995.

– : *Rudolf Steiner. Eine Biographie.* 2 Bde. Stuttgart: Verlag Freies Geistesleben, 1997.

Lissau, R.: Geistige Schau und irdischer Ausdruck. In: R. Steiner: *Geistige Schau und irdischer Ausdruck*, Hrsg. J.-C. Lin. Stuttgart: Verlag Freies Geistesleben, 2001.

Mahnke, D.: *Unendliche Sphäre und Allmittelpunkt*. Beiträge zur Genealogie der mathematischen Mystik. Halle: Niemeyer, 1937.

Matile; H.: Die Urnenstreit-Szene des «Sturz des Antichrist» und der Urnenstreit vom 3. April 1925. In: *Hinweise und Studien zum Lebenswerk von Albert Steffen*. Heft 18/19 / Winter 2003/2004, S. 27–32.

Matile, H. und A. Meister: *Zu den sogenannten Polzer-Hoditz-«Aufschreibungen»*. In: Nbl., Nr. 45, 9.2.1997, S. 260–263.

Meffert, E.: *Mathilde Scholl und die Geburt der Anthroposophischen Gesellschaft 1912/1913*. Dornach: Philosophisch-Anthroposophischer Verlag am Goetheanum, 1991.

Meyer, Th.: *Ludwig Polzer-Hoditz. Ein Europäer*. Basel: Perseus Verlag, 1994.

– : D.N. *Dunlop – ein Zeit- und Lebensbild*. Basel: Perseus Verlag, ²1996.

English edition: D. N. Dunlop, A Man of Our Time. London: Temple Lodge Publishing, 1992.

Neugebauer-Wölk, M. (Hrsg.): Aufklärung und Esoterik. Hamburg: Meiner, 1999.

Plato, B. v. (Hrsg.): *Anthroposophie im 20. Jahrhundert. Ein Kulturimpuls in biografischen Porträts*. Dornach: Verlag am Goetheanum, 2003.

Pomian, K.: *Europa und seine Nationen*. Berlin: Wagenbach, 1990.

Prokofieff, S. O.: *Menschen mögen es hören. Das Mysterium der Weihnachtstagung*. Stuttgart: Verlag Freies Geistesleben, 2002.

English edition: May Human Beings Hear It!, The Mystery of the Christmas Conference. Sussex: Temple Lodge Publishing, 2004.

Ravagli, L./Röschert, G.: *Kontinuität und Wandel. Zur Geschichte der*

Anthroposophie im Werk Rudolf Steiners. Stuttgart: Verlag Freies Geistesleben, 2003.

Röschert, G.: Anthroposophie als Aufklärung. München: Trithemius, 1997.

Sam, M. M.: *Im Ringen um eine neue Sprache. Rudolf Steiners Sprachstil als Herausforderung*. Dornach: Verlag am Goetheanum, 2004.

Schefer, Ch.: *Platons unsagbare Erfahrung*. Basel: Schwabe, 2001.

Selg, P.: *«Ich bin für Fortschreiten». Ita Wegman und die Medizinische Sektion.* Dornach: Verlag am Goetheanum, 2002.

– : *Die letzten drei Jahre. Ita Wegman in Ascona 1940–1943.* Dornach: Verlag am Goetheanum, 2004.

– : *Geistiger Widerstand und Überwindung. Ita Wegman 1933–1935*. Dornach: Natura Verlag im Verlag am Goetheanum, 2005 (a).

– : *Die Briefkorrespondenz der «jungen Mediziner». Eine dokumentarische Studie zur Rezeption von Rudolf Steiners «Jungmediziner»-Kursen*. Dornach: Natura Verlag im Verlag am Goetheanum, 2005 (b).

Steiner, M.: *Briefe und Dokumente vornehmlich aus ihren letzten Lebensjahren.* Privatdruck der Rudolf Steiner-Nachlaßverwaltung, Dornach 1981.

Steiner, R.: *Theosophie. Die Textentwicklung in den Auflagen 1904–1922 in vollständiger Lesefassung*. Rudolf Steiner Studien Bd. IX. Dornach: Rudolf Steiner Verlag, 2004.

Stuckrad, K. v.: *Was ist Esoterik? Kleine Geschichte des geheimen Wissens.* München: C. H. Beck, 2004.

Szlezák, T.: *Platon lesen*. Stuttgart-Bad Cannstatt: frommann-holzboog, 1993.

Templeton, R.: *Carl Unger. Der Weg eines Geistesschülers*. Dornach: Verlag am Goetheanum, 1990.

Vickers, B. (Hrsg): *Occult and Scientific Mentalities in the Renaissance.* Cambridge a. o.: Cambridge University Press 1984.

Villeneuve, C. *Rudolf Steiner in Britain. A Documentation of his Ten Visits*. 2 Vols. Sussex: Temple Lodge, 2004.

Vreede, E.: Kurze Geschichte der ersten Wochen nach R[udolf] St[einers] Tod. Abschrift eines unveröffentlichten Manuskripts (Oktober 1934). Archiv Goeth.

Werner, U.: *Anthroposophen in der Zeit des Nationalsozialismus (1935–1945)*. München: Oldenbourg, 1999.

Wiesberger, H.: *Marie Steiner – von Sivers. Ein Leben für die Anthroposophie*. Dornach: Rudolf Steiner Verlag, 1988.

– : *Rudolf Steiners esoterische Lehrtätigkeit. Wahrhaftigkeit – Kontinuität–Neugestaltung*. Dornach: Rudolf Steiner Verlag, 1997.

– : Rudolf Steiner: Bewusstsein – Leben – Form. Ein Beitrag zur Werkbiographie. In: *Das Goetheanum*, 2001, Nr. 25, S. 455–457.

Yates, F. *Giordano Bruno and the Hermetic Tradition; The Rosicrucian Enlightenment*. Routledge, 1999.

Zeylmans van Emmichoven, J.E.: *Willem Zeylmans van Emmichoven. Ein Pionier der Anthroposophie*. Arlesheim: Natura, 1979. *English edition: Willem Zeylmans van Emmichoven*. Sussex: Temple Lodge Publishing, 2002.

– : *Wer war Ita Wegman. Eine Dokumentation*. Bd. 1: Edition Georgenberg, 1990. Bd. 2 und 3. Heidelberg: Edition Georgenberg, 1992. *English edition: Who Was Ita Wegman*. New York: Mercury Press, 1995.